SUSTAINABLE POWER

'Having journeyed with Simon Holley and the supernatural community at the King's Arms Church, Bedford for more than five years now I am so happy to see this book in print. It is a template for the miraculous and living in the reality of the kingdom of God now. I know of no other person more qualified to write on the subjects covered in this book than Simon Holley. His insights and theological truths are matched by his experience of living and developing a people who are more aware of God's presence and his ability to act than they are of the possibility of defeat. These are robust, practical and deeply moving words which will change your life and your church forever. Simon Holley is the most authentic person I know and what is contained in here will leave you wanting more of God and greater displays of his power! This book is a must for pastors, leaders and anyone who wants to see heaven invade earth.'

Julian Adams, Founder of Frequentsee Trust,
speaker and author of Gaining Heaven's Perspective

'Simon Holley has been a huge blessing to me personally, and a great provocation to many evangelicals who want to see more of God's kingdom here on earth. Simon's winsome style, raw authenticity, childlike faith and biblical wisdom appear throughout this powerful and stirring book, with insights, stories and fresh approaches to Scripture that will challenge you to think differently and live differently.'

Andrew Wilson, Teaching and Training Pastor at King's Church
Eastbourne and author of Incomparable *and* God Stories

'Simon's ministry communicates a combination of love, compassion, faith, integrity and courage. He is building a growing church reflecting these values. You will be blessed as you gather insights from this his first book.'

Terry Virgo, Founder of the Newfrontiers Family of Churches and author of books such as God's Lavish Grace *and* The Tide is Turning

'Simon Holley is both provoking us and encouraging us to continue to seek more of the tangible presence of God amongst us by his Spirit. This book is full of faith, honesty, humour, both avoiding hype and demonstrating genuine integrity – all characteristics that I have valued in Simon himself.'

David Devenish, international church planter, leader of the Catalyst Network of Churches within Newfrontiers and author of Demolishing Strongholds, Fathering Leaders *and* What on Earth is the Church For?

'Endorsing a book for a man who is "doing the stuff" is so much easier than for someone with just good ideas. Simon is a doer of the word and has written from that perspective. I particularly love the chapter on culture. I believe that, while doctrinal statements are important, intentional culture is to this apostolic move of God the most vital component. This book will help us all to create an intentional culture, and by very definition culture is passed from generation to generation. It is much more than just a good idea, it becomes a way of life – and Christianity was always intended to be a way of life that transforms the culture of earth into the culture of heaven.'

Paul Manwaring, Director, Global Legacy, Bethel Church, California and author of What on Earth is Glory? *and* Kisses from a Good God

TESTIMONIES OF HEALING

'Ever since I was 16 years old, if I stood still for longer than ten minutes I would get a crushing pain across the lower part of my back. This was diagnosed as being due to a prolapsed disc. I am a carpenter, so it makes my job very difficult at times and I have often had prayer for my back. While I was attending a course at King's Arms Church, a young man prayed for me during a meeting. The following week at work I was on a building site shovelling about two tonnes of clay into a skip, which would normally cause me to collapse in pain after about an hour. Instead I lasted all day without a single twinge. I knew then that God had healed me! Since then I have had no pain in my back and can stand for hours without a problem. God is so good! This isn't just any book on miracles. This is a story of God at work in our time and in incredible ways. Reading this book will inspire you to expect God to move in new and exciting ways through his power and healing.'

Adam, healed from a prolapsed disc, 2012

'Many people have a fear of death but mine was specific – I was terrified of dying in a natural disaster. During thunderstorms I would suffer panic attacks; in heavy winds I would hide in a windowless room and turn my music up. In 2011, whilst on a mission trip, I was physically sick with fear as there was a thunderstorm during the flight home. My fear even stopped me from being able to get excited about my honeymoon, as I was so frightened of flying through another thunderstorm. My fear was controlling my life and I was desperate for breakthrough. One

Sunday at King's Arms Church I responded to a word about someone with a fear of death. I was prayed for and God totally set me free! Never settle for a life with fear. Reading this book will show you how there is freedom to be had.'

Rachel, set free from a fear of death, 2012

'Eight years ago, as the church pressed in for more intimacy with God and growing in faith for the miraculous, I experienced incredible freedom from depression, pride, cynicism and unbelief. It's amazing how much my life has changed! Previously I had to continually fight the blackness of depression and negative thoughts about myself: now I am free to enjoy God, to take him at his word, and to see him work powerfully in situations which used to seem impossible. I'm so grateful to God for what he has done in my life and I'd recommend this book to anyone who wants to know more of God's love for them and his desire to come and bring healing and freedom.'

Ali, set free from depression, 2005

'I was born with a deformed eardrum. When I was five years old I had a test that showed that I only had 10 per cent hearing in my bad ear. I was tested again when I started secondary school and yet again when I started university and discovered that I had less than 10 per cent hearing in that ear. During a training course which was part of the leadership training programme that I am undertaking, and at which Simon Holley was speaking, God healed me! I got a doctor at work to look at my eardrum and she confirmed that it looked physically fine with no sign of deformity. As far as I can tell, my hearing has been fully restored in my bad ear. When I shared my testimony of healing one Sunday at my home church, a woman who had deafness in one ear received healing as well, praise God! Now I have faith to pray for others both in and out of church.'

Aidan, hearing restored and another lady healed after hearing his testimony, 2013

SUSTAINABLE POWER

CREATING A HEALTHY CULTURE OF THE SUPERNATURAL IN THE CHURCH TODAY

SIMON HOLLEY

Authentic

Copyright © 2013 Simon Holley

20 19 18 17 16 15 14   8 7 6 5 4 3 2

First published 2013 by Authentic Media Limited
52 Presley Way, Crownhill, Milton Keynes, MK8 0ES.
www.authenticmedia.co.uk

British Library Cataloguing in Publication Data

A catalogue record for this book is available from the British Library.

ISBN: 978-1-86024-884-9
978-1-78078-327-7 (e-book)

Unless otherwise stated Scripture quotations are taken from the
HOLY BIBLE, ENGLISH STANDARD VERSION,
published by HarperCollins*Publishers*, © 2001 Crossway Bibles, a
publishing ministry of Good New Publishers.
Used by permission. All rights reserved.

Cover design by Toby Cosh
Printed and bound by CPI Group (UK) Ltd., Croydon, CR0 4YY.

Contents

ACKNOWLEDGEMENTS

There are so many that I want to thank for helping me on the journey that led to the writing of this book.

Thank you to Mum and Dad for your amazing generosity, prayers and love over the years. Thank you to all of the leadership at King's Arms, past and present. Without your support, courage and encouragement none of this would have been possible. Thank you to the King's Arms Church for faithfully walking this out so that I have a story to tell.

Thank you to all of those within our family of churches, Newfrontiers, who have partnered with us and given us space and encouragement to explore these things in God. Thank you to Terry Virgo, David Devenish and Bill Johnson, the three men that have taught me most about living life as a godly leader, hungry for more!

Thank you to Laura, Ali, Andrew, Toby, Mike, Peter and Liz who have all played a major part in putting this book together.

Thank you to my three wonderful kids, Kiah, Caleb and Ethan – you guys keep me pressing on for the sake of the next generation. Lastly, and most importantly, thank you to my beautiful, talented and amazing wife Caroline. This is the fulfilment of something that was promised to us together all those years ago and it is as much your story as mine. I love you!

1

AMBUSH

God is predictably unpredictable. You'd think this wouldn't be
the case. The sun comes up every day. The grass keeps growing.
Surely the God who created all of that would be a predictable
kind of God? He's not. He likes surprises. I've found this out
through bittersweet experience on many occasions. On one
of these I stood to the side of a room, anxiously waiting for
my turn to speak. I had been asked to contribute at a meeting
before the main speaker gave his message. I wasn't totally sure
what I was going to say and my mind was wheel-spinning,
grappling for the right words. Suddenly the guest speaker
turned to me and said, 'Simon, I feel that God has something
to say to you.' He asked me to move to the centre of the room
and Caroline, my wife, to come and stand with me. At least I
wasn't being divinely ambushed alone.

'Simon and Caroline, the Lord is going to put miracles in
your hands and your heart and your mouth and your mind.'
As he began to speak, what felt like a strong electrical current
began to flow over my body. I doubled over on the floor. It
didn't seem to bother him, and he continued: 'You're going
to pray like John G. Lake and John Hyde and other men
who threw themselves into the miracle-working presence of
God. I hear him say that it all comes from his presence. And

I hear the Lord say, "Equip, train and send out as many as you can. Give them what you've got." You're going to come to the Lord and ask him, "Is there another message?" And he will say, "I am the Lord who heals. I am the Lord who heals. I am the Lord who heals." I prophesy tonight that you will see diseases that have been untouched and you will see them healed in the coming days. The Lord says, "Pray and expect AIDS to dissolve and disappear. Ask for cancer to go." I see a book coming out of this. Between the two of you there are going to be things that are written from your own experience and placed in the hands of other people. You are to get into the hearts and the hands of people what God has done inside the two of you.'

Throughout this, the feeling of electricity flowed through my arms, over my lips and in my stomach. It wasn't painful, but it wasn't comfortable. It was a physical demonstration that God was endorsing these words and that they were significant for our lives. A holy ambush.

Fast-forward fifteen years, and now in 2012 I am leading the senior leadership team of the church that I was part of all those years before. This prophetic word, among many others, has shaped my life and our church community, and it has provoked this book. This is the book that God said we must write; it's about the things he has taught us on this journey to create a supernaturally-natural culture in our lives and in a local church. It's the story of a group of people with an insatiable hunger to encounter a living God and take his life-giving and powerful gospel to the world around them. Is it possible to see God's power that we read about in the book of Acts at work in the church today? Is it possible to see God touch and anoint not just one special individual but a whole community? We believe that it is, and this is the story of our pursuit of him.

Church Now and Then

First let me backtrack to the beginning of the story. My home church when I was growing up was a small church in south-east London. Although the gospel of salvation was faithfully preached every Sunday evening, few were saved and little breakthrough was seen in people's lives. As far as I know, the church didn't believe God's power could work today, or didn't know how to see it. At the back of the church was the church bookshop. It was actually little more than two shelves, and the books were not new but second-hand donations. Strangely, the shelves were stuffed with books about Charles Finney, Smith Wigglesworth, Andrew Murray and the like. Each of these men saw significant demonstrations of God's power. What's more, each of these books was available for the princely sum of ten pence. I was an avid reader and devoured them. I read the stories of when God used Smith Wigglesworth to heal people with stomach cancer and raise people from the dead. Of when Charles Finney walked into a factory and the power of God fell so strongly that people stopped their work, dropped to their knees and cried out, asking what they must do to be saved. I actually felt bad about taking most of the stock, embarrassingly sometimes for less than ten pence, until I realized that no one else was reading them. I read on.

The church I found in the library, as opposed to the church I found in the flesh, caused me to grow up with spiritual double vision. One church that I could see was filled with energy, healing, mass salvations and whole communities experiencing the power of God. It looked like the things I read about in the book of Acts. The other, the one I actually lived in, was filled with faithful people who loved Jesus. To be honest, though, it made little more than a dent in the local community. I soon became disheartened. I longed for the library-church that I saw reflected in the pages of Scripture, and I studied the Bible endlessly to try to rediscover the way back to it.

The Journey Begins

I learned on the journey that by definition God is a supernatural being. He exists beyond and within the natural universe that he has created. This is part of what makes him God. He has created natural laws and properties that control and regulate the universe that we live in. Part of our joy and delight is to study, understand and harness those laws for our benefit and advancement. However, the God who created those laws will not be contained by them. We see this throughout Scripture. From the very first story of God walking with Adam in the cool of the day right through to the final stories of angelic battles in the book of Revelation, it is clear that God's supernatural realm co-exists with the natural realm that he has also created. The problem is we just don't see it.

I once saw a guy wearing sunglasses in a nightclub. I could tell he felt pretty cool. To everyone else he looked like a prize plum, and it was clear he could hardly see where he was going. In a similar vein, the Apostle Paul says: 'For now we see in a mirror dimly, but then face to face. Now I know in

part; then I shall know fully, even as I have been fully known'
(1 Cor. 13:12).

Like the man in the nightclub, we see the supernatural
world 'in a mirror dimly'. In Paul's day, mirrors were made
of highly polished metal and gave a limited or dim view of
the subject. We see into the heavenly realms in a similar way,
living with a limited perspective on the true reality. Paul
looked forward to the day when heaven, God's supernatural realm, will be in full alignment with earth. Then we will
see clearly, 'face to face', all that God has made, and we shall
know God and his entire realm fully.

Before we despair, in the meantime we see God's supernatural realm at work most evidently in his people. The Bible
is filled with stories of supernatural events as God moves
with, appears to, speaks to, orders and organizes his people.
Abraham is visited by angels, and his wife receives a supernatural conception. Jacob, his grandson, wrestles with an angel
and has open visions of the supernatural realm. Moses' supernatural events are too many to list but include hearing the
audible voice of God, eating with God himself, crossing large
bodies of water on dry ground and having food appear out
of thin air. The rest of the Old Testament continues with the
same theme. From prophetic visions to audible voices, from
handwriting on walls to walking through fiery furnaces, from
visible angelic armies to food provided by birds. The list is
extraordinary in the truest sense of the word. Any uninitiated
reader honestly reading through the Old Testament cannot
help but come away with a sense of awe and the realization
that we follow a supernatural God to whom the supernatural
is, quite frankly, natural.

Instead of decreasing, the pace of supernatural activity actually picks up in the New Testament. Supernatural conceptions, an angelic choir, a moving star, a virgin birth, mass healings, the dead being resuscitated, and on and on it goes. Jesus' whole ministry seems to be based on two major components: preaching and acts of power (italics here and in all Bible quotations are mine):

- 'And he went throughout all Galilee, teaching in their synagogues and proclaiming the gospel of the kingdom and *healing* every disease and every affliction among the people' (Matt. 4:23).
- 'And Jesus went throughout all the cities and villages, teaching in their synagogues and proclaiming the gospel of the kingdom and *healing* every disease and every affliction' (Matt. 9:35).
- 'When the crowds learned it, they followed him, and he welcomed them and spoke to them of the kingdom of God and cured those who needed *healing*' (Luke 9:11).

Along with using this as a mark of his unique Messianic claims, he trains his followers to do similar things. On several occasions when commissioning his followers to preach the gospel, Jesus says this should be accompanied by signs and wonders: healing the sick, driving out demons or even raising the dead (see Matt. 10:7–8; Luke 9:2; 10:9). It seems fairly clear that God's intention for the church was that it would be a place where his power was evident. The Apostle Paul even declared: '*By word and deed*, by the power of signs and wonders, by the power of the Spirit of God – so that from

Jerusalem and all the way around to Illyricum I have fulfilled
the ministry of the gospel of Christ' (Rom. 15:18b–19).

This would not be limited to healing alone: Paul writes
to the Corinthians that they should expect such a level of
prophetic revelation that if an unbeliever entered the meeting
the secrets of his heart would be disclosed, 'and so, falling on
his face, he will worship God and declare that God is really
among you' (1 Cor. 14:25).

COME AND ENCOUNTER GOD

Until recently, not one church that I have been part of
regularly experienced these things. Unbelievers who came
would usually receive a warm welcome and maybe even an
invitation to lunch, but rarely if ever would they encounter
God in a tangible way. In recent times things have changed.
A lady in our church was out in town when she felt God ask
her to look for a person with a certain name: Janet. Throughout her time in town she was expecting to find this lady but
never did. That Sunday she was serving on the ministry team,
and at the end a lady who was there for the first time came
up for prayer. She said that her name was Janet. Our ministry
team member became very excited and said, 'Janet, God told
me that I would meet you, and I've been praying for you this
week!' Having already been moved by the sermon, the lady
wanted to receive Christ, and the ministry team member was
only too glad to oblige! Another young man came to church
after an invitation from someone in his football team. As far
as I know he had never been to church before. A word of
knowledge was given about a knee injury.[1] The young man

responded, was prayed for, became free of pain and gave his life to Christ.

On another occasion, I took a friend to another church where I was speaking so that he could help me pray for people. During the meeting I asked him if he had any prophetic words for the people gathered. He asked a young man to stand and said to him, 'You don't belong here.' Inwardly I groaned. This was not a good start. My friend continued, 'What's more, you don't belong in this country. I feel God is calling you overseas – maybe to Africa. No! I get the word "Lebanon".' There were a few more words that were a little more encouraging, and then the young man sat down. A few weeks later we heard the rest of the story. This was the first time he had been to the church: he was visiting family. The night before coming to the meeting, he had said to his grandfather, 'Grandad, I don't know if you think it's weird, but I don't feel like I belong in the UK. I feel like I should go travelling. Would you think I was crazy if I went to Lebanon?' We also found out that at the end of the meeting he had given his life to Christ.

These are not isolated incidents. We have regularly seen Christians and not yet Christians who come among us having some kind of encounter with God. Grown men who don't even believe in God weep uncontrollably in worship. Children are healed. People experience peace. Recently one lady visited our night shelter and was prayed for. The lump in her breast vanished immediately and her painful back condition disappeared. She gave her life to Christ and was at the Alpha course the next evening, telling everyone, 'I didn't believe this stuff, but listen to what's happened to me!'

Jesus, Paul and the model of the early church teach us that these things should be the regular experience of every local church. The early church flourished against all the odds in a society with a huge variety of competing religious ideologies. Surely this was because they followed the simple formula that Jesus had given them: preach the gospel, heal the sick, love God, love one another. If we want to have the same impact on our planet we would be foolish to try to succeed in any other way than that laid out by Jesus. Yes, the church should be incredibly loving. Yes, it should be incredibly servant-hearted. Yes, it should be relevant to its culture and yes, it should be pure and devoted. All these things should be true of the church today. But if it should be all those things, it should also be a place where the power of God is evident. It should be a place where the gospel is preached and demonstrated in both a practical and a 'God must have done that' kind of way. There are a multitude of competing philosophies and religious ideas, and Christianity is just one of them. Why should anyone believe that we speak the truth as opposed to any other sincere believers of another faith? The truth, love and power of the church must be head and shoulders above that which can be found anywhere else.

Many churches today could tick all of these boxes, apart from the last one. Where the New Testament disciples seemed to preach a very simple gospel backed up by the Spirit's power, it seems that the church today, particularly in the West, often preaches a very complicated gospel backed up with little power. Where have we gone wrong?

WORLDVIEW WARS

Since the Enlightenment of the eighteenth century, Western culture has become increasingly naturalistic in its worldview. This view believes that only natural forces exist in the world: there is nothing supernatural. In the Enlightenment, many of the false superstitions that had dogged previous generations were rejected. At the same time, however, our forefathers also rejected any possibility of supernatural intervention in the natural world. This thinking has even infected the church. It's hard to become a Christian without some belief in the supernatural: the idea of God raising Jesus from the dead as a foundational reality makes this a tough feat to pull off (even though some have tried). For many, though, even after coming to faith in Christ it is hard to let go of naturalism completely. Often God's supernatural activity is reduced to one period in history when the Bible was being formed. It is claimed that he no longer intervenes in this way.

To confuse things further, those who have pressed through to embrace a biblical belief in the supernatural activity of God have had a difficult time on their hands. Recent years will illustrate it well enough. The Pentecostal movement of the early twentieth century was marked by incredible supernatural power, but also by many excesses and unbiblical practices. Among other things, children died when their parents denied them medical help and waited instead for God to heal them. The healing movement of the 1940s saw some of the most powerfully anointed men and women that have been documented in recent years. Yet many of these too fell, with unbiblical theologies, moral failures or excesses. For example, A.A. Allen, one of the greatest healers of that period, who regularly saw chronic cases healed by God's power, was reported to have died at the age of 59 of liver failure caused by acute alcoholism.[2] This and other similar horror stories caused people to grow weary and move to 'safer' models. Even some recent moves of God have added to the confusion and withdrawal, when clear power has been seen to be mixed with moral failure and unhelpful practices and preaching. The history books show that the church can and at times does move in power, but this has rarely been demonstrated in a sustainable model. Moral failure, unbiblical teaching or simply pure exhaustion has derailed moves towards restoring the church to its former glory and significance. Equally, even when the church has got it right, it seems that only one or two people have moved in significant power, while the rest warmed seats and watched.

Is it Even Possible?

With this backdrop, our God-given mandate to facilitate a church where the presence and power of God are seen is a sobering and humbling one. Is it even possible without blowing up the church? It's hard enough to see God's power move in church meetings in a sustainable way, but our instruction is to see it break through the walls of the church and out onto the streets. After all, that is where most of the New Testament miracles are documented as having happened, and if we really want to see that kind of church established again it couldn't possibly just involve a Sunday morning. Also, I would not have been satisfied with just one or two people 'doing the stuff', as this was clearly not the biblical pattern. I had long been fond of John Wimber's phrase 'Everyone gets to play,' and it must surely apply to this ministry as much as to any other area. I was discussing this a few years ago with a friend, who exclaimed, 'Simon, pretty much anyone who moves in this stuff ends in either moral failure or theological error.' I couldn't deny his analysis of history. Many of those who tried before have been shipwrecked. It was therefore with some trepidation that we embarked on this journey.

The journey is still in process. I do not write this as one who has arrived. But I have observed a significant shift in our church community. Our culture has shifted in love, generosity, joy and honour in dramatic ways. Fear, disappointment and unbelief have started to give way to courage, hope and faith. Deliverance, prophecy, healing and acts of God's power, along with an increase in salvation response, are now a far greater feature of our life together.

For example, at the beginning of 2008 we set some five-year goals as a church. One of them was that we would see thirty miracles on the streets. As we announced the goal, the whole church audibly gave a gasp: not one of faith, but a gasp of unbelief. The reason was simple: at that point we had not seen anyone healed on the streets and only very few in church meetings. How would it be possible to see thirty people who were not Christians healed, one every other month over the course of five years, and not in church meetings? We pressed on. January and February came and went, and soon we were in the middle of March. I began to panic slightly – we were behind already! Then suddenly we got one. A guy in the church was sitting on a train on the way home from work when he noticed the woman opposite was popping pills. He began to sweat, as he knew the Holy Spirit was prompting him to pray. After a few moments he found the courage to ask her what was wrong. She said that her neck was in agony. He stumbled out a brief explanation and offered prayer. Much to his surprise she accepted! After a brief prayer, he asked her to move her neck, and she said it was now completely pain-free. He related later that he was not sure who was most shocked. As they alighted from the train, coincidentally at the same station, her husband met her on the platform. She ran up to him and proclaimed, 'This man just healed me,' thus verifying that she wasn't simply being polite on the train as he had feared. He falteringly tried to correct her theology and gave glory to God![3]

One soon became two, and then we saw a third. Momentum built when we saw a whole group of teenagers healed in the town centre. The impossible had suddenly become possible. What really excited me was that it was not just a few leaders but people right across the church who began to pray for friends, strangers and colleagues. At the end of the year we took stock. We had been asking God for thirty in five years, but we realized that we had seen sixty-nine unbelievers healed outside the context of Christian meetings in just one year. Our culture had shifted. We quickly updated our goal to three hundred people healed on the streets in five years, and we were delighted to exceed it by far, losing count on the way.

It has not all been plain sailing. There have been ebbs and flows, good times and struggles, wins and losses. However, this book attempts to tell the story of the culture shift that has begun to take place in our lives. It is written for every church leader, small group leader or individual who's passionate about transforming their church, family or personal culture to such an extent that they see whole communities of individuals moving in power and advancing the kingdom of God. This is not a book of magic formulas. I'm simply attempting to write as faithfully as I can the journey of culture transformation that we have experienced, in the hope that God will use some of the principles to spur you on in your own journey. It began in an unexpected way: repentance.

Notes

[1] When God speaks to us and gives us information that we could not possibly have known, we believe that this is the word or 'utterance' of knowledge, a subset of the prophetic gift, that Paul talks about in 1 Corinthians 12:8.

[2] There is some dispute over the circumstances of Allen's death, as he was a target of much criticism and attack and, as some have suggested, it is possible that the facts surrounding his death were manipulated to discredit him. However, I think this is the most likely explanation of his death.

[3] You can listen to this story, as originally told, at http://www.kingsarms.org/cm/content/view/123/78/.

2

MAN IN THE MIRROR

From that time Jesus began to preach, saying, 'Repent, for the kingdom of heaven is at hand.'

Matthew 4:17

Although we firmly believed that God's power and activity should be the hallmark of every healthy local church, we had few models to follow. When you have never seen anyone healed of a physical sickness it's hard to know how to start. Like a bleary-eyed reporter hunting for the big scoop, I began to track down stories from anywhere and everywhere, dragging them back to Bedford to inspire and provoke. During one Sunday sermon I told the story of a family who had all been healed of food intolerances. The entire family of six had suffered from wheat and dairy intolerances, and they were all very limited in their diet. One day they had received prayer and were all instantaneously healed. To check out the healing, they went to a pizza restaurant that night and ate themselves into deep-pan oblivion: a true test of a genuine miracle, no doubt! 'If God is doing these things elsewhere in the UK,' I declared, 'we can have faith for him to do the same things here.' It sounded good in a sermon, and the church was suitably inspired – so much so that after the meeting a lady approached me. 'I have food intolerances,' she said. 'Would you pray for me?' My initial response on the inside was disappointment: I felt like saying, 'Why do you have to ruin a great story by asking me to do the same thing?' There I was, stewing in the glory juices of my own wonderful sermon, and someone was bringing me down to earth with an uncomfortable thud. With the echo of my own words, 'Believe God,' resounding in my head I could hardly refuse to pray, could I? The lady later told me that the look on my face was more fear than faith. However, I dutifully prayed, expecting nothing to happen, just as I had many times before. The next Sunday she came running up to me. 'Simon, God has done something amazing. I've eaten things this week that I've never eaten before in my life.' 'Really?' I said, incredulously. Neither before nor after did I have any faith, but God had still worked.

As I walked away from the lady, the Holy Spirit placed his red-hot poker of a finger into my heart. 'You are riddled with unbelief,' he prodded. 'Ouch.' But I knew that he was correct in the way that God has a habit of being. How could I lead the church forward into these things when my own heart was so sceptical? I had many promises that God would heal. I had every confidence from Scripture that God could heal. Yet my heart remained stubborn and hard. The reality sank home: before I could help others to change, I had to change. Before I could be used by God to transform the outside world I had to let God transform my inside world. I have subsequently learned that when God wants to use a person or a group of people, he will often start in this place. The biblical word for it is one we do not savour: repentance.

REPENTANCE IS FOUNDATIONAL

This place, repentance, is where Jesus began his work with his disciples. 'Repent, for the kingdom of heaven is at hand,' declared Jesus, echoing what his cousin John had said previously. We see this theme repeated in Scripture again and again (Matt. 11:20; Mark 1:15; Luke 13:3–5). James summed it up when he wrote, 'Draw near to God, and he will draw near to you. Cleanse your hands, you sinners, and purify your hearts, you double-minded' (Jas 4:8). This is written not to unbelievers but to believers. Far from repentance being a 'once at conversion' experience, it is an ongoing process for the follower of Christ.

There is a common misunderstanding concerning the meaning of repentance. Most people, when asked to define it, would say that it means 'to say sorry to God' for something that we have done wrong. One dictionary definition of the word expresses this as 'to feel or express sincere regret or remorse'.

While it's not a bad thing to say sorry, and feeling or expressing remorse is to be applauded, this actually does not get to the heart of what Jesus or John the Baptist meant when they talked about repentance. The word used in the gospels is exclusively the Greek *metanoeo*, which means 'to think differently, to reconsider'. It has less to do with saying or being sorry and more to do with changing the way you think about things. In the context of Matthew 4:17 it is concerning God and the kingdom of God that Jesus is calling for new thinking. Repentance is a total mind-shift concerning the things of God. If we are to see the expression of the kingdom in our day that we desire to see, our thinking must change. And not just our thinking: John the Baptist called the religious leaders who came to him 'a brood of vipers' because they simply wanted a quick-fix 'get right with God' rather than the complete mind-shift that would lead to a total change of behaviour. That stings.

THIS IS FOR ALL OF US

We saw the effect of such a mind-shift illustrated in our church when I began leading in 2003. The previous senior leader had left to start a new church in another town. Neither Paul nor I, the other two on the leadership team, felt that we were capable of being the senior leader, but we thought that we could perhaps do a passable job if we were to lead it together. There did not seem to be a better option, so we began. The church had grown very quickly when it started in 1992, but in more recent years the growth had levelled off. The church was not growing, and we had no idea why. During a prayer time the Lord spoke quite clearly to us: 'The kingdom, like a seed, has life within itself. Remove everything that is stopping it growing, and it will grow.' This thought was revolution-ary enough for us to know it could not have originated from us. Over the next few years we systematically went through every area of church life and removed or changed the things that we thought might be preventing the church growing. We changed the preaching style, the welcome process, the team structure, the leadership structure, the children's ministry, the youth ministry, the small group structure and style, and the worship. In fact there wasn't much that we didn't change.

Sure enough, just as God had said, the church began and has continued to grow.

This principle of kingdom growth applies just as much to the individual believer as it does to the corporate church. John's gospel records the occasion when Jesus attended the great feast of Pentecost. At a significant moment Jesus stood up and cried out, 'If anyone thirsts, let him come to me and drink. Whoever believes in me, as the Scripture has said, "Out of his heart will flow rivers of living water"' (John 7:37b–38). John also adds his own explanatory comment: 'Now this he said about the Spirit, whom those who believed in him were to receive, for as yet the Spirit had not been given, because Jesus was not yet glorified' (John 7:39).

Jesus' promise, then, is that every believer will have these rivers flowing out of his or her heart. These rivers are the rivers of the Spirit, promised for every follower of Christ.

As I travel around various churches, however, I find that most Christians are hungry for a greater reality of these Spirit-rivers flowing through them. Their experience, many would confess, feels more like a trickle than a multiplicity of rivers. Did Jesus lie? Not possible. Did he exaggerate? No. So if we have the rivers as Jesus promised that we would, but it feels more like a trickle than multiple rivers, only one thing is possible. Something must be blocking the Spirit's flow. Just as rivers in the natural can be blocked or dammed with large rocks, I believe it's these spiritual 'rocks' that Jesus was talking about when he called for those who would follow him to repent in order to see the kingdom. I believe this is the reason why Jesus started with the message of repentance. He knew that once he was glorified, everyone would have their own 'river source' placed within them in the form of the indwelling Holy Spirit. However, those who had not had the full depth of repentance would always block the flow of the living river source placed inside them. Those who experienced the fullest extent of repentance and 'mind-shift' would have a powerful, saturating, satisfying river flowing out of them. Leave the rocks in place, however, and the river will be little more than a trickle.

Does this align with the rest of Scripture? Do we, mere humans, have the ability to block or resist the almighty Holy Spirit? The answer is a resounding yes. Again and again, Scripture warns us not to resist the Spirit (Acts 7:51), not to quench the Spirit (1 Thess. 5:19) and not to grieve the Holy Spirit (Eph. 4:30). Clearly, although he is sovereign, in some ways and in some areas the Spirit is expecting and wanting a level of partnership with us, without which he will not move to the full extent that he desires to. It's the same principle expressed in another way: the kingdom has life in itself, and we just need to get everything out of the way of that life.

We often and correctly associate repentance with salvation: a massive mind-shift is required before we can even begin this new life with God. But the mistake made by many in the church is to feel that once this initial repentance has been undertaken, our repentance is over. Scripture and experience should show us otherwise. Paul demonstrates this truth when he says (writing to Christians), 'Be transformed by the renewal of your mind' (Rom. 12:2). An ongoing mind-shift (repentance) is necessary for the fullest transformation possible.

In the matter of the power of the Spirit in my own life, my mind certainly needed renewing. I was in a mess! For many years I had been confused about why the church in the UK in particular and the Western church in general seemed to be lacking the same vibrancy and demonstrable power that I read about in the Bible. Clearly there had been a few individuals who saw such power, and even some seasons of revival, but my everyday experience of church did not in any way match the one that I read about in the pages of Scripture. As I began to read more about the church in the developing world, I began to see that they were experiencing the power of God today. This left me even more puzzled. Was it because they had more faith? Was it because they were poor and so needed supernatural assistance, while we didn't because we had modern medical science? I just couldn't figure it out. It wasn't just in the area of healing that I saw little evidence of God's power. The gifts of the Spirit that I saw demonstrated were good but often not in the 'fall on your knees' category. The sense of awe often reported in the Scriptures was something I had rarely seen. This was no criticism of the Christians that I met, many of whom were hungry for more. It was as though we had our foot on the accelerator, but the engine was simply not delivering. Eventually I assigned the whole area to the box labelled 'God has sovereignly withheld his power from us right now and I don't know why.' In my mind, the problem was clearly at God's end. Although I had a hunger for more of God's presence and power, I had no idea how to get it and knew no one in the UK that I could learn from. There were some models, but they all seemed to be 'travelling ministries' who would come to the occasional meeting. Mostly I observed that the church had a brief 'blip' of faith for the duration of a meeting or two but was then back to 'business as usual'.

THE TRANSFORMATION

Two incidents began the transformation and mind-shift that I needed. The first came through a story I heard from a church in America. I was in a meeting when I heard what has since been affectionately named 'the doughnut story'. A young man went late at night to buy doughnuts at a local supermarket. While in the checkout queue he noticed that the lady in front of him was wearing two hearing aids. He felt the Lord prompt him to ask her if he could pray with her for healing. The lady agreed, and as the young man prayed her hearing immediately improved to the point where she removed the aids and, weeping, began to declare, 'God has healed me.' The lady serving at the checkout had observed this and was also overcome with emotion, saying, 'Surely this is God.' The young man agreed: 'Yes, this is God.' He also said, 'I believe God wants to heal some others in this supermarket. Can I use your loudspeaker?' She agreed, and he spoke to the supermarket. 'Attention, shoppers. God has just come into this supermarket and healed a lady at checkout 10.' He asked the lady to share her story over the loudspeaker system. He then declared, 'God wants to do more. There's someone here who needs a new hip, and God is speaking to me about "carpal tunnel syndrome".' It was late at night, and this incident was so peculiar that all twenty to thirty people in the store gathered to witness it. A lady in a wheelchair pushed through the crowd, saying, 'I'm the new hip.' The young man prayed for her and she leapt out of the chair, declaring that she was free of pain. Another man said that he had carpal tunnel syndrome and needed healing. He, too, was prayed for and became pain-free. A few others were healed, and then the young man decided that as he had a crowd he was going to share the good news of Jesus. He spoke to those gathered, complete with an 'eyes closed, heads bowed' response time. The young man led seven people to Christ that day.[1]

When I heard this story, something shifted in me. I know the USA quite well, including small-town American life. It's not so very different from life in the town where I live. I suddenly realized that if God can do this in America, he can do it anywhere. Every argument as to why God was moving in other centuries and other locations than our own evaporated. The light dawned as I realized that the problem was not at God's end but at mine! The mind-shift had begun.[2]

The second incident occurred in my own family. My wife had a serious back condition in the early days of our marriage, and it was exacerbated by pregnancy and the birth of our first two children. Her back would regularly lock up and she would be bedridden, sometimes for seven to ten days at a time. I had to take time off work to look after our young children every three months or so. We were recommended an excellent osteopath who soon diagnosed the problem. One of Caroline's legs was one inch shorter than the other. The small group that we belonged to had been challenged by stories that we had heard from elsewhere, and so we began to pray. Caroline told her osteopath about this, and the osteopath, who was not a Christian, said, 'I'm afraid you can pray as much as you like, but I wouldn't hold out much hope, because your problem is "actual".' When asked what that meant, she explained that sometimes legs are different lengths because of tightness in the muscles. In Caroline's case, however, the bone in one leg was shorter than that in the other. This posed a significant problem. We continued to pray, finding strength in God after every disappointment when she wasn't healed. I told our church that I would continue to pray for Caroline even if it meant doing so for the rest of our lives. We were committed.

In the coming weeks I became aware that Terry Virgo, the leader of our family of churches, was speaking in Cambridge, a city very close to ours. I had recently seen Terry pray for a whole row of people one at a time, many with one leg shorter than the other, and had seen several legs grow in front of my eyes. These were the first 'miracles' that I had actually witnessed. I knew that I had to take Caroline to the meeting and ask Terry to pray for her. I remember vividly walking down a street in Cambridge, wrestling with the potential disappointment. 'What if she's not healed?' 'But what if she is?' 'But what if she's not?' Back and forth rebounded my thoughts. At the end of the meeting there was no space or time for a ministry time, so I begged Terry to pray for my wife. He took us into a side room and sat Caroline down. He lifted her legs, and the small group gathered could clearly see a difference in their length. I decided to keep my eyes open to see what would happen. As Terry prayed, right before my eyes I saw the leg move. First it grew longer than the other and then it shrank back to the same length! To confirm it, Caroline immediately opened her eyes and said that she had felt what seemed like a finger run down the top of her thigh, from the hip to the knee. Terry had been holding her feet and I was watching the whole time, so I knew that no one had touched her leg at all. With great celebration we returned home. This was not just a healing; it was a miracle, something impossible without divine intervention.

Days later Caroline visited the osteopath again and begged her to re-measure her legs. She was very reluctant but agreed to do so, more to humour Caroline than anything else. With shock she was able to confirm that Caroline's legs were now the same length. She also confirmed that it was Caroline's thigh-bone that had needed to grow, something we had not known before and the exact location of the curious sensation that Caroline had felt during prayer. The osteopath attended church that Sunday, and although she has not yet become a Christian she has subsequently seen two other people who are part of King's Arms have the same miracle! Again my mind shifted as I realized that seeing the active power of God was possible, even in small-town England.[3]

These two incidents illustrate something of our journey. A journey that has been punctuated by experiences of repentance or 'mind-shifts' throughout its course that have radically transformed the way we think and removed some major rocks that were blocking the flow of the river of God in our lives. As I've subsequently looked at the way that Jesus led his disciples to repentance, I've observed some surprising parallels.

D.L. Moody wrote, 'I believe firmly, that the moment our hearts are emptied of pride and selfishness and ambition and self seeking, and everything that is contrary to God's law, the Holy Ghost will come and fill every corner of our hearts;

but if we are full of pride and conceit, and ambition and self seeking, and pleasure and the world, there is no room for the Spirit of God; and I believe many a man is praying to God to fill him when he is full already with something else. Before we pray that God would fill us, I believe we ought to pray Him to empty us.'[4]

He expresses the same point that we've discovered. The Spirit of God wants to flow like a river through you and me. If we are filled with the Spirit and the river is not flowing as fast or as powerfully as we want it to, the problem is not at God's end, it is at ours. Something must be blocking the flow of the river. These rocks in the river must be removed if we want to become churches filled with sustainable power.

IT'S CONTAGIOUS

We have seen the remarkable transformation of ordinary believers through this repentance process. One retired gentleman was travelling down to our church for training. He knew his car mechanic well, and after a service the man asked him why he was suddenly putting so many miles on his car, given that he was retired. Our friend replied that he was doing a training course in Bedford. 'What are you being trained in?' the mechanic inquired. Our friend paused. He would definitely describe himself as reluctant in sharing his faith. But several weeks of training had led him on this journey of repentance and he was beginning to change his thinking. 'Well,' he began, 'suppose in the future you were sick. Suppose you wanted someone to pray for you. This course is preparing me so that you could call me and I would come and pray for you.' 'How interesting,' the mechanic replied. 'What if I was sick now? Would you pray for me now?' 'Er, I guess so,' faltered our friend. 'Do you expect God to heal you?' 'Of course,' replied his mechanic, 'why shouldn't I?'

It's events like these that convince me that God has a sense of humour. A non-Christian mechanic provoking a Christian to faith is a moment of pure comedy genius. It turned out that the mechanic had a shoulder injury from which he had suffered for many years. Our friend laid hands on it, prayed as quick a prayer as possible, and left as soon as he could to save further embarrassment. A number of weeks later he decided to return to the garage to check with the mechanic. 'How's the shoulder?' he dared himself to ask. 'Do you know what?' the mechanic exclaimed. 'A short while after you prayed I noticed that I had no more pain from my shoulder, and I haven't had any since. My wife couldn't understand how it could go away on its own, as I've had it for so long. Then I remembered you had prayed for me. I've also got a bad wrist: would you pray for that too?' And so he took a small step forward on his journey to find Christ.

This is just one story from literally a hundred or more that I could use to illustrate the change that has taken place during and following this journey. I've divided this book into two parts. In the first part we shall look at this issue of repentance and how we have been led to remove some significant rocks from our hearts. In the second part we'll look at the other key transformations that we have seen over the past five or six years as we've sought to become a community of people who see sustainable power. The first part of this book is 'destruction' – tearing down the rocks and barriers of the heart that would prevent a people from living the life God has called them to in a sustainable way. The second part is 'construction' – building on a foundation that can sustain this life. Let's go to work.

NOTES

[1] A version of this story is recorded in an interview with the young man concerned at
http://www.missionsmag.com/heartHole.htm.

[2] A better reading of Scripture could have taught me this before. Most of Jesus' most powerful works were not done in Jerusalem but in very small-town Israel.

[3] Although vastly improved, Caroline still suffers from back pain and is not completely healed, as yet.

[4] D.L. Moody, *Secret Power* (Fig, 2012). Many evangelical and some charismatic Christians believe that the Spirit is given fully to every believer at conversion as a gift of grace. To them, Moody could be accused of taking away God's grace in the gift. Other charismatic and most Pentecostal Christians believe that while there is a deposit of the Spirit at conversion and the Holy Spirit dwells within all believers, there is also a second 'filling' or empowering that happens after conversion. They would say this is again a gift of grace, freely given in response to our faith. Do Moody's comments and the things that I am saying somehow undermine the fact that it is by grace and through faith that we receive the Holy Spirit? Without shrinking back from necessary debate and conflict, I want to leave room in this book for Christians of both

theological convictions. I would align myself with this second group, but whichever view you take, I believe Moody's comment can fit into your theology and help explain the massive disparity between the power that we see in the New Testament church and what we see in much of the church today. It's not just how the river of the Spirit is placed within us that is at stake – this is clearly by grace through faith. The point is that once the river is there, how powerfully is it able to flow through you and me?

3

LEAN ON ME

If you then, who are evil, know how to give good gifts to your children, how much more will your Father who is in heaven give good things to those who ask him!

Matthew 7:11

In 2004, the church seemed to be flourishing. Paul and I had been leading for a year or two together, and although there were the inevitable areas to improve, overall we were in a healthy place. Sunday attendance was strong for the UK, and the church was growing both numerically and in the quality of disciples. People were becoming followers of Jesus fairly regularly, and finances were stable. The quintessentially bland English expression 'not too bad' would be a fair assessment of church life. Of course, good can so easily be the enemy of great, and as a community we had a deep desire for more. We had an overriding sense that surely there must be more than this. Was this all that God intended for the church? The number of lost people coming to faith was a trickle compared with the ocean of need in our town. The night shelter and follow-on hostel that we ran for the homeless were excellent, but too many of those coming through needed greater breakthrough than we were seeing happen. Our Sunday meetings were strong, but too often they lacked that sense of vibrant life that one expects when reading the pages of Acts. The sense of awe, the sense that 'God is in the house', was not there to the same degree that deep down we longed for.

One area of my personal life also stood out as being in need of help: my marriage. Caroline and I had been having difficulties since we were married in 1999. Not huge difficulties, but enough to leave us with a general sense of dissatisfaction. It had taken us five years to work out that she thought most of the major issues were mine. I, in turn, was absolutely confident that my issues were a paper-cut compared to her open-heart-surgery-requiring problems. In the summer of 2004 Caroline went to visit her parents in Oklahoma City and during her stay decided to receive some personal prayer ministry from Diane, a lady known in her parents' church as a 'guru' in these things. Caroline went expecting to air many of her grievances against me, in response to which Diane would agree with her and then give her some wisdom on how to deal with her difficult English husband. As it turned out, the Lord had other ideas. My name was mentioned during the numerous sessions, but Diane, led by the Holy Spirit, gave Caroline what can only be described as spiritual and emotional open heart surgery. As I suspected! However, such was the lasting change in my wife when she returned from the USA that even though on the outside I was smugly vindicated, on the inside I knew that whatever had happened to Caroline also, and almost definitely more so, needed to happen to me.

Six months later I had my chance. It was Christmas 2005. Diane had agreed to see me over two days in the run-up to Christmas. I made myself comfortable on Diane's sofa and waited to begin. I can only describe this day as the spiritual version of the time when I deep-cleansed the barbecue after I had forgotten to clean it before the winter and opened the lid six months later to find two inches of green 'hair' growing in the bottom of it. Hard work, but what a difference! Layers of grime and muck that had stained my soul and been encrusted after years of neglect in the deep recesses of my heart were cleaned out that day, and I still feel the effects of it as I write this some years later. The next morning Diane had invited another man, Brother Nelson, to pray with us. I'm not sure why he was called Brother Nelson, because he wasn't a monk, but we happily settled into calling each other Brother Nelson and Brother Simon. After an hour of talking, Brother Nelson came to what he had discerned was a key issue for me. 'Have you ever repented of the sin of pride, Brother Simon?' he asked. My immediate response was, 'But I'm not a proud person.' He did not look pleased. Apparently, this was the wrong answer. 'It's not the pride of haughtiness or arrogance,' he pressed, 'but the pride of self-reliance.' In a moment it seemed as if the room grew very still. The presence of the Holy Spirit was palpable as I had a flashback of the first time in my life when I had taken the road of self-reliance. I knew that it was the first of many. Whenever I had read about pride in the Bible I had always presumed that it meant arrogance and neatly slipped myself off the hook. Suddenly, horrendously, on Diane's sofa I realized that I was guilty of pride, and in a mountain-sized way. I fell on my knees under the conviction of the Holy Spirit and received massive freedom from a spiritual stronghold that I had never seen was there.

I returned home transformed. Some people even said that I looked different. I'm hoping that they thought I was more handsome. As a leadership we decided that for the sake of authenticity I should tell the church what had happened, and that Sunday I did so. Breakthrough occurred for many as they began to see that it was acceptable in Christian community to be open about your failings and weakness. The Apostle John wrote that if we walk in the light as Jesus did, it opens the way for a deep level of fellowship with one another and also in some way enables the blood of Christ to have its full effect in cleansing us from sin (1 John 1:7). We've observed this, as our culture moved to a new place of authenticity that day.[1] As I've told this story on many occasions since then, I've found that many, especially pastors and leaders, walk into a new level of freedom from the pride of self-reliance. We shall see in this chapter how it relates to the issue of sustainable power.

Self-reliance is not a term that we find in Scripture. However, the evidence of it is seen throughout the lives of the disciples, and if we look carefully we can see how Jesus dealt with it. It's rooted in an orphan heart, a heart that sees itself as being alone in the world. It is not possible to sustain the power of God within the church while living as functional orphans. Firstly, the orphan heart has not truly connected to the source of life and power: the Father. Secondly, the orphan heart is cut off from the Father's love that makes a safe context for power. When a Samaritan town rejected Jesus, his disciples James and John, flushed with ministry success and an understanding of their new-found power, wanted to nuke the place (Luke 9:54). They had power, but their orphan hearts were still remote from the Father's love for lost people: a deadly combination. Jesus worked hard to lead his disciples to the place of repentance or mind-shift on this issue. We see it primarily through his teaching that God is a Father. Although Jesus wasn't the first to call God Father, he was the most extensive and radical in his use of this name. In the Old Testament God is called Father fifteen times; in the New Testament he is called Father 245 times. A foundational revelation that Jesus brought was that we are not alone: we have a Father. Interestingly, the only story we have from Jesus' childhood is the incident when he identified that his primary calling was to be in his 'Father's house' (Luke 2:49).

THE DISCIPLES' JOURNEY

Jesus sought to bring his disciples into the fullness of the revelation of the Father. He taught them that they needed to think differently when relating to unbelievers: they were to love their enemies. The reason? 'So that you may be sons of *your Father* who is in heaven' (Matt. 5:44–45). They were representing their heavenly Father.

He told them that they must think differently about where they looked for approval and not look to be applauded by men. Instead, he told them, 'Do not let your left hand know what your right hand is doing' when they were giving to the needy. Why? Because then '*your Father* who sees in secret will reward you' (Matt. 6:3–4).

He told them that they must think differently about how they prayed, because they were not trying to impress a distant deity with long, rambling prayers. Why not? Because '*your Father* knows what you need before you ask him' (Matt. 6:8).

He taught them that they needed to think differently about provision. Why? Because even a flawed dad looks after his kids to some degree, and so 'how much more will *your Father* who is in heaven give good things to those who ask him' (Matt. 7:11).

He taught them not even to worry about life and death, because not one sparrow 'will fall to the ground apart from *your Father*' (Matt. 10:29).

When faced with a massive food shortage, Jesus told the disciples to feed the crowd, clearly in an effort to demonstrate that they had the resources available if they would just think differently about the Father. When they balked, Jesus showed them how it was to be done. The first thing he did was to look up to heaven, to his Father (Luke 9:13–17).

When Jesus was dealing with a difficult healing of a deaf man with a speech impediment in a public place, Mark records again that 'looking up to heaven, he sighed and said to him, "Ephphatha," that is, "Be opened." And his ears were opened, his tongue was released, and he spoke plainly' (Mark 7:34–35). Again we see the first look is to the Father.

When he sends the disciples out on a ministry trip for the first time, he tells them not to take anything with them. Why? Perhaps to show them that the Father will provide (Mark 6:8).

Lest they become confused about the source of his wisdom and power, Jesus declares that he only ever does what he sees the Father doing and says what he hears the Father saying (John 5:19).

The list goes on and on, culminating probably in Jesus' most powerful parable of all, that of the prodigal son, which might perhaps be better named the parable of the prodigal or 'extravagant' father (Luke 15:11). This journey of mind-shift was to teach the disciples that they were not orphans but had an intimate connection with a loving and benevolent Father. Even if they strayed, the Father would be there for them when they returned. They did not have to rely on themselves, because they could lean on God their Father. In fact, at the end of his earthly ministry, perhaps out of concern that this foundation might be undone, Jesus makes the declaration, 'I will not leave you as orphans; I will come to you' (John 14:18).

FUNCTIONAL ORPHANS

Even though many Christians know these truths, they live as functional orphans. In my experience, this is especially true of those in church leadership. I know, because I've spoken to many, and because I was one. The story of my 'session' with Brother Nelson at the start of this chapter should be enough to illustrate something of the journey of repentance that I have been on. Since that moment I've realized how often I switch into 'orphan' mode. This issue is critical for the church on the journey towards sustainable power, because when we initially begin to see success, greater needs will arise. If we have not dealt with the issue that the source of provision and life is the Father rather than us, it will be very easy to lose our way or even be crushed under the weight of the need.

Recently the stress concerning the financial situation of our church building began to escalate. I knew that God had promised to provide, but time was running out. Where was he? What was the delay? It was here that I stumbled again upon

a story that I had read many times before. It was the story of
George Müller, the man who started numerous orphanages in
the Bristol area of England long before it was fashionable to
do so. One incident jumped from the page. It was the famous
story of when Müller comes down to breakfast in the orphan
house with three hundred or so orphans present and realizes
that there is nothing for breakfast. He gathers the children to
pray, and then there is a knock at the door. Outside is the local
baker, who says that God woke him at 2 a.m. and told him that
the orphans had no breakfast and that he was to bake bread for
them. A few minutes later there is another knock. It's the milk
delivery man, whose cart has broken down outside the orphanage and who asks if Müller can use the milk in his orphanage,
because he needs to offload the weight of the milk from the
cart. Thus breakfast is provided. I've read this story many times
before, but this time one line jumped out at me and pierced me
to the core. When Müller comes downstairs and realizes that
there is no breakfast, the first thing he says is, 'Come and see
what God will do.' He then gathers the children to pray and
simply says, 'Dear God, we thank you for what you are going
to give us to eat. Amen.' As I read these words afresh, I realized
my orphan heart was still not fully transformed. My mind
was not fully shifted. Müller's heart had so changed, his mind
had so shifted, that his first, default response when presented
with a massive problem was, 'Let's see what the Father will do.'
Instead of spiralling into self-pity, or hurrying into activity and
self-reliance, Müller's transformed mind saw this difficulty as
an opportunity for his Father to demonstrate his goodness.
He knew that the source of everything that he needed was not
himself but his Father.[2]

Self-reliance and the orphan spirit are massive rocks obstructing the river-flow of the Holy Spirit, because they push us back into our limited resources instead of God's unlimited supply. As we repent and mind-shift from this place, the river begins to flow and things begin to change around us. William Booth, writing of how he was inspired to help the starving, jobless millions of England in the mid-nineteenth century, said, 'If I did not feel my Father's hand in the darkness, and hear His voice in the silence of the night watches bidding me put my hand to this thing, I would shrink back dismayed. But as it is, I dare not.'[3]

ORPHAN SYMPTOMS

Living as a functional orphans has a dramatic effect on our behaviour as Christians. The gospels give us prime examples of this in the differing ways that Jesus and the Pharisees respond to and think about God, others and themselves:

Jesus saw God as *his generous Father*, but the Pharisees viewed him as a *hard master*. Jesus exposed this in the story of the talents when the servant replies, 'I knew you to be a hard man' (Matt. 25:24).

Jesus was *dependent* on his Father, saying, 'the Son can do nothing of his own accord' (John 5:19). The Pharisees lived *independently* of God, plotting and scheming to achieve their ends (Matt. 12:14).

Jesus lived in the *security* of his Father's favour and love, saying, 'the Father who sent me has himself borne witness about me' (John 5:37). This meant that he could reach out to society's rejects like the tax collectors and prostitutes. The Pharisees, from their *insecurity*, despised him for it (Mark 2:16).

Jesus *did not look for approval from man* 'because he knew all people' (John 2:24). Jesus *did not need to seek his own glory* because his Father was seeking it for him. 'Yet I do not seek my own glory; there is One who seeks it, and he is the judge' (John 8:50). The Pharisees were *always looking for approval from man* rather than from God.

Jesus' *self-image* was based on *what the Father said* about him, saying, 'the Father loves me' (John 10:17). The Pharisees' self image was based on *their own comparison* with others. Jesus illustrates this in his story when the Pharisee prays, 'I thank you that I am not like other men' (Luke 18:11).

Jesus gave *self-giving love to others* and brought life. The Pharisees were *jealous of others*, especially Jesus, and brought death. Even Pilate could see that 'it was out of envy that they had delivered him up' (Matt. 27:18).

Jesus was able to *offer mercy* when others failed, the woman caught in adultery being a prime example. In the same situation, the Pharisees *offered judgement* (John 8:7).

Jesus was warm and *affectionate in his love*, especially to the vulnerable such as the sick and children (Matt. 19:14). The Pharisees were *cold and hard*, even using a vulnerable man like the one with the withered hand, for their own ends (Matt. 12:10).

Jack Frost, who inspired my study of this through his excellent book on the subject, *From Spiritual Slavery to Spiritual Sonship*, makes the following point: 'Acknowledging your orphan heart is the first thing necessary toward embracing sonship.'[4] It's as we look at the life of Christ and the lives of the Pharisees in the light of our own attitudes and behaviour that we can begin to step away from living like orphans and into our destiny as sons of the Father.

THE SOURCE OF ORPHAN THINKING

For many, this orphan thinking begins at an early age. Our view of God as Father is often formed by our relationship with our earthly father.[5] The great reformer Martin Luther, who had immense biblical knowledge and theological understanding, is alleged to have once said, 'I have difficulty praying the Lord's Prayer because whenever I say, "Our Father", I think of my own father, who was hard, unyielding and relentless. I cannot help but think of God that way.' Imagine that! A man who had spent years studying the things of God could not pray the most basic prayer from his heart because of wounds that he was carrying from his relationship with his earthly father. These wounds act like filters and cloud the lens of our view of our heavenly Father so that we cannot see him as he is. Some common filters are listed in this table.

Orphans see God as one who . . .	But the Father . . .	
loves conditionally based on our performance	loved us before we were created and even when we were lost in sin	Romans 5:8: 'But God shows his love for us in that while we were still sinners, Christ died for us.'
communicates poorly or only when he wants us to do something	loves to speak to his children and guides, counsels, rebukes and cherishes them with his voice	Psalm 73:24: 'You guide me with your counsel.'
delights in control and manipulates purely for his own ends	leads his children into increasing freedom, joy and life through following him, for their good and his glory	Galatians 5:1: 'For freedom Christ has set us free; stand firm therefore, and do not submit again to a yoke of slavery.'

sets an unreasonable standard and is harsh and critical when we miss it	is compassionate to his children, knows that they are frail and failing and has covered their sin with the blood of his Son	Psalm 103:13–14: 'As a father shows compassion to his children, so the LORD shows compassion to those who fear him. For he knows our frame; he remembers that we are dust.'
is fickle and unreliable and fulfils his word when he feels like it	is completely trustworthy. In eternity no one will accuse him of letting them down for his ways and plans will be evident	Isaiah 26:4: 'Trust in the LORD for ever, for the LORD GOD is an everlasting rock.'
is cold, aloof and unable to display affection	is warm and affectionate, using people, creation and his voice among many other ways to convey it	Psalm 63:7: 'For you have been my help, and in the shadow of your wings I will sing for joy.'
is unforgiving and merciless	is quick to forgive and merciful time and time again, dealing so thoroughly with our sin that we never run into it again	Psalm 103:12: 'As far as the east is from the west, so far does he remove our transgresions from us.'
is stingy and holds out on his children	is lavishly generous spiritually and materially	James 1:5: 'Ask God, who gives generously to all without reproach, and it will be given him.'

Let me illustrate how this works. One of my children would get a look of fear in his eyes whenever he did anything wrong. Even though our discipline was rarely harsh, the mere fact that he had done something wrong would mortify him. Caroline and I began to pray about this and realized that he was beginning to believe the lie that our love for him was conditional. If it were left unchecked, he would begin to see God that way. From that point on, whenever there was a discipline issue, before and after we would say, 'Buddy, there's nothing you can do to stop us loving you.' The transformation in his little heart could be seen as he was able to receive discipline without the same terror.

A lady that I was praying with relayed to me that she felt that God was controlling.[6] We asked the Holy Spirit to show us when this had begun. She clearly had a memory of her father, who would become angry at the slightest provocation. Even a spilt glass of water would elicit his wrath. As she walked into forgiveness, she has come into a new place of knowing the joy of being under her heavenly Father's care, not control.

A pastor I was praying with told me that although he knew these things about God, he never felt the warmth and affection of God. He had no personal experience of the God whom Paul clearly describes when writing to the Corinthians as the 'God of all comfort' (2 Cor. 1:3). Rather, he saw God as cold and aloof. It was not rocket science to work out that the reason for this was that his parents had never hugged, comforted or encouraged him in any way. Although he knew that they loved him, neither parent had ever told him so. As he stepped into forgiveness and freedom, he felt the love of God embrace him. He tells me now that he regularly experiences this affection from his heavenly Father.

These are just a few stories to illustrate the process of repentance or mind-shift. Firstly we have to realize where our mind needs shifting. This material on the symptoms and sources of orphan thinking, by the inspiration of the Holy Spirit, may help with that journey. Then we need to ask the Saviour to lead us to freedom. This is what he does best. Often there is forgiveness, both received from Jesus and given to others, and a connection with emotion that we have not felt for many years.

Ongoing Journey

The journey to freedom has been long and arduous for me. This thinking runs very deep in my heart. I have found that I have to keep coming back again and again to these truths to be sure they are 'sticking' and that my thinking is genuinely changing. The Holy Spirit has been so gracious with me on the journey, bringing me into divine encounters on the way that have propelled me several steps forward. On one such occasion I was visiting a church and noticed as I walked into the meeting an older gentleman and a boy of about 13. The boy had very severe cerebral palsy. He was sitting in a wheelchair with a head restraint and clearly had no real ability to control his limbs or even to hold his head up. I smiled at the gentleman as I sat down. I later found out that he was the boy's grandfather. We stood to sing, and I forgot about those around me as I began to worship God. About halfway through I sat down, and as I did so I noticed that the man had lifted the boy onto his lap and was cradling him in his arms, with the boy's head on his shoulder. He was looking right into the boy's eyes, his face only inches away. As he held him, rocking backwards and forwards, I could clearly hear what he was saying. Over and over he was telling the boy, 'God loves you and I love you. You're a really special boy. God loves you and I love you. You're a really special boy.' The boy could do nothing, not even stop the dribble running down his chin. As I watched this scene I was overcome with emotion and began to weep. I saw in an instant a picture of the unconditional love of God. I really could do nothing for him or anything of any account for myself. Yet he loved me. I was special to him. The tears came like a flood as years of orphan thinking began to be stripped away from my heart.

It's in moments like these that, if we will allow him, the Father will begin to speak into the deepest places of our hearts and move us from acting like orphans to being sons and daughters of the living God. Raniero Cantalamessa, preacher to the papal household, once wrote, 'The love of God is the answer to all the "whys" in the Bible: the why of Creation, the why of the Incarnation, the why of Redemption . . . If the written word of the Bible could be changed into a spoken word and become one single voice, this voice, more powerful than the roaring of the sea, would cry out: "The Father loves you!"'[7]

It's so critical that we take this journey from self-reliance and the orphan heart to a place of freedom. If we do, great fruit will begin to be produced as the river begins to flow. Instead of us striving to produce fruit by our own efforts, the abiding life that is connected to the Father will start to bear the fruit on its own.

We run a night shelter where homeless men and women can sleep with a roof over their heads and receive a warm bed and a hot meal while we help them to relocate to more permanent accommodation.[8] One day one of our team members was preparing food for the evening meal that the evening shift team would later cook. The large pot of potatoes had only two-thirds of the required amount, so she left a note for the team: 'You need to go to the supermarket to buy some potatoes, but before you do, check the pot, because I have prayed.' The next team came in, lifted the lid on the pot and found that there was exactly the required amount of potatoes for that meal. The person who prays like this is a person who has begun the mind-shift from an orphan to a child of an amazing Father. In this new way of thinking, every difficulty becomes an opportunity to 'see what the Father will do'.

Another lady was on a yacht with a backslidden friend. The friend had paid for the trip, and this lady was wishing she had some way to repay her. While sitting on the deck, she noticed that her friend seemed to be in some considerable pain with her back. She asked her if anyone had ever prayed for her. 'There's nothing that can be done, because I have one leg shorter than the other,' said the lady. Her friend replied that this was not a problem, as she had seen and heard of legs growing before by the power of God. 'Would you like me to pray for you now or later?' she asked. The lady reluctantly agreed to receive prayer now. With a group of friends gathered round, she lifted the lady's legs onto a chair: everyone could see the clear difference in length of an inch or so. She began to speak to the leg, commanding it to grow. The recipient of the prayer began to laugh mockingly: 'See? I told you, nothing is happening.' At that moment, our friend later said, she felt the Spirit of God come on her. She held up her hand. 'Stop,' she declared. 'God is working.' As she spoke the words, everyone gasped as they saw the leg grow literally in front of their eyes. Quite shocked, the lady stood up to test it. She said that it felt completely different and that all the pain in her back had gone.[9] As she knew the captain of the yacht she then set about helping out on board, having no pain for the rest of the week. More than a year later she was still pain-free, marvelling at what had happened to her.

The point is this: what the Father orders, he pays for – whatever it is. Self-reliance and orphan thinking are rocks in the river for any believer or community that wants to move in sustainable power. We must repent, change our thinking and begin to enjoy the goodness of our Father!

Notes

[1] This was actually a very important decision in the life of our church. Authenticity is critical to spiritual growth, and when leaders set a model of living open and transparent lives, it helps others overcome their inhibitions and fears of sharing the areas where they are battling. It helps to deconstruct the 'Sunday' mask and create genuine community where we can all grow and be changed into Christ's image together.

[2] Janet and Geoff Benge, *George Müller: The Guardian of Bristol's Orphans* (Christian Heroes: Then & Now), (YWAM Publishing, US, 1999).

[3] William Booth, *In Darkest England and the Way Out* (1st Edition, The Salvation Army, 1890).

[4] Jack Frost, *Spiritual Slavery to Spiritual Sonship* (Destiny Image, 2006) p. 120.

[5] It is also massively affected by our relationship with our mother and other authority figures.

[6] We were praying with a third person, as I avoid praying for ladies on their own.

[7] Raniero Cantalamessa, *Life in the Lordship of Christ* (Sheed and Ward, US, 1990), pp. 3–4.

[8] For more information about our work with the homeless, please visit www.kingsarmsproject.org.

[9] Sometimes with this type of healing the pain does not immediately disappear. I think this is because the muscles need to readjust to the new shape of the body.

4

SCAREDY CAT

And do not seek what you are to eat and what you are to drink, nor be worried. For all the nations of the world seek after these things, and your Father knows that you need them. Instead, seek his kingdom, and these things will be added to you. Fear not, little flock, for it is your Father's good pleasure to give you the kingdom.

Luke 12:29–32

Helen Berhane, a persecuted believer who had to flee her native Eritrea to live in Denmark, said, 'The Western church does not make the most of its freedom. You have religious freedom but you don't exercise it. The Western church is not free. It is full of fear. This needs to be overcome.'[1]

This was certainly true for me. Fear has always featured in my life in one major, life-controlling way. For some reason, from a young age I have had a physiological reaction to stress, whereby the skin on my face and neck turns bright red. This is particularly prevalent when I speak in public to a small or large group, and it reached the point where I would avoid public speaking at all costs. The real problem was that I knew that I had something to say. Like Jeremiah, who spoke of a feeling like fire in his bones (Jer. 20:9), I couldn't seem to keep silent.

It came to a head one day while I was praying and worshipping. A vivid picture came to mind: I saw myself standing before Jesus and for some reason I knew that the scene was from the end of my life. Jesus was standing facing me, and we were about ten feet apart and surrounded by a large group of people. All were looking at us. Curiously, I noticed that the men and women surrounding us were all injured in some way. Some were on crutches; one was missing an arm and one the lower part of one leg. Most were bandaged and bruised. Jesus spoke, and I looked at him: 'Simon, have you done everything I asked you to do?' As I thought about my answer, I looked around and realized who these people were. They had all been wounded in the service of Jesus. These were ones who had been tortured and beaten for Christ. I knew immediately what my answer should be. I was going to say, 'No, Lord.' Then Jesus would ask me, 'Why not?' It was at that point that in front of a group of people who had been tortured or murdered and had probably lost loved ones for the sake of Christ, I was going to have to say, 'Because I was afraid of going a bit red.' I wept as I realized that I must never allow myself to get into that position. As the picture ended I made a decision, one that I have held to over the last fifteen years or so. I decided that I would never again turn down a speaking request because of the fear of what people would think of me if my skin turned red, aubergine, green or any other colour! By the grace of God, from that day until now I never have, even though the symptoms have varied in their intensity.

We found on this journey of repentance that the second major rock that the Lord wanted to detonate in our hearts was the rock of fear. Much kingdom extension simply does not happen because God's people are locked up in fear. Paul wrote to his disciple Timothy, 'Fan into flame the gift of God, which is in you through the laying on of my hands, for God gave us a spirit not of fear but of power and love and self-control' (2 Tim. 1:6–7). Clearly Timothy had received a spiritual gift through Paul's ministry, but it had fallen into disuse through Timothy's fear. The rock in his life was stopping the river flowing. E. Stanley Jones, the great missionary-statesman to India, once said, 'Fear is the sand in the machinery of life.'[2] It is a major block to the flow of the river of the Spirit through you.

The gospels are full of examples of Jesus calling his disciples to repent of fear. He relentlessly corralled them into a change of thinking. A brief scan through the gospels shows the following examples:

- He helped them repent of their fear of others when he told them that just as he had been maligned and called 'the devil', so they would too. 'So have no fear of them, for nothing is covered that will not be revealed, or hidden that will not be known' (Matt. 10:26). He was saying that people can think or call you what they like, but there will come a day when justice will be done and the truth will be heard.
- He helped them shed the fear of death when he said, 'Do not fear those who kill the body but cannot kill the soul' (Matt. 10:28).
- When a recent follower who had asked Jesus for a miracle received the news that his daughter had just died, Jesus helped him break the fear that God wouldn't come through when he said, 'Do not fear, only believe' (Mark 5:36).

- As we saw in the last chapter, he confronted the disciples' fear that God would not provide, saying, 'Fear not, little flock, for it is your Father's good pleasure to give you the kingdom' (Luke 12:32). Clearly, when your Father owns everything and has given it to you there is no need to have anxiety over the trivial things of life!

What's clear is that, like us, the disciples were paralysed by fear in many areas of their lives. All these fears, left unchallenged, would affect their hearts, crippling them and preventing them from accomplishing the things that Jesus was leaving them to do.

A *Peanuts* cartoon shows Charlie Brown going to Lucy for psychiatric help. She tries to pinpoint his particular fear. 'Perhaps,' she says, 'you have hypengyophobia, which is the fear of responsibility.'

Charlie Brown says, 'No.'

'Well, perhaps you have ailurophobia, which is the fear of cats.'

'No,' replies Charlie.

'Well, maybe you have climacophobia, which is the fear of staircases.'

'No.'

Exasperated, Lucy says, 'Well, maybe you have pantophobia, which is the fear of everything.'

'Yes,' says Charlie, 'that is the one!'

Although we might not quite be suffering from pantophobia, there are many other common fears that trouble the body of Christ. Here are some common ones that I have come across:

- *Fear of rejection*, which stops us doing what the Holy Spirit is asking us to do, out of fear that people will reject us for being 'weird' or annoying. The truth is that we will be rejected by some, for as Paul says, 'Indeed, all who desire to live a godly life in Christ Jesus will be persecuted' (2 Tim. 3:12). But we are not to fear this, because our security is in Christ.

- *Fear of failure*, which hinders us from going to the next level of the things of God. Instead we stick with what we know, because we believe that if we make a mistake we are somehow less loveable. The truth, of course, is that in God's eyes success consists of obedience and faithfulness, and to avoid situations where we might make mistakes is probably the biggest mistake of all.

- *Fear of poverty*, which stops the generosity of the kingdom, because we fear that God will not provide. One of the key things that happen in most revivals is an amazing outpouring of generosity from the people of God. This fear blocks God's kingdom activity through us, because the principle 'Give and it will be given to you' gets clogged up with our fear.

The Apostle John wrote, 'There is no fear in love, but perfect love casts out fear. For fear has to do with punishment, and whoever fears has not been perfected in love' (1 John 4:18). As we repent of living under fear, we enter more fully into the Father's perfect love. We no longer fear him as the one who can ultimately punish us, for we realize that his love in Christ has made a way for us. Fear loses its grip on us, and we in turn are able to do the things that our loving Father is asking us to do.

We see that the disciples of Jesus were aware of the power of fear to block the kingdom advance that they were seeking. In Acts 4, when they gather to pray, they ask for two things: firstly that God would give them boldness to declare the message of the kingdom, and secondly that he would stretch out his hand to perform signs and wonders. They realized that both God's presence and power and their ability to overcome fear would work together to extend the kingdom in the way that God desired (Acts 4:23–31).

On our journey, we realized that we were so locked up in fear that the power of God was not able to flow through us in the way that the Father wanted. We were not taking the opportunities around us to do the good works that the Father was setting us up for. Instead we were shrinking back in fear. It has been a long and sometimes painful journey for us to walk into greater freedom in this area. But what an incredible difference we have seen already.

When we began, I challenged the church that the kingdom must be expressed wherever we go. I mentioned that if they were too nervous to pray for someone who was not a Christian, they should feel free to call me and I would come and pray with them. A few days later I received a call from a lady in the church. She said that a guy was cleaning her oven and that he had tendonitis in his wrist. He was in constant pain, his wrist and arm were badly swollen, and he had limited mobility. Even though the doctor had told him that he needed to take time off work to rest it, he had continued to work, as he was self-employed and needed the income to feed his family. The lady asked if I would speak to him. It was a slightly awkward conversation, but he was open for prayer. He said that although he wasn't sure if he believed in God he was desperate and would try anything. We arranged to meet at the same house the following week. As I was talking with him on the phone, by chance another member of the lady's small group arrived at the house. When he had finished speaking with me they together plucked up the courage to ask him if they could pray there and then. They prayed, but there was no immediate improvement. That night he told his wife about the strange events of the day, and they were both shocked the next morning when the man found that he had about 40 per cent improvement in the pain and mobility. 'You'd better go back,' said his wife, now suddenly enthusiastic. Later that week we met as agreed. I'm not sure who was more nervous! He had only been prayed for once before, and I had never seen a non-Christian healed before. The lady's husband and I prayed for the wrist again. Immediately the wrist became extremely hot to the touch in a localized area – far more than normal. The man was astonished and mentioned that his wrist was feeling extremely hot. Even though it was the first time that I had ever felt supernatural heat, I responded as nonchalantly as I could, 'Oh, that's just God touching you,' as though it were a daily occurrence. On the inside I felt like screaming and jumping up and down. He began to move his wrist, and to his amazement found he had full mobility and zero pain. He told us that he had been an atheist for forty-one years, but that Sunday he came to church for the first time and gave his life to Christ.[3]

This is just one illustration, from those that I know personally, of the breakthrough that begins to come as the rock of

fear is dismantled in the hearts of believers. I have observed
several stages in this breakthrough.

LEADING BY EXAMPLE

I found that our community particularly needed to hear
the personal stories of their leaders as they also broke free.
I remember one occasion when I saw a young lady with a
seriously damaged leg. I felt the compassion of Jesus as I saw
her bravely hobble through town, and I sensed the tug of the
Spirit to go over and offer to pray. However, courage failed
me and I watched her walk away. That Sunday I felt convicted
that I should tell the church how I had disobeyed God and
had let them down because of fear. I asked them to pray
for greater boldness. Instead of their being discouraged by
the timidity of one of their main leaders, I found it actually
encouraged them that I was facing the same battle as they
were, failing at times but getting up and having another go.

On another occasion the Lord prompted me to pray for a
lady in a wheelchair. This has always been a big fear for me.
I fear disappointing people who so clearly need a touch from
God and who have probably been prayed for many times
before. I gently asked the lady if she would like prayer, and
she responded positively, asking for prayer for her severe fibro-
myalgia. We prayed together for around forty-five minutes.
Although she wasn't healed completely, she felt some pain
relief and improvement and said that she had felt so loved
that I had taken so much time to pray for her. This first prayer
for someone in a chair was a breakthrough for me. Suddenly
I could respond to the Father if he wanted me to pray again,

because the rock of fear had been shifted from the Spirit-river of my heart. I recently prayed for another lady who had been in a wheelchair for a few years. She had pain in every part of her body, but particularly in her back and knees. By the end of thirty minutes she was walking around completely pain-free, and the three of us who were praying celebrated as we saw a touch of the King who can 'see the lame leap for joy'.[4]

BREAKING THROUGH IN 'SAFE' PLACES

We observed that using 'safe' church meetings as places to break through was also key to breakthrough in our everyday lives. Worship is a great way to facilitate freedom from fear, because so many are bound up in fear in their worship. If fear of what people think of you dominates you in that most central and arguably most accepting and loving environment in your life (at least that's what it should be), then no wonder it runs riot in every other area. In contrast, find freedom in worship first, and it naturally flows out into every area of your life. At one conference, a visiting speaker encouraged us to come and sing a song to God, using the microphone, 'especially if you are terrified of doing it'. Cautiously and slowly, one person, then another, stepped forward. The songs began, nervous and wobbling at first but slowly giving way to bolder and bolder songs to God. Voices were wavering, sometimes even out of tune. But it didn't matter. Everyone knew that the Spirit of freedom was in the room, and breakthrough was happening. Many people fell to the floor after bravely stepping up to sing and were set free from spiritual oppression, while others wept as people gathered round to pray for them. After each person was set free, the room erupted in spontaneous applause, people enjoying the moment of freedom. These things seem simple, almost trivial, but we have seen a tremendous increase in boldness to share the love of Christ and demonstrate his power in many places because of the breakthroughs that happened in meetings like this. Encouraging people to dance, lie on the floor, kneel, sing, share or do anything that breaks them out of their comfort zone as they respond to the Spirit's prompting will have a similar effect.[5]

Courage Buddies

At times we have found the idea of 'courage buddies' a helpful way of moving us out of our comfort zones and into greater freedom from fear. One couple of ladies, desperate for greater courage in their everyday lives, agreed together to go into the town centre to see where God would lead them. Individually they had been procrastinating for some months, but together they found renewed courage to do what they knew God was asking of them. This 'teaming' model is actually very biblical, and it's notable that Jesus always sent his disciples out in twos, perhaps for this very reason. On one occasion, the ladies noticed a stranger as they walked into the town centre. Five minutes later they saw her again, felt that God wanted to speak to her, and so followed her into a store. As she spent time looking for DVDs, they spent time trying to hear from God about things to do with her current situation. When they 'compared notes' they had a fairly similar sense, so they approached her and explained that they were Christians and that they felt God had spoken to them about her to encourage her. As they started to share with her, tears began to well up in her eyes. They had particularly felt that she was worried about her job situation (which they felt might be teaching) and that she was very lonely in it. They told her that God wanted to pick her out to tell her he was with her. She could barely hold it together, telling them that she had only recently arrived in the country, knew hardly any people and was feeling very lonely even though she had a new job as a teacher! It took two ladies of courage to break free from fear together to enable the Spirit's river to flow.

Organization and Spontaneity

For a number of years we sent people from the church out 'treasure hunting' into the town centre.[6] This is a time when people in groups of no more than four meet briefly to pray, asking God to speak to them about individuals that they might meet. They write down these clues about people's appearance or illness, or even the place where they are likely to meet them, and then go out looking for God's 'treasure'. Some people have disagreed with this. Calling it a 'Christian fad', they criticized us for undertaking such a foolish endeavour, declaring, 'You won't even be doing this in five years' time.' My response was simple. I didn't mind if it was a fad or if we were not doing it in five years' time, because I could see the effect it was having on Christians. They were facing and overcoming two of their greatest fears: speaking to strangers about Jesus and offering to pray for someone in a public place. They were facing fear in a massive way and overcoming it! I knew that there was much greater fruit to be had, because in everyday life members of our church were encountering sick and broken and hurting people *everywhere* and *every day*. Why, then, were we not having more stories of breakthrough and encounter on the streets in our everyday lives? The answer that came to me time and time again was simple: fear. How do you overcome this fear – not just in ones or twos but in a whole community? Nothing we had tried before had worked. But this was working, and in spades! I said to people, 'Look, I don't care if you never go treasure hunting again. That's fine. Just go once. Face those fears once and see what God will do.' The fruit was astounding.

One team prayed and wrote down what they felt God had given them: the words 'eye problems', 'Felix' and 'fish'. They went to a nearby fish and chip shop and found a young man who was obviously blind. They approached him sensitively and asked his name. 'Felix,' he replied. They were astonished, and this experience together with another opened him up to want to know more about God. He came to church on several occasions to learn more.

TAKING A STAND

Billy Graham once said, 'Courage is contagious. When a brave man takes a stand, the spines of others are often stiffened.'[7] There are many places in society where the church has withdrawn through fear of persecution or loss. In his book *Tortured for Christ*, Richard Wurmbrand tells the story of his imprisonment in a communist Romanian prison:

It was strictly forbidden to preach to other prisoners . . . whoever was caught doing this received a severe beating. A number of us decided to pay the price for the privilege of preaching, so we accepted their terms. It was a deal: we preached and they beat us. We were happy preaching; [the guards] were happy beating us – so everyone was happy. The following scene happened more times than I can remember. A brother was preaching to the other prisoners when the guards suddenly burst in, surprising him halfway through a phrase . . . After what seemed an endless beating, they brought him back and threw him – bloody and bruised – on the prison floor. Slowly, he picked up his battered body, painfully straightened his clothing and said, 'Now, brethren, where did I leave off when I was interrupted?' and he continued his gospel message![8]

The church must overcome its fearfulness and regain the courage that many of our persecuted brothers and sisters have found. We've seen that looking for the places where the church has withdrawn from society and, as the Lord directs, seeking to take a stand is a key to shifting this rock of fear.

One lady was at a family gathering and heard the sad story of a baby suffering from leukaemia and a large, inoperable stomach tumour. The people present would have been sceptical of prayer, and she was torn between the urge to pray and the fear of the scorn of family members. In the end she could not resist discreetly laying hands on the baby while no one was looking, commanding the cancer to leave. She was thrilled to hear later that not only had the leukaemia disappeared but the tumour had shrunk, without radiotherapy, to the size of a walnut. The surgeons were then easily able to remove it, and the child is happy and healthy to this day.

Overwhelming Odds

In the television series *Band of Brothers*, about soldiers in the Second World War, one soldier complains to his commanding officer, 'Sir, we're surrounded.' His commander replies, 'You're an Airborne Ranger. You're meant to be surrounded.' So it is, too, for the follower of Jesus. It is often when we face overwhelming odds that fears which we thought we had dealt with rise to the surface.

I've battled with the fear of God not providing right through my life. I had it relatively under control until a number of years ago, when we felt God speak to us as a leadership team about buying a building. We are not a wealthy church, and it seemed the amounts that would be required would be immense, far beyond anything we could raise. Having never really asked people to give money before, I felt that we should set a small target of around £10,000. One of our senior leaders felt that we should attempt something a little more ambitious and suggested £200,000, 10 per cent of the £2 million we expected that we would need. In the run-up to the gift day I felt nauseous. Was it possible for us to raise that amount of money? My fears pounded against my soul day after day. I would often wake up with a sick feeling, and sleepless nights were frequent.

A week or so before the offering date, I received an email from one of our prophetic guys who had dreamed that we were holding a cheque with the sum of £146,000 written on it.

He was encouraged that this was an indication of the amount we would receive, well on the way to our goal. The day of the offering came and we counted the total. Many people had given monthly pledges over a number of years. Taking those aside, the amount actually given on the two gift Sundays was £146,343! Within 0.3 per cent of the figure prophesied.[9] Who could predict the amount that 200 or so people would give with such accuracy but God alone? I knew from that point that God was in this project and had us covered financially. Jokingly we of course rebuked our prophetic friend for his inaccuracy and told him to do better next time. Amusingly, in his defence he said that the last three digits were actually blurred and he just assumed they were zeros. Six years and seven gift days later, after seeing £1.5 million given to the project, we opened the doors of a 30,000-square-foot converted warehouse now named King's House. Against overwhelming odds, God had fulfilled his promise.

When we hear the call of God and refuse to see overwhelming odds as any barrier, our Father is able to provide the most extraordinary means of fulfilling his word.

Looking For a Fight

When we live in fear, we often avoid kingdom breakthrough even when a clear opportunity presents itself. We so easily walk past the work of the enemy and 'keep our heads down' rather than getting stuck in. Once fear has shifted, however, courage looks for a fight! We read in the gospels that very quickly Jesus had a nice little revival going on in Capernaum. Many were healed and delivered, and he became something of a local celebrity overnight. Peter encouraged him to stay and continue the work, but Jesus replied that they must move on to others towns, 'For that is why I came out' (Mark 1:38). He was not content to settle, but had a drive to push on to new places to bring this kingdom message to those trapped in his enemy's kingdom.

C.T. Studd, the missionary to India, China and Africa, wrote to the churches in the UK to try to inspire them for mission:

> Last June at the mouth of the Congo there awaited a thousand prospectors, traders, merchants and gold seekers, waiting to rush into these regions as soon as the government opened the door to them, for rumour declared that there is an abundance of gold. If such men hear so loudly the call of gold and obey it, can it be that the ears of Christ's soldiers are deaf to the call of God? Are gamblers for gold so many, and gamblers for God so few?[10]

It's time again for the church to start looking for fights. Kingdom fights, I mean! The streets, towns and workplaces of our nations need the church to step back out and witness for Christ again. We will face threats and intimidation, but God is raising up an army of faith and power, unlike any that has been seen on the earth before.

When I was praying with a group of teenagers on the streets, one girl with very thick glasses approached me for prayer. She said that she had acute astigmatism and other eye issues that were causing her eyesight to gradually fail. Could God heal her? I offered to pray, but before I could, her boyfriend began to mock me.

'You wear glasses yourself, you fool,' he said. 'How can you heal her?'

'I don't know,' I replied with a shrug, 'Let's see what Jesus will do.' I began to rebuke the disease in her eyes. Immediately she took off the glasses and started to read car number plates across the town centre. She said that the blurriness was vastly improved. Often right before a breakthrough the enemy loves to intimidate, to try and cause us to shrink back. No matter what he does to threaten and intimidate us, 'the earth shall be filled with the glory of the LORD' (Num. 14:21).

Someone once said, 'A ship in the harbour is safe, but that is not what ships are for.' This struck me as the battle that we all face as believers: to move out of the harbour into uncharted and sometimes dangerous waters. Although this blockage of fear was an area in which it was hard for us to achieve a mind-shift, we've been so encouraged over the years by the small but significant changes in our community. God is beginning to move in great power across the world. What we are seeing is just the beginning. If we want to sustain and host this, we have to deal with the rock of fear in our hearts.

NOTES

[1] Helen Berhane as quoted in *Release* magazine Issue 62 p. 15 (available online http://www.releaseinternational.org/media/Release_magazine/2011/RELEASE%20MAG%2062.pdf).

[2] Quoted at http://quotationsbook.com/quote/14789/.

[3] While as far as I know he is still a believer, I understand that for various reasons this man is currently not part of a church.

[4] I had no other contact with this lady and so do not know if she was healed completely.

[5] We will discuss this more fully in a later chapter but it is worth noting that discernment is needed in the context of the meeting. Explanation will be important for those not used to these things, especially unbelievers, and we have found that less explanation is needed for conference and prayer meetings as against a regular Sunday. Having said this, Jesus said and did some fairly controversial and unexplained things in the public setting which proves that there are no formulas to this, but we must learn to follow the leading of the Holy Spirit. We must beware of both overly formulaic meetings devoid of Spirit life and of allowing any manner of excess which can be a hindrance to people's response to the gospel. Remember that we are talking here of walking into freedom so that we can follow the Holy Spirit to reach more lost people!

[6] For more information about 'treasure hunting', see K. Dedmon, *The Ultimate Treasure Hunt* (Destiny Image, 2008).

[7] Billy Graham, 'A Time for Moral Courage', *The Reader's Digest*, July 1964.

[8] Richard Wurmbrand, *Tortured for Christ* (Living Sacrifice Book Company, 2010).

[9] The actual total for the offering, including pledges that would come in over time, went well beyond the £200,000 we were looking for.

[10] Norman Grubb, *C. T. Studd: Cricketer and Pioneer* (Lutterworth Press, 2006).

5

STEP AWAY FROM THE GAVEL

Judge not, that you be not judged. For with the judgement you pronounce you will be judged, and with the measure you use it will be measured to you.

Matthew 7:1–2

At first glance these strange and seemingly out-of-place words of Jesus seem to have little to do with cleaning out the river of our hearts. What does judgement have to do with anything? How could it stop the flow of God's life and power through our lives? Rather than an irrelevance, we found it to be a critical area of blockage that God wanted us to deal with. In one particular series of meetings one of our leaders was struggling with how others were responding to the Holy Spirit. I remember him talking with me during one of the breaks, insistent that many were simply attention-seeking or worse. He had no evidence of this but was sure that he was right. However, during the next meeting the power of God fell on him. He was shortly weeping on the floor with great cries of soul-pain as God powerfully dealt with him. During the next day we began one of the meetings with an opportunity for people to share what God had been doing in them. When there are unusual or loud manifestations of the Spirit's power,

I like to leave space for testimony to 'earth' and to demon-strate that it is not really about the external experience but the internal transformation of the heart. This same man who had been touched stood to share. He confessed the hardness of his heart, particularly towards those who had experienced things in earlier meetings. He confessed that he had judged them as attention seekers and that he was truly sorry for doing so. 'How can I know what is in your heart, and what right do I have to judge you?' he said. This was all well and good, but then he added: 'If you would also like to repent of similar judgements, I'd like you to stand with me.'

'This will be interesting,' I thought to myself. As I looked around, one-third of the people in the room had stood up to signify their repentance. There was a holy breakout of the Spirit's power in that meeting, with unusual freedom. In fact I am not sure that our church has ever been the same again.

STANDING IN THE PLACE OF GOD

In reality, a major area in which Jesus led his disciples into a mind-shift was to do with judgements. Jesus realized that if his followers were ever to see the kingdom of God advance they had to clear this rock out of the way, otherwise the very power of God that should be working for them would end up working against them. This is the way that judge-ments work: when I proudly put myself in the place of God, making judgements over others that I have no right to make, justice demands that I be judged by my own stand-ard. Even if I am right, I can find that I am horribly wrong. It is clear that Jesus was not calling his disciples to avoid discerning right from wrong. Jesus himself discerned, and Paul reminded us that we are to 'try to discern what is pleasing to the Lord' (Eph. 5:10). However, the judgement that Jesus was warning about was very different. The difference between judgement and discernment is that judgement concludes with a feeling of superiority over the person that I am judging. I can rightly discern that my friend's sexual promiscuity is wrong and sinful. This is correct. However, it becomes a judgement if I end up feeling superior to my friend. I can easily tell where I have stepped over the line from discernment to judgement, because I will be saying or thinking things like this:

'I would never do something like that.'
'Can you believe what he did?'
'What on earth was she thinking when she . . . ?'
'Did you hear what those people do?'

These thoughts and expressions expose a heart that is judgemental. Judgemental hearts often enjoy judging and take joy in exposing others' faults, because it makes them feel more significant. They expose a heart that has forgotten the grace that has been shown it, and like the servant forgiven a debt of ten thousand talents who still extracts a paltry sum from another, such a heart will soon come under the judgement of God (Matt. 18:24–35). It is the heart that is critical here. Different people can say identical words, one operating out of judgement and the other out of discernment.

Charles Spurgeon, the great nineteenth-century preacher, wrote:

It does us much hurt to judge our neighbours, because it flatters our conceit, and our pride grows quite fast enough without feeding. We accuse others to excuse ourselves. We are such fools as to dream that we are better because others are worse, and we talk as if we could get up by pulling others down. What is the good of spying holes in people's coats when we can't mend them? A friend's faults should not be advertised, and even a stranger's should not be published. He who brays at an ass is an ass himself, and he who makes a fool of another is a fool himself![1]

When writing to the church in Rome, the Apostle Paul says, 'Why do you pass judgement on your brother? Or you, why do you despise your brother? For we will all stand before the judgement seat of God' (Rom. 14:10).

The word translated 'despise', *exoutheneo*, has within its meaning to treat someone or something with contempt and scorn or as worth nothing.[2] The New International Version gets a good sense of it when it translates this as 'Why do you look down on your brother?' and the King James Version uses 'Why dost thou set at nought thy brother?' This is what judgement does. It causes me to despise and look down on another human being, one made in the image of God, as either having an opinion that is worth nothing or more critically as being themselves worth nothing. This is the spirit of judgement: it robs people of their value.

When we see this, we realize the potent and destructive effect that judgements have on the church and why they act as a block to the river of the Spirit that wants to flow through us. How can God use me to bless when internally I am cursing? How can he use me to bind up when internally I am breaking up? How can he use me to heal one to whom I show no value? How can he use me to draw close when internally I am pushing away? How can he use me to show mercy when internally I am full of judgement? How can I lead someone to his righteousness when I am full of self-righteousness?

The story of the woman caught in adultery is a case in point (John 8:1–11). This woman, caught in the act of adultery, is brought to Jesus. Notably absent is the man caught with her, but we won't get into that. The difference between the way that Jesus and the Pharisees apply the law is remarkable. Both agree that she has done wrong. But where the Pharisees self-righteously want destruction, Jesus, the only one who actually has a right to judge her, gives her time to repent. Notice that he does not say she is forgiven, as he does in many other cases, because she has not asked for it. He simply says, 'Go, and sin no more.' He gives her time to clean her life up, space to choose a different path, a second chance. This is the contrast between judgement and discernment: one brings down the axe as soon as possible, the other holds it back as long as possible.

Jesus said that his disciples, his servants, were to have the opposite spirit to this judgement. Even though he had the right to judge, he said that he was laying down the right to do so right now because he had a different agenda: 'If anyone hears my words and does not keep them, I do not judge him; for I did not come to judge the world but to save the world' (John 12:47).

How much of the church has accepted this mandate? The sinners and tax collectors had spent years being judged and condemned by the religious leaders of their day. This is why they were so attracted to Jesus. Where they expected judgement, they received the offer of forgiveness and mercy. Where they expected, even knew that they deserved, to be pushed away, they were allowed to draw close.

But So What?

What has this to do with a community that longs to move in supernatural power in a sustainable way? Unrepentant hearts and minds that are not shifted will inevitably withdraw from the power of the Spirit or misuse this power, causing others to withdraw from them. God's power flows in a healthy and sustainable way when it flows from hearts that are like his – full of mercy, grace and compassion. The Bible says a number of times that Jesus was moved with compassion directly before he moved in power (e.g. Matt. 14:14). Judgement in the heart blocks us from genuine mercy and compassion and so acts like a rock in the river of the Spirit. Paul also makes the point that a heart that is not full of love can possess massive power and revelation yet is empty and ultimately worthless (1 Cor. 13). We have all seen what happens when a sinful individual gets hold of power and it ends in disaster. I believe that God wants to raise up in our generation a church that is both powerful and pure. It will be a world-changing combination. But before we get to growing in power, there is more repentance to be endured!

The point is this: the power of the Spirit cannot bring the breakthrough that God intends if people cannot get close enough to encounter it. Where judgement keeps us at arm's length from the very people we have been sent to minister to, Jesus wants us to draw close enough for his power to bring freedom. This will only happen if we lay down the right to judge. 'Freely you have received,' Jesus said to his disciples, 'freely give.' We cannot live with this generous spirit and the spirit of judgement at the same time.

We make things worse for ourselves when we simultaneously break another of God's laws: 'Honour your father and your mother' (Matt. 15:4). When we dishonour our parents by judging them, we open ourselves up to the judgement of God breaking us open on the rock of our own attitudes. It is good and necessary to discern that Mum or Dad made mistakes and sinned. In fact it is essential to do so, or you are actually in denial and cannot truly forgive them. Discernment is one thing, but having a superior judgemental feeling and believing that 'I would never do something like that' is completely different. The truth is we do not know what we would have done or how we would have behaved if we had been given the life that our parents had. We don't know what choices we would have made. Apart from the grace of God, who knows, we might have made worse choices!

As a community, we came to understand that judgements are one of the things that God hates most of all. Here we were, trying to please God with our lives and yet falling into one of the sins he hates most. The author of Proverbs writes: 'There are six things that the LORD hates, seven that are an abomination to him: haughty eyes, a lying tongue, and hands that shed innocent blood, a heart that devises wicked plans, feet that make haste to run to evil, a false witness who breathes out lies, and one who sows discord among brothers' (Prov. 6:16–19).

The first thing on the list is directly connected to this spirit of judgementalism! 'Haughty eyes' are eyes that look down on or despise others. Notice we don't even have to say anything! The last item in the list is also connected, for one who 'sows discord among brothers' is often one who comes with a judgemental spirit.

Repentance was needed, and quickly! One lady in our church found that the husband she had married was not able to lead her even though she longed for him to. Strangely, I knew the guy, and knew that he was trying his best to lead, but it seemed that his efforts would all go wrong in the process. During prayer it was revealed that her mother and father had a similar relationship. The lady clearly remembered judging her father for his apathy and lack of leadership. As the Holy Spirit brought this to mind she was able to repent (change her thinking), renouncing this way of thinking and the judgements she had made. Amazingly, the marriage turned around as the power of the judgement was broken and together they found a fresh power to respond differently to one another.

Another man told me how he had judged his mother and father because he felt that they had always treated him as the favourite. His childhood had been spent feeling bad for being 'the good boy' while his sister was continually compared to him. It had made him hold back from truly excelling or even enjoying praise for the things that he was good at, because he felt that if he did receive praise it would be at someone else's expense. Freedom came as he forgave and released his parents and repented of his judgements, and a reconciliation with his parents has since been possible.

We found that just as Jesus led his disciples to repent of judgements, so too he led us to repent of the same things. If honour releases the life of the kingdom, judgements act like a rock to stop that life flowing. We found that we had to repent of judging friends, leaders, pastors, other churches, denominations and streams, parents, youth leaders, spouses, grandparents, police officers, siblings, children and more. The list seemed never-ending as we followed the Spirit's leading and as he exposed the hardness and judgemental nature of our hearts. The big shock for me was just how superior and judgemental I was. This was not a one-off sin. This was a lifestyle, a mindset. But it was wonderful to feel the grace that flowed as we released people, forgave and walked away, trusting Jesus to be the perfect judge. It's ironic that the only one who could feel superior to us all is not judgemental at all, even though he will one day judge all humankind. What an amazing reality it is that our perfect Saviour will judge truly but does not delight in judgement. He would much rather that all people found his mercy (Ezek. 18:23).

The Fruit of Repentance

The effect has been wonderful. The uptight, proud, self-righteous and haughty spirit that is so repellent to the Spirit of God is slowly being dealt with. In its place is flowing the joy, kindness, mercy and compassion of Jesus. Some feared that it would make us soft on sin. But the reverse is true. Whereas in the past our judgemental spirit would cause people to run when their sin was brought into the light, now they are able to stick around to find forgiveness and genuine life-change. Laying down the judgemental spirit creates an atmosphere where people are willing to be open about their junk, and this in itself creates a platform for God's Spirit to draw people to genuine repentance. Repentance naturally flows far more easily and more powerfully in such an environment. I have seen whole meetings where people are on their faces before God, spontaneously repenting of their sin, in a way they had never known before. A recent youth group meeting dealt with this subject with dramatic effect. Friendships were restored and some who had left the group now wanted to return.

The psalmist writes, 'Behold, how good and pleasant it is when brothers dwell in unity! It is like the precious oil on the head, running down on the beard, on the beard of Aaron, running down on the collar of his robes! It is like the dew of Hermon, which falls on the mountains of Zion! For there the LORD has commanded the blessing, life for evermore' (Ps. 133).

Oil in Scripture is usually a symbol of the Holy Spirit. We see here a prophetic picture of Christ and his body, represented by Aaron. Like Aaron we stand before God as a royal priesthood, the body of the Great High Priest, Jesus. Just as Aaron was anointed with oil, so Jesus was anointed with the Holy Spirit. That anointing wants to flow onto his body, but look first at the prerequisite: the unity of brothers. It is on a unified body that the Father will bring his ultimate blessing, the presence of the Holy Spirit. Jesus, of course, reflected this same understanding in his prayer in John 17, much of which is focused on this unity:

'I do not ask for these only, but also for those who will believe in me through their word, that they may all be one, just as you, Father, are in me, and I in you, that they also may be in us, so that the world may believe that you have sent me. The glory that you have given me I have given to them, that they may be one even as we are one, I in them and you in me, that they may become perfectly one, so that the world may know that you sent me and loved them even as you loved me' (John 17:20–23).

It doesn't mean that we need to agree on every issue. This is not an issue of the head, but of the heart. Without unity we have little to say to the world. The reality is that many, many great moves of God have begun well but ended in splits and division in the church. The world may be impressed by the power, but this feeling soon grows old and cold when people see the division in the church. As we prepare for a church that can walk in sustainable power, it's critical that we sort out the number one cause of disunity: judgements. As we learn to walk judgement-free, good relationship and brotherly unity can be sustained across many secondary theological and practical issues that would otherwise divide Christ's body.[3]

NOTES

[1] Charles Haddon Spurgeon, *John Ploughman's Pictures* (Passmore & Alabaster, 1890).

[2] '*Exoutheneo*: to make light of, set at naught, despise, treat with contempt and scorn.' William D. Mounce, *Mounce Concise Greek–English Dictionary of the New Testament* (Oak Tree Software).

[3] Of course, there are primary theological divisions across which unity cannot be maintained: the deity of Christ, the physical resurrection, etc.

Control Freak

At that time Jesus went through the grain fields on the Sabbath. His disciples were hungry, and they began to pluck ears of corn and to eat. But when the Pharisees saw it, they said to him, 'Look, your disciples are doing what is not lawful to do on the Sabbath.' He said to them, 'Have you not read what David did when he was hungry, and those who were with him: how he entered the house of God and ate the bread of the Presence, which it was not lawful for him to eat nor for those who were with him, but only for the priests? Or have you not read in the Law how on the Sabbath the priests in the temple profane the Sabbath and are guiltless? I tell you, something greater than the temple is here. And if you had known what this means, "I desire mercy, and not sacrifice," you would not have condemned the guiltless. For the Son of Man is lord of the Sabbath.'

Matthew 12:1–8

A few years ago the Lord spoke to me very clearly about control. He said, 'Simon, the number one thing that resisted the spirit of Christ when he walked the earth was the religious controlling spirit. If you think that it's not affecting you and your church, you're kidding yourself.' I am quite a blunt person, but these words seemed unfairly blunt even to me.

'Surely not, Lord,' I felt like saying. 'We're the good guys.' I just could not see it. We were a relatively 'free' church with very few of the trappings of what I saw as formalized religion. Surely God had the wrong target?

When you look at the gospels, it's clear that the primary opposition to Jesus came from the religious leaders of the day. Several incidents in the gospels illustrate the struggle that Jesus was involved in. In one story, Jesus and his disciples were walking through some fields on the Sabbath when his disciples decided to pick some heads of corn for a snack. The Pharisees who were walking with Jesus immediately turned on the disciples, claiming that they were breaking the religious law (Matt. 12:1). What they were doing, in the Pharisees' eyes, was classed as 'work', which was illegal on the Sabbath. Jesus soundly defended his disciples, making the point that others had broken the Sabbath when required to by their need and that in any case, he was Lord of the Sabbath and so had the freedom to decide what could and could not be done.

In another incident, Jesus was speaking to a group in the synagogue when he observed a man with a disabled hand (Matt. 12:10). The Pharisees had also seen the man and were waiting to see if Jesus would heal him on the Sabbath. Jesus was appalled that they were so hard of heart as to create and defend a legal system that would limit the display of mercy, and in the name of God. He exposed the faulty foundation on which they are standing by asking whether it is better to heal or destroy on the Sabbath. He also revealed the hypocrisy of their position by asking them if they wouldn't rescue a sheep that fell into a pit on the Sabbath rather than waiting for the next day. With no response coming from them, he healed the man and sent him on his way.

Self-control is an important fruit of the Holy Spirit. It sets us free to obey, it avoids sin, it helps us say no to things that displease the Holy Spirit. Jesus, full of the Holy Spirit, was filled with self-control. Yet notice how unpredictable he was. Notice how willing to break away from expected behaviour.

Religious control is the counterfeit of self-control. These stories clearly show what religious control does in the people of God. It takes God's intention to bring life and freedom to people and twists it around until it becomes bondage. Jesus summarized the effect of it in a blistering attack on the mindset of the religious leaders of his day. You can read the full dialogue in Matthew 23, but let me summarize Jesus' exposure of the main effects of religious control. Firstly he accused them of *hypocrisy* because they 'preached but did not practise'. He called the religious leaders 'whitewashed tombs', a dramatic picture of the *outer appearance of purity encasing a rotten core* (Matt. 23:3,27). He complained that they *overloaded people with religious instruction*, 'They tie up heavy burdens, hard to bear, and lay them on people's shoulders' (Matt. 23:4). He provoked them because they were more *concerned about 'looking good' to people than about how God saw them* (Matt. 23:5). He was grieved that they *made it more difficult than necessary* for people to enter the kingdom of God (Matt. 23:13) and that they *twisted Scripture to their own ends* (Matt. 23:16–22). He said that their fundamental mistake was *exalting human priorities over God's priorities*, declaring that they *minimized the most important things to God* and maximized those least important, 'straining out a gnat and swallowing a camel' (Matt. 23:24). Finally, he gave a powerful indictment because he knew that they were *outwardly accepting of previous moves of God* but inwardly carrying the same spirit as those who had resisted previous moves of God: 'Thus you witness against yourselves that you are sons of those who murdered the prophets' (Matt. 23:31). What a damning list! What was worse was that the Lord was telling me that this same spirit or attitude was warring for my heart and the heart of our church.

There is some slight comfort in the fact that it is clear from Scripture that Jesus' battle against religious control did not end with the Pharisees. His own disciples were riddled with it. In one instance, Peter had to be rebuked for attempting to resist God's plan because he felt he had a better path for the Messiah to follow, indicating that he'd fallen into the trap of doing things that looked good to people rather than to God (Matt. 16:23). Martha had to be gently rebuked because she was busy making sandwiches that Jesus did not order and complaining that others would not be controlled into helping her (Luke 10:40). She'd fallen into the trap of minimizing the things that are important to God (spending time in his presence, learning from and being with him) and maximizing those that are less important (getting tasks done).

Of course, Judas' heart is exposed through the incident with the woman who poured a valuable jar of perfume on Jesus. The huge expense 'wasted' on Jesus was more than Judas could bear (Matt. 26:6–13; John 12:1–8). This radical act of worship exposed that his motivation to help the poor was really 'man-made' rather than God-inspired. It also exposed the hypocrisy of his religious control: in reality he wanted the money for himself rather than for the poor. We see this often where something good, such as 'helping the poor', gets corrupted by religious control in people's hearts. It then becomes an issue to beat others up with ('You're not doing enough for the poor') and the only standard by which something or someone is evaluated.

Even after the church was established, religious control resumed its assault on God's people and had to be dealt with, even in the highest levels of church leadership. Paul confronted Peter for hypocrisy after his refusal to eat with the Gentiles when influential Jews were around (Gal. 2:11–12). Paul also had to battle for his apostolic authority when it was challenged because he was not the best public speaker (a human priority), even though Christ had clearly anointed him and sent him for the job (God's priority) (2 Cor. 10:10). And of course, Paul's letter to the Galatians is fighting along the lines of this battle with religious control over Spirit-inspired life. These stories, captured for us in the gospels and in Paul's epistles, demonstrate the far-reaching impact of religious control in the people of God.

Religious control wants freedom, but on its own terms. One of the most tragic verses in the gospels has to be the one in which Luke writes, 'But the Pharisees and the lawyers rejected the purpose of God for themselves, not having been baptized by him [John the Baptist]' (Luke 7:30). The Pharisees wanted a move of God. They were desperate for God to set his people free and return Israel to its former glory. But when God came to visit them, they rejected him because of the packaging he used. John the Baptist was not what they were expecting, and when he asked them to be baptized, a rite reserved for Gentiles converting to Judaism, they balked at his audacity. How could this poorly dressed peasant command them, of all people, to undergo baptism? They clearly saw something of the Spirit of God on John (or they wouldn't have come to hear him), but the packaging that God had used and the message that he brought caused them to reject God's purpose for them. Isn't it shocking that God had a purpose for the Pharisees? The ones who later became the greatest enemies of Jesus could have ended very differently had they just swallowed their pride and allowed John to baptize them. This baptism was a test of their hearts. They had surely prayed for God to come, but did they really want to submit to God's way? With the 'packaging' of John, God offended their minds to reveal their hearts.[1]

It was clear to me that God was right – that habit of his! I knew that this control must be in my heart and our community, but where was it? I honestly struggled to see it until the Holy Spirit began to point it out.

1. MEETING AGENDAS

In one conference we hosted at King's Arms, the visiting speaker spoke for two and a half hours in the first session. I was devastated. I was already nervous about this conference, and for him to speak for so long at the first session filled me with disappointment. A few sessions later, when I was putting the recording device on his lapel right before he was to speak, I said (in the earshot of everyone), 'You can speak as long as you like now, because this thing will record for ever.' Everyone laughed, including the speaker, as we settled in for the session. I returned to my seat, and as I sat down the Lord said, 'Simon, you have a spirit of control. Lie on the floor.'

I protested, 'Lord, not *now*. Let's deal with this later.'

But his words were insistent.

'Lie on the floor *now*.'

I had no idea what people would think but I knew that I had to obey. As discreetly as I could I slid to the floor and lay there for the rest of the session. At the end of the session I took the guest speaker back to my house, as he was staying with us for the weekend. I felt that I needed to confess what had happened during the meeting: particularly that my comment had not been a joke but a controlling comment meant to manipulate him into speaking for a shorter time. He graciously forgave me, and I felt the Spirit of God break me free from a spiritual oppression that had been dominating me for a long time.[2]

Planning meetings is important. The Holy Spirit was not denying this practical need. Planning is a wonderful servant but a terrible master. When the plan becomes the master, fairly soon the Holy Spirit will want to mess with the plan to see who is really in charge. Does he have room to do what he wants to do? Of course, the Holy Spirit can move through our plans if we put him in charge of them. It can be just as much the flesh to have no plan because we can't be bothered to plan! On this journey of walking free from religious control it is critical that we learn the ways of the Spirit in these things. Someone once said, 'A great worship service is the same thing as a good vacation. A good vacation is the right balance of preparation and spontaneity. Be prepared so that you're confident but be ready for when God walks into the room.' This outlines a tremendously important principle.

2. Worship

During the same conference, the visiting speaker also instructed the church that he felt we should dance a 'conga' during the worship. For the uninitiated, a conga is a dance where people line up behind one another with hands on the waist or shoulders of the person in front. The leader then starts to move forwards and the whole long line follows behind, dancing and having fun. The problem was this: we were the King's Arms! We're a cool, hip, young church. We don't *do* that sort of thing in life . . . or in worship. We are passionate in worship but we don't conga! It's so cheesy!

Anyway, under his leadership of the meeting there was little choice. So we conga'd (not sure if that is a verb, but you get the idea). At least, most of us did. I personally was nonplussed about it. I'm not a big conga fan; I can take or leave my congas. I could see, however, the point that the speaker was driving at. Our worship was passionate but a little too 'serious', a little too 'uptight'. He felt led by the Spirit to help us break free from some of that. No one could accuse us of being 'seeker-insensitive', because there weren't any seekers there; it was purely a conference for believers. However, in the coming days and weeks we had a wall of complaints from people in the church who were there on that night. Angry people! Again and again I had to tell people, 'Look, if you didn't like the conga that's fine. If you never do a conga again, that's fine. But if it makes you angry that other people were enjoying the conga then something's wrong. What's really going on?' Again and again religious control was exposed in hearts as people realized that what they had felt was 'our freedom in worship' had become bondage because of religious control in the heart that made any other type of worship somehow wrong. What was most important to God (his children freely worshipping him and enjoying doing so) had been sacrificed on the altar of what was important to us: 'looking cool' in worship. Many people were able to come to repentance and get free. Do we conga in worship now? Sometimes we do. People are free to join in or not, as they desire. What I've noticed is that those who don't join in are usually smiling and happy that everyone else is enjoying themselves and God. The conga is not the point; the attitude of the heart is.[3]

Scripture makes the point over and over again: 'Make a *joyful noise* to the LORD, all the earth! Serve the LORD with *gladness*! Come into his presence with *singing*' (Ps. 100:1–2). '*Clap your hands*, all peoples! *Shout* to God with loud songs of joy' (Ps. 47:1). 'Let them praise his name with dancing, making melody to him with *tambourine* and *lyre*' (Ps. 149:3). 'David *danced* before the LORD with all his might' (2 Sam. 6:14). 'Then our mouth was filled with *laughter*, and our tongue with *shouts of joy*; then they said among the nations, "The LORD has done great things for them." The LORD has done great things for us; we are *glad*' (Ps. 126:2–3). 'Rejoice in that day, and *leap for joy*' (Luke 6:23). 'For the *joy* of the LORD is your strength' (Neh. 8:10).

There's something about worship that's meant to be free, joyful and celebratory! George Müller, a man responsible for the care of 10,000 orphans, who established 117 schools and travelled more than 100,000 miles preaching the gospel, said, 'I saw more clearly than ever that the first great and primary business to which I ought to attend every day was, to have my soul happy in the Lord.'[4]

3. MANIFESTATIONS

The third major area that the Lord has used to expose religious control is manifestations of the Spirit. Throughout Scripture, when the Spirit of God falls on people there is evidence of his presence. John on the island of Patmos falls on his face to the ground (Rev. 1:17), as do the guards at Jesus' arrest (Matt. 28:4; John 18:6) and Ezekiel on the banks of the Chebar canal (Ezek. 1:28). The people shake when Ezra reads the Law (Ezra 9:4); the psalmist witnessed similar things (Ps. 96:9), as did Moses when he stood before God (Heb. 12:21) and the guards at Jesus' resurrection (Matt. 28:4). Various disciples in Acts and the Thessalonian church all had the experience of laughing in the Holy Spirit (Acts 13:52; 1 Thess. 1:6).[5] Weeping, of course, is experienced right through Scripture.

This list is not exhaustive but it will suffice to illustrate the point. Clearly there are degrees of God's manifest presence. Sometimes he is more evident than at other times. This does not mean that if the room is not shaking, an angel has not appeared and there is a decided lack of awe, God is not there. The point is that these signs of God's manifest presence should be expected and enjoyed as part of normal church life. They might not happen in every meeting, but signs of God's presence should not surprise us, because we follow a supernatural God. We see from the experience of the early church that believers were not just to believe by faith that God was present in their meetings (although of course faith is a good thing), but were also actively experiencing the manifest presence of their super-natural God in a variety of ways. We have seen that when this manifest presence of God increases, there are often physical manifestations in human bodies. The reason for this is unclear, and Scripture does not explain it but merely reports it. I liken it to placing your finger in a power socket. It's surprising at first that an invisible flow of electrons should cause such immense physical results, such as throwing you across a room. In the same way God's power, far more potent than electricity, can have similarly unusual physical effects.

This pattern of manifestations has been repeated through-out church history, and there are many good books that document the evidence for these things.[6] They range from the shaking, falling and trances that accompanied Jonathan Edwards' revival to the weeping and shaking that accompanied John Wesley and George Whitefield and many others. On 30 April 1739, Wesley wrote in his journal:

> We understood that many were offended at the cries of those on whom the power of God came: among whom was a physician, who was much afraid, there might be fraud or imposture in the case. Today one whom he had known many years, was the first (while I was preaching in Newgate), who broke out 'into strong cries and tears'. He could hardly believe his own eyes and ears. He went over and stood close to her, and observed every symptom, till great drops of sweat ran down her face, and all her bones shook. He then knew not what to think, being clearly convinced, it was not fraud nor yet any natural disorder. But when both her soul and body were healed in a moment, he acknowledged the finger of God.[7]

Whitefield was so concerned about these manifestations that
Wesley noted in his journal:

> I had an opportunity to talk with him [Whitefield] of those
> outward signs which had so often accompanied the inward work
> of God. I found his objections were chiefly grounded on gross
> misrepresentations of matter of fact. But the next day he had
> an opportunity of informing himself better. For no sooner had
> he begun (in the application of his sermon) to invite all sinners
> to believe in Christ, than four persons sunk down close to him,
> almost in the same moment. One of them lay without either
> sense or motion. A second trembled exceedingly. The third had
> strong convulsions all over his body, but made no noise, unless
> by groans. The fourth, equally convulsed, called upon God, with
> strong cries and tears. From this time, I trust, we shall all suffer
> God to carry on his own work in the way that pleaseth him.[8]

Our problem is that we find these things uncomfortable.
Even Wesley felt the same way when he prayed, 'Lord, send
us revival without defects, but if this is not possible send
revival defects and all.'[9]

The wisdom of proverbs confirms this approach: 'Where
there are no oxen, the manger is clean, but abundant crops
come by the strength of the ox' (Prov. 14:4). The nature of life
on this earth seems to be that there is always a little mess and
untidiness around production and life. If you do not have an
ox, your feeding trough is completely clean. But you don't
get nearly as much done without the ox! In the same way,
a certain degree of spiritual mess and untidiness will always
surround spiritual life and productivity.

For many of us, the rocks of the heart stopped us assessing correctly and rejoicing appropriately in what the Lord was doing. When I first came across these things I was living in Exeter in 1994. I sat in a meeting as I had many, many times before. This meeting was different. There was a sense of something; an excitement, electricity in the air. At the end of the worship, the speaker stood to begin, and almost immediately a lady a few rows behind and to the right of me began to laugh. It started as a chuckle but soon began to rise in frequency and hilarity. As the speaker was saying nothing particularly humorous, her laughter soon became irritating to me. 'Why doesn't someone shut her up?' I thought to myself. 'She's clearly mentally ill or attention-seeking.' I shifted uncomfortably in my chair. In a few moments she was laughing so hard that she fell off her chair and onto the floor. As she lay there prostrate, laughing, I inwardly sighed. This was the most ridiculous thing I had ever seen. A grown woman laughing so hard that she fell from her chair. Finally some of the ministry team moved to her. I was expecting them to pick her up and throw her out of the meeting. Instead they began to pray for her. It was then that I realized that maybe this was God at work. Could it be?

Roland Allen once said, 'Many welcome spontaneous zeal as long as there is not too much of it. We pray for the wind of the spirit but not for a mighty rushing wind. I believe in a rushing wind and pray for its presence at all costs to our restrictions.'[10]

Interestingly, it seems that most of the powerful moves of God have had something about them that caused offence. Many rejected the Holiness movement of the nineteenth century because people would often 'fall' in the Spirit during the meetings. The manifestation was nicknamed 'being slain in the spirit' and created much controversy in the body of Christ.[11] The Methodists, as we have seen, were criticized both for preaching in the open air and for the falling and shaking of people under the conviction of sin. The massive revival under Charles Finney in America was criticized for the weeping and noise during the meetings, as was the move of God under Jonathan Edwards. More recently the Pentecostals were criticized for speaking in tongues, the Jesus movement because it was bringing uncouth hippies into church, the charismatic move because there were many Catholics who were touched, and the move of God in Toronto because of the laughter and reported animal noises.

The point is this: life can spring up from anywhere. Protestants had to humble themselves to learn about healing from a Catholic priest named Francis MacNutt. Everyone had to humble themselves to learn from the Azusa Street revival and sit in a railway shed under the preaching of a one-eyed man named William Seymour.

This is not to say that every manifestation is good. We must learn to look for the life of the Spirit. I can learn from Amos without becoming a goat herder. I can receive from King Saul without betraying God. I can learn from David without becoming a murderer and adulterer. The psalmist best sums up God's attitude, I think, when he writes, 'Our God is in the heavens; he does all that he pleases' (Ps. 115:3).

The sooner we get over it, the better!

Over the years I became familiar with some of the ways of the Holy Spirit and not as uncomfortable with them. I realized that there are four primary sources of these manifestations: the Holy Spirit, a demonic spirit, attention-seeking and a physical reaction due to suppressed emotional pain. What was critical was discernment of the source. Wesley again wrote, 'Careful people will assess the fruit of manifestations. Wise people will rejoice at what can be rejoiced in but will be slow to put all the phenomena down to God. It seems we are going to have to live in the tension of rejoicing with caution.'[12]

When these things first began to happen in the King's Arms in 2006 there was a similarly mixed reaction. Some jumped in and some wanted to jump out! Again, issues of the heart were exposed on both sides. When we host conferences I have learned to start most sessions with stories of what God has been doing. To me, especially when there are lots of physical manifestations, it's important to 'earth' what God is doing by hearing what is happening in the heart. As the Pentecostals used to say, 'It's not how you go down that matters, it's how you get up.' I also find these times helpful to reassure those who experience little physically that God is still at work. During these times I usually tell the story of Randy Clarke, who has been in these meetings more times than I have eaten at McDonald's (I have three children – that's a lot!) and has only laughed in the Spirit on four occasions.

Of course, it is very important to discern the source of a manifestation. We must also be conscious of those who are unfamiliar with these things, especially unbelievers who may be present. I will talk more on this in a later chapter. The main point here is that I honestly believe that one of the major reasons why God allows and provokes physical manifestations is that they expose the religious control in our hearts in a massively effective way. Freedom comes as we allow the Spirit to do what he wants to do and enjoy looking for the fruit.

We have seen much fruit. One lady in a meeting said to the Lord, 'I've been weeping for forty years, God: surely it's time for me to laugh.' At that point the Holy Spirit fell on her, and she recounts that she laughed on and off for two days as joy filled her heart. Another friend of mine was impacted by the Spirit and laughed for three days on and off. He changed overnight from a shy introvert to a bold preacher and was preaching to his youth group within days. Many others have been transformed by similar encounters with God, from tears to joy to falling under the power of God to feeling electricity all over their bodies. Many others, of course, have been transformed with no outer manifestation at all. The experience is secondary; the fruit of the experience is what the Holy Spirit is seeking.

In addition, church history tells of the fruit of these manifestations in the lives of some of the great men and women down the ages. From Finney to Moody, from Wesley to Sundar Singh, the stories of God's transforming power and its often peculiar manifestations have been told throughout the history of the church.[13]

Freedom from Control

It's time for the followers of Jesus to clear out the rock of control and again become true followers of the one who came to set us free. The fruit of this freedom has been evident in our community. The whole church has a freedom about it that was missing before. More joy is evident, more laughter, a greater ability to love the body of Christ no matter what our differences are. A welcome for those who are not 100 per cent sorted. Barriers have dropped as the church has learned to reach the lost and make it as easy as possible for people to come and be part of us. There's a greater freedom in worship and a greater openness and hunger of heart. We're not there yet, but a major rock blocking the flow of the river of the Spirit has begun to shift from our hearts.

Notes

[1] This is not a biblical phrase, but I believe the principle is very biblical, and this phrase concisely sums it up.

[2] I am not saying that everyone who is bored when a speaker speaks for too long has a control issue. This is my story, but the Lord must speak to you!

[3] I am not saying that you have to conga in worship! I'm sure that some people who did conga on that night also had issues of control that manifested in other ways.

[4] George Müller, *The Autobiography of George Müller* (GLH Publishing, 2012).

[5] Some may say that being filled with joy in the Spirit does not mean that they laughed. I agree it does not necessarily mean that they laughed, but that is most probable. Given the exuberance and general level of joy found in most Middle Eastern cultures it's unlikely that being filled with joy did not include laughing.

[6] For example, Eddie L. Hyatt, *2000 Years of Charismatic Christianity* (Charisma House, 2002).

[7] John Wesley's Journal as quoted in Jeff Doles, *Miracles and Manifestations of the Holy Spirit in the History of the Church* (Walking Barefoot Ministries, 2007), p. 196.

[8] John Wesley, *The Journal of John Wesley* (Christian Classics Ethereal Library, 2009).

[9] Frank Bartleman, *Frank Bartleman's Azusa Street* (Destiny Image, 2006).

[10] Roland Allen, *The Spontaneous Expansion of the Church – and the causes which hinder it* (Lutterworth Press, 2006).

[11] I dislike the term 'being slain in the spirit', as nobody dies and it is confusing to the uninitiated.

[12] John Wesley, *The Journal of the Rev. John Wesley* (Ulan, 2011).

[13] Eddie L. Hyatt, *2000 Years of Charismatic Christianity* (Charisma House, 2002).

7

HELP MY UNBELIEF

'Is not this the carpenter, the son of Mary and brother of James and Joses and Judas and Simon? And are not his sisters here with us?' And they took offence at him. And Jesus said to them, 'A prophet is not without honour, except in his home town and among his relatives and in his own household.' And he could do no mighty work there, except that he laid his hands on a few sick people and healed them. And he marvelled because of their unbelief.

Mark 6:3–6

On one occasion while speaking at a church I noticed that one particular man was looking very sceptical as I told stories of healing and salvation that had come about through the power of God. I am not unfamiliar with this myself. My own heart was swimming in so much unbelief that I recognize it in others without too much difficulty. I pressed through and kept preaching, and at the end of my message the team and I gave several words of knowledge of conditions we felt that God was going to heal. The man responded to a word about an issue with an Achilles tendon. I saw him receiving prayer at the back, and the next thing I was aware of was that he was asking to give testimony at the front of the meeting. 'When

Simon was speaking, I was very cynical,' he said, 'but four years ago I severed my Achilles tendon. The surgeon sewed it back together, but it was too short and it has left me able to walk but not run. I have had to give up all sport, and I was an active sportsman. However, I received prayer and have been running around the room with no pain.' We subsequently heard that he had started playing football again.

God is so gracious that he can and does work even in the middle of the swamp of our unbelief. But the clear message from Scripture is simply this: Jesus responded to faith and applauded it wherever he saw it. If we want to be the church that Jesus desired, and if we want to sustain it over the long haul, it's critical that we get this rock of unbelief out of our hearts.

As we began this journey, the sad reality was that I knew that my own heart was full of unbelief and cynicism. I just didn't know what to do about it. Whenever I read Jesus' words commending someone of 'great faith', on the inside I would groan and feel demotivated. The truth is that if reading Jesus' words results in demotivation, we must have read them incorrectly. I knew that something had to change in my heart concerning faith, but first I had to deal with my cynicism and unbelief.

We see from this passage that Jesus had a hard time helping his friends, family and followers to remove the rock of unbelief from their hearts and minds. So powerful was its effect that it even meant that Jesus himself could do no mighty works in his home town (Mark 6:5): a startling statement. It's easy perhaps to think that once we become 'believers' we are immune from unbelief, but nothing could be further from the truth. Several passages illustrate that even supposed believers can be impacted by unbelief. In Mark's gospel we read the story of the disciples who, having had minor success in ministry 'Jesus-style', were blocked from setting the boy free by their lack of faith (Mark 9:19). Apparently the human heart has the ability to believe and yet disbelieve at the same time. The father in this story has probably the most accurate assessment of the state of his own heart: 'I believe; help my unbelief!' he cries (Mark 9:24). A helpful prayer for us all! Even this admission seems to be enough faith for Jesus to partner with, and he promptly sets the boy free. Clearly we must deal with this rock of unbelief if we are to create churches with sustainable power.

Unbelief has many effects on the hearts of people. These are documented in the Scriptures for us:

- It breaks us off from God's plan for us (Rom. 11:20).
- It stops us from fully entering the rest of God (Heb. 3:18–19).
- It causes us to fall away in part or in totality (Heb. 3:12).
- It acts as a spiritual poison (Acts 14:2).
- It defiles the conscience (Titus 1:15).
- It can affect a whole region (Mark 6:5).
- It limits the power of God not only over my life but also over the lives of those I love (Mark 9:19).[1]

FAITH AND REVELATION

Paul wrote to the church in Ephesus, 'I do not cease to give thanks for you, remembering you in my prayers, that the God of our Lord Jesus Christ, the Father of glory, may give you a spirit of wisdom and of revelation in the knowledge of him, having the eyes of your hearts enlightened, that you may know . . . what is the immeasurable greatness of his power towards us who believe' (Eph. 1:16–19). This reveals why unbelief is such a huge problem in the heart of the believer and why it is critical that we ask for the Spirit's help to remove it from our hearts. Notice that Paul is writing to believers but is still praying for revelation in their hearts. Why? So that they may know this 'immeasurable greatness'. Paul's contention was that their experience of God's power would come after they had had a revelation of it and had combined that revelation with faith. This power works 'towards us who believe', he wrote. The point is that revelation mixed with belief is the dynamic combination that releases the power of God onto the planet. This is why our enemy goes to such lengths either to stop us hearing God's word, which blocks the revelation, or alternatively to fill our minds with cynicism, which blocks the faith. He knows that, like a bottle of Coke on a roller-coaster, revelation and faith together are an explosive combination that will shower our lives with the very power of God!

SOURCE, IDENTITY AND PURPOSE

I've observed that there are three primary areas in which the enemy seeks to use unbelief to block God's power:

1. Our source: the revelation of who God is.
2. Our identity: the revelation of who we are in Christ.
3. Our purpose: the revelation of what I can do by the Spirit.

It is critical that our source, identity and purpose are founded on truth if we are to exercise faith. Our experience has been that they are key areas where the enemy would want us to operate out of unbelief.

Source

If the enemy can cause me to doubt who my Father is or if he can make me believe that he is distant or stingy, lacking in love, harsh, or not good all the time, I will not come to him as a humble child. Instead I will live partly disjointed from him in my heart and will have an area of separation from the one who is the source of all true life.

At a gift day for our new building a few years ago, one church member wrote: 'I had struggled under the weight of almost £12,000 of debt lingering from student days and an irresponsible lifestyle. Whilst life had changed after I became a Christian, paying the interest on my loans and credit cards without really denting the total was all I could do. I felt a huge burden, shame and guilt from my mistakes. In March 2007 I received a prophetic word about the removal of debt. I laughed it off, thinking that it wouldn't be possible, but prayed that somehow I'd be free from debt by the end of that year. The months passed and I got engaged, bought a ring, travelled abroad and paid into the building fund, yet astonishingly, when working out where various accounts and cards were, for the very first time in about nine years on the first day of January the following year I was in the black. New clients had appeared out of the blue, people had offered to pay money up front for work I hadn't yet done, and other work opportunities had arisen. It was incredible, and the figures didn't seem to add up, *but* God did what he said he would and cleared the entire personal debt in just nine months.' The Father is our source, but unbelief will sever us from this revelation if it can.

Identity

The movie *The Lion King* provides a powerful illustration of the importance of knowing my identity. A friend of mine calls Rafiki 'the prophetic monkey' because of his ability to see the true identity of Simba, the hero of the story. In their first encounter together Simba has little understanding of his destiny as the future king. Rafiki provokes and cajoles him, eventually prodding him into action with the statement, 'You don't even know who you are!'

Simba replies, 'Oh, and I suppose you know?'

Rafiki responds, 'Sure do. You're Mufasa's boy!'

As he begins to believe in his identity as the son of a king, Simba finds courage that drives out his fear and starts to change the world around him.

If the enemy can cause me to doubt my identity in Christ, I will not live in the fullness of all that Christ has purchased for me. Instead of living as an adopted son of God, delighting in my Father and enjoying and looking forward to the inheritance I have in Christ, I will live as an orphan. Instead of living as a royal priest, helping to stand in the gap between God and people with my big brother Jesus, I will live as one still cut off from God. Instead of living as a heavenly citizen, knowing and walking with heaven's resources and living for a world yet to come, I will camp out in this slum and act no differently to the other slum-dwellers around me. Instead of living as an ambassador of Christ, appealing to others to be reconciled to God, I will see myself as not worthy of such a great mission and will content myself with living for some lesser purpose.

Purpose

If the enemy can cause me to doubt what I can do by the Spirit, I will be forever trapped within the limitations of an earthly man instead of soaring into the impossibilities of the world to come. I will not beat sin as powerfully or as fully as I could; I will not move in the gifts of the Spirit as fully as I could; I will not bear and demonstrate the fruit of the Spirit as beautifully as I could. I will hinder the power of God that could work so powerfully in me, and limit its effectiveness.

Wretched unbelief! Who can free me from its curse? Now, perhaps, we understand why Jesus went after this particular rock with such determination and relentlessness. While Jesus never rebuked a sufferer who came to him for their lack of faith, he regularly rebuked his disciples for theirs. At times he seems almost brutal in his assessment. When Peter sinks as he tries to walk on water, Jesus' response, 'You of little faith' (Matt. 14:28–31), seems more than a little harsh! Yet like a surgeon faced with a tumour, Jesus knew the toxic effect of unbelief in the heart of one who would follow God and partner in bringing God's kingdom onto the earth. He knew that these leaders of the early church would soon be filled with an extraordinary power. If that power ran up against rocks of unbelief in their hearts it would surely be dissipated and not have the planet-changing effect it was designed to have. Hence, a full exposure of this rock, provoking a full repentance, was necessary.

HOW CAN WE TELL IF UNBELIEF IS AFFECTING US?

We found that the following list, adapted from Jesus Ministry International, was a helpful tool to identify how strongly unbelief had grabbed our supposedly believing hearts.[2]

As you read through the list, try to see how many points you identify with:

- I find myself disappointed and let down by God when he doesn't seem to work or answer my prayers as I believe he should.
- When I hear of others' experiences of God's presence or power my default response is 'cynical' and I often try to analyse, minimize or disprove their claim.
- Others call me critical, but I feel that they are naive and I am discerning.
- I first perceive situations as 'impossible' rather than 'possible with God'.
- Prayer is usually a last resort for me.
- I doubt that God speaks to others as they claim, because he doesn't speak to me in that way.
- I'm reluctant to receive prayer, because it hasn't worked before.
- I think my situation, my sins, my fears, my _____ (fill in the blank) will never change.
- I have a tendency to worry, and have anxiety and fear about many things.
- I often control people and situations, because I'm afraid to let go and trust God even when I know I should.

Ouch! When I use this list at conferences and seminars, there is very often a 'knowing look' as people confirm to one another that they have seen themselves in more of these questions than they would like. The reality is this: unbelief is rampant in the church, and it's time to deal with it. But first, how does unbelief get in?

GATEWAYS TO UNBELIEF

We have found that the pathway to freedom starts with identifying which door in our lives the unbelief first walked through. Children are by nature believers, which is perhaps one of the reasons why Jesus identified them as suitable role models for those who would become children of their heavenly Father. Somewhere along the road, the faith of children is gradually replaced by cynicism and unbelief. Unbelief is usually rooted in a lie or lies that we have believed, and identifying those lies is the key to a renewed mind. How does it happen? I've observed several ways.

1. Unbelief comes in when we take offence at God

This happens when we don't like what God is doing or how he's doing it. The story in Mark's Gospel that we read at the beginning of this chapter tells of the people of Nazareth who at first were amazed by Jesus' teaching and miracles. However, cynicism soon came in to rob them of the benefit they could have had, because they could not cope with the fact that they knew Jesus' family. They liked what God was doing but did not like the person he was using to do it. They therefore rejected him and missed out on the things that God wanted to do in their midst. Alternatively, it could happen when we get disappointed with God and don't deal with that disappointment healthily (more on this in Chapter 8).

2. Unbelief comes in when we refuse to believe the witness of others concerning the things of God

In Mark's Gospel we read the story of one of Jesus' post-resurrection appearances to his disciples. Instead of giving them warm and fluffy words, Jesus actually rebuked the disciples for their unbelief because 'they had not believed those who saw him after he had risen' (Mark 16:14). In those days the testimony of women was not considered reliable enough to present in court. Yet the disciples knew these women, and Jesus required that the disciples believe them. He rebuked them when they did not. God will often send us the revelation that we need in a package that we do not like. How often do we reject God's message for us because we do not like God's messenger? We've seen already how the Pharisees did this with John the Baptist.

It's clear that the saying 'God offends the mind to reveal the heart' reflects a scriptural truth. God feeds those who are hungry enough to ignore the packaging and go for the food! The starving never complain about the lack of tomato ketchup. It seems that he often delights to hide his messages in unpalatable packages in order to expose and weed out those who are fuelled more by their own glory than by his and those who are truly willing to humble themselves before him, not just pay lip service to humility. This also exposes hearts that are hard and stubborn, which is another breeding ground for unbelief. We see throughout the Old Testament that one of God's major issues with his people was that they were stubborn. He repeatedly challenged them on this issue (e.g. Deut. 9:6; Judg. 2:19). In the New Testament, Jesus had the same issue with the Pharisees, and in Acts we see that Paul had to withdraw from the Jews because of their persistent stubbornness (Acts 19:9).

I remember a time when I was at university and had become an atheist. Four or five of us were sitting in our dorm room one day when a dowdy-looking girl from the Christian Union arrived, brandishing a clipboard and asking if we would take part in a survey about belief. Having nothing better to do, we agreed. What she didn't know was that I was an atheist who had been to church several times a week for nearly eighteen years. I knew the Bible back to front and inside out. Over the next fifteen minutes I verbally tore her arguments apart as I pointed out supposed contradictions and the foolishness of her beliefs. As she walked away, even though I had clearly won the argument, I had to admit to myself that she was brave to be doing what she was doing. At the same time, even in my unbelieving state, I knew that something had died within me. I could feel something spiritual going on even though I didn't believe in spiritual things. Years later, when I was praying about the state of my heart and asking the Holy Spirit why it was so hard and unbelieving even though I was a Christian and a church leader, the Lord reminded me of this specific incident. I wept as I recalled it and knelt in repentance before him, specifically renouncing the words I had said in naming myself as an atheist. As I did so, a stronghold was broken, and unbelief began to be disentangled from my heart.

3. Unbelief comes in through mockery

While I can find no direct biblical evidence for this, I've observed that unbelief and cynicism often exist in an atmosphere of mockery. In Psalm 1, David says that he avoids hanging around mockers, as he had obviously realized their toxic effect on the soul. My whole sense of humour was based on mockery: if it moved, I'd mock it! As I was praying about this I found the Holy Spirit was not pleased with my mockery and began to expose two areas for repentance. Firstly, my identity was in part founded on the lie 'If I am funny, people will love me.' This lie came in during my teenage years, when as the youngest member of my youth group I was desperate for acceptance. I soon realized that my humour would win me the approval I craved. Now, at 35, what had been a wonderful servant had become a terrible master. Repentance for this has been long and painful, and I've often had to come back to the Lord for power to change.

Secondly, I realized that mockery, while sometimes used by God and his prophets in judgement, is deadly when it gets out of hand. I found that in any situation you can choose to mock the negative or rejoice with the positive, and by always choosing to mock the negative I was in some way aligning myself with evil rather than good. My thoughts in every situation were looking for the thing to mock rather than the thing to rejoice in. It was a major mindset that needed deconstruction and repentance, and it took a long time and many failures to see even some change. But the fruit has been powerful. Instead of immediately jumping to the potential negative aspect, the foolish part or the shameful area and looking for something about it to mock or make a joke of, my mind now more often than not naturally looks for the good, the positive and the honourable.

4. Cynicism is a form of unbelief

In the past, when I heard a healing story my default response would be along the lines of 'They're probably not healed,' or 'It probably won't stick,' or even 'I wonder if they're sharing this because they need the attention.' Truly a toxic combination, even if there are indeed some attention-seekers around! Sometimes, when I realized that expressing some of these thoughts was seen as 'extreme' I would say, 'I guess I'm just a cynical person.' For many, and in particular many men, our greatest fear is being naive or having others think that we are naive. I realized that to guard against this fear I had surrounded my heart with cynicism as a defence mechanism. While being naive is not a good thing, it is not necessary to go to the extreme of cynicism to avoid it. A pastor I was talking to recently came out with the 'I guess I'm just a cynical person' line. I asked him how he had become so cynical, and he replied that he didn't know. 'Let's ask the Holy Spirit,' I said. 'He knows.' As we waited, the man was reminded of seeing a 'faith' healer on TV who had later been exposed as a charlatan. 'Have you forgiven this man?' I asked. He replied that he hadn't thought that he needed to. I led him through the process of forgiveness, and he was amazed as he felt differently after the prayer time. Months later he came to me to tell me how dramatically that moment had affected him and his faith. His normal response of cynicism and inner mockery had dramatically changed, and he found himself much more humble and open-hearted towards people, especially those who were different from him.

RECOGNIZING UNBELIEF

Once we've identified the source of the unbelief in our hearts, repentance is critical. While the sin of unbelief is our own responsibility, I have found that forgiveness for others who unhelpfully fostered the sin in us is also key. As I have begun this journey and have been determined in following the Spirit's leading, I've found amazing freedom from clinging unbelief. No longer is my first thought to mock, scoff or not believe. When I hear something that is not plausible to me I am still keen to research and find the truth. But I do it in a way that honours rather than tears down. My responses to bad news have changed, and I am more likely to say or feel that this might be an opportunity for the Father to do something.

One young man who attended our nine-month training course had been abandoned by his father. For his whole Christian life he'd had the feeling that God was going to abandon him in the same way. As God spoke to him during the course and removed the unbelief, he testified that his whole life had been transformed: 'Where I had my deepest wound, God has now laid a strong foundation. I know that I am his son and that he will not abandon me.'

BEYOND THE PERSONAL: FREEING A WHOLE CHURCH FROM A CULTURE OF UNBELIEF

As well as identifying cynicism in individuals, I have observed that many whole churches have a culture defined by it. When I speak at such places I can actually feel it in the atmosphere within about fifteen minutes and sometimes change my talk on the spot to deal with it. In our church, we realized early on that we needed to create a culture where people could learn to trust again. Many recognize that their churches are filled with unbelief but they don't know how to dismantle it. Here are a few things that we have found helpful in creating a culture of people who are stepping into freedom from unbelief:

1. Exaggerate nothing; celebrate everything

Firstly, we must understand that we do not have to become naive, gullible people to stay clear of unbelief. There are many people who do not tell the truth for various reasons: wanting approval, fear of others, manipulation, or a genuine but misguided belief that God needs a little 'help' to magnify his name. God does not need our help. The God of the Bible is not afraid of telling the story as it happened, with all the mess and honesty that it entails. The gospels are so honest. Matthew records in his that even just before Jesus ascended to heaven 'some doubted' (Matt. 28:17). How easy would it have been to leave that part out? But such is his passion for the truth that the Holy Spirit wants a faithful account rather than the glossy version that would, in our eyes, 'give God greater glory'. We tell stories regularly in our gatherings, and we have learned that one of the most important things is honesty. On one occasion, a man was telling of his miraculous recovery from pleurisy, a very painful condition that affects the lungs. He'd had it for many months and was losing hope because of its ongoing effects. He was at the back of the room, and the meeting was dragging on. He told the church, 'I was sweating so badly and I was in such pain with only a third of my lungs working that I thought to myself, when is he going to get on with the healing?' I loved the rawness of the testimony and I believe it gives far greater glory to God when we tell stories with all their earthy humanity. To complete the story, the speaker said that people should look to Jesus, and the man did so. His temperature had been very high and he was sweating badly, but suddenly he was hit by an icy blast. He thought the air-conditioning had been switched on but then realized that it was God. Immediately his temperature returned to normal, the pain left his body and he felt better than he had done in months. A doctor's visit and a blood test later confirmed that he was now well, with 100 per cent lung capacity and a heart that was completely healthy.[3]

2. Allow time to percolate

We tell stories on most Sundays of people who have been healed or have seen or received other kingdom breakthroughs. These are sometimes stories of what has happened in the current meeting, but more usually they are from three or four weeks ago. Why? The reason is that I've seen many cases where people thought they were healed but it later turned out they were not. In most cases, we like a little time to go by to ensure that the healing is permanent. Obviously you can only take this so far, and some in their unbelief would rather leave it years! We must examine our own hearts to find what motivates our actions, but I've found that a good balance is three to four weeks. Recently at a big guest service we had arranged for someone to share their testimony of healing. The lady who was interviewing the person ran up to me right before the meeting and said, 'The person is saying some of the symptoms have come back today. What should we do?' We both knew immediately that despite the disappointment we had to change the interview, because it was such a large and high-profile meeting. We wanted to take time to pray for this person again and allow them to share when we were confident that the healing was done.

3. Don't hype

I was recently looking through our website at some of the healing stories and came across one that said someone had been 'given a new bone'. The story was clearly a healing, but I was uncomfortable with the expression 'new bone' as we did not know that the bone was new. It might simply have been repaired. We quickly had the record amended. When I tell stories from the streets I'll often use the expression 'All the pain left and they had full mobility' rather than 'They were healed.' The reason is simply that the first is exactly what happened, as reported by the person we prayed for. They may well have been healed, but unless we see the person again to verify it we can't know for sure. I've found that these kinds of decision create a culture in the local church where people know that to the best of our ability we are relaying trustworthy information. Of course, mistakes are made, but these are unintentional rather than intentional deceptions, carelessness or hype. Sadly, so many of these have permeated the church and led to a high level of cynicism.

4. Hear with faith

In the past, when someone told me a story that stretched my 'credibility meter' I would immediately have dismissed it. More recently I've trained my heart to deal with such stories in a more healthy way. Usually I won't repeat the story to others, especially publicly, until I've heard a little more. Often these stories are third-hand. In that case I'll ask if I can see or speak to the original source. God is doing amazing things on the planet, and I don't want to get left behind in cynicism or unbelief. I also want to guard myself and our church from the many false or exaggerated stories that circulate on the Internet.

5. Don't judge and withdraw

In recent times some high-profile ministers have fallen into sin and brought the healing ministry into disrepute. They had appeared to be moving in such anointing that the whole body of Christ was shocked to learn of their sin. I have noticed that many have subsequently 'backed off' from the area of signs and wonders because of these incidents. It is as if their faith 'burned out' as a result of being raised so high and then dashed so low. King David illustrates to us that falling into sin is not an indication that a previous anointing was phony. Equally, the very fact that there is a counterfeit points to the reality that there is something to copy. We must continue to press in for the genuine in a sustainable and healthy way. It's time to rid believers of their unbelief!

NOTES

[1] Some might argue that these verses are speaking of the unbelief that a non-Christian has, i.e. a lack of saving faith. This is true. My response would be that while a pint of rat poison will kill you, a mouthful will surely make you seriously ill. It is the same with unbelief in the life of the believer. All of these symptoms

can be experienced in part by believers if we allow unbelief to go unchecked.

2 Mike Riches, *Foundations of Jesus-Ministry* (Revalesio Ministries, 2007), p. 34.

3 You can listen to this story at http://www.kingsarms.org/cm/content/view/267/78/

8

Step Out of the Prison

My wife Caroline was in the local gym when she saw a lady who was limping. She asked her what was wrong. The lady responded that her ankle had just 'gone out' and that she did not know how she was going to get to the car. Caroline asked if she could pray for her and, although surprised, the lady agreed to be prayed for there and then. Caroline bent down, placed a hand on her ankle and spoke to the pain, commanding it to leave. (By the way, there is no need to shout in these situations. Try to be as normal as possible! The quiet voice of one who knows her authority is more powerful than the raised voice of one who does not.) Caroline asked the lady how her pain level was after the prayer, and the lady said that there was no improvement. She offered to pray again, and again nothing happened. On the third prayer, the pain decreased from a level of around eight out of ten to six out of ten, and then after further prayer it went down to two out of ten, with much more mobility.[1] Although the work was not complete, the lady thanked Caroline and was clearly keen to go on her way. Caroline saw her a week or so later, and the lady said that after leaving she had realized that she was completely pain-free and that she had done all her usual sport with no pain since they had prayed.

A few months later Caroline was in the stretching room, chatting to a number of friends, none of whom were Christians. The same lady ran up to her and said, 'Caroline, can you do that thing you did on my ankle again, on my knee? I've busted my knee playing football.' Caroline was a little nervous. 'You mean you'd like me to pray for you?' she said. 'Yes,' said the lady, 'put your hands on it.' This was an awkward situation, but Caroline had little choice. Bending over in front of her friends, she laid hands on the knee and again spoke to the pain, commanding it to leave. The lady immediately stopped her. 'Let me test it out,' she said, more aware of the 'drill' than most Christians. She began to bend and twist it, quickly declaring, 'Yes that's fine now. All the pain has gone. Thanks, Caroline, you should come and stand on our touchline and pray for all my injured teammates.' Caroline slowly rose from the floor, observing the open-mouthed expressions on the faces of her friends, who had watched it all.

This story, though, cannot be told alone. Caroline now regularly sees people touched by God, but that was not always the case. When we first began to see healing on a regular basis, Caroline did not see anyone healed. As she was speaking to the Lord about this one day, she had a vivid memory of a time when she was in her late teens. A friend, Julie, had been killed in a car crash, and Caroline and Julie's brother went to the hospital to ask God for a resurrection. They stood around her body crying out for God to raise her from the dead. But it was not to be, and Julie was buried shortly afterwards. Now, years later, God brought this back to Caroline's mind and said to her, 'You are offended with me.' Even though it had happened many years before, Caroline realized that in her heart she did not have peace over this incident. She had been 'holding God to account' for it in some way, and she knew that this was decidedly unhealthy. She repented and to this day believes that this was a critical moment in her journey towards walking in the living river of the Spirit.

We have found that overcoming disappointment and offence with God is critical on the journey to sustainable power.[2] We see this with the disciples in the aftermath of the crucifixion as they struggle to reconcile the things that have happened. We see it most poignantly perhaps with John the Baptist. John was the first to have the revelation that Jesus was the promised Messiah who had come to usher in a new expression of the kingdom of God. He excitedly heralded this news and used his influence to give Jesus a platform upon which to do all that he had come for. But things did not work out in the way John had anticipated. He was thrown into prison, and Jesus clearly did not manifest the kingdom in a fashion that met with John's approval. Languishing in prison, John sent messengers to Jesus, asking him if he really was the Messiah or if John had made a mistake and they should be expecting someone else. Jesus replied, 'Go and tell John what you have seen and heard: the blind receive their sight, the lame walk, lepers are cleansed, and the deaf hear, the dead are raised up, the poor have good news preached to them. And blessed is the one who is not offended by me' (Luke 7:22–23).

John was offended, and Jesus seeks to pull his relative back on track, urging him not to lose the plot at the final hurdle. We can only speculate at the source of John's offence, but I think it is probably obvious. What was one of the first things that Jesus had declared? 'I have come to set the captives free.' Where was John? In prison. The turmoil of a man who had believed so strongly, even given his life to that belief, is evident in John's desperate question. But although he was in prison physically, Jesus was urging John to step out of a spiritual prison to which he himself held the key. That's what disappointment or offence with God is: a self-enforced spiritual prison. We've seen on our journey that many had to choose to walk out of it before they were able to see God's power at work through their lives. Certainly, the road to a life of sustainable power is littered with the abandoned attempts of those who started well but were derailed by disappointment before genuine sustainable momentum could be achieved. I believe that Jesus faced the ultimate, extreme form of disappointment when he cried out on the cross, 'My God, my God, why have you forsaken me?' (Matt. 27:46). Christ, our big brother, suffered without limits, but his victory in this area is a sure guarantee that we, too, can walk free even in the worst or most disappointing circumstances.

Not only is it possible to walk free from disappointment, it is absolutely critical. My own story is one of someone who 'backed off' from praying for the sick for many years because of the disappointment of those unhealed. Since repenting and changing my mind, I've prayed for tens of leaders and probably hundreds of Christians who have been in a similar position. Disappointment resists the flow of the Spirit through us in a most deadly way. How, then, is freedom possible?

1. BETTER OUT THAN IN

Before we can even take hold of the key to this particular prison, we have to realize that we are in one. Pretending that this rock is not in our hearts will not help us. Many in the church will not admit that they are disappointed with God, covering their disappointment with pseudo-spirituality far from human or even biblical reality. A friend once told me that most Christians, when faced with a situation, tend to jump over it right to the 'solution'. 'God is perfect,' 'I know he can't do anything wrong,' 'So I just need to get on with it.' These thoughts are not conscious but they form a thick rug under which it is possible to sweep many of life's pains without really dealing with them. Jesus' example to us is far from this. His cry on the cross, 'Why have you forsaken me?' expresses the depth of his pain. Did he believe that the Father had ultimately forsaken him? Clearly not. He knew and had already told the disciples that he would rise again (Luke 9:22). Why say it, then? Jesus was expressing the depth of pain in his soul in a similar way to that of the psalmists. When reading some of the Psalms, one could question the Holy Spirit's wisdom in allowing such uncensored thoughts into the Bible. A few examples:

Why, O LORD, do you stand far away? Why do you hide yourself in times of trouble? In arrogance the wicked hotly pursue the poor (Ps. 10:1–2).

How long, O LORD? Will you forget me for ever? How long will you hide your face from me? How long must I take counsel in my soul and have sorrow in my heart all the day? How long shall my enemy be exalted over me? Consider and answer me, O LORD my God (Ps. 13:1–3).

My God, my God, why have you forsaken me? Why are you so far from saving me, from the words of my groaning? O my God, I cry by day, but you do not answer, and by night, but I find no rest (Ps. 22:1–2).

I don't know about you, but I can't remember ever being in a prayer meeting with songs or prayers like those! There's something of a healthy earthly reality in the Psalms and the example of Jesus that is intended to be a model for us. The Apostle Paul sets a similar example:

Five times I received at the hands of the Jews the forty lashes less one. Three times I was beaten with rods. Once I was stoned. Three times I was shipwrecked; a night and a day I was adrift at sea; on frequent journeys, in danger from rivers, danger from robbers, danger from my own people, danger from Gentiles, danger in the city, danger in the wilderness, danger at sea, danger from false brothers; in toil and hardship, through many a sleepless night, in hunger and thirst, often without food, in cold and exposure. And, apart from other things, there is the daily pressure on me of my anxiety for all the churches (2 Cor. 11: 24–28).

This was from a man who was on God's mission! One can perhaps excuse the persecution. After all, we know that our mission will be resisted by the unrepentant. But shipwrecks? Surely those are under God's direct control, and a little peaceful sailing for a man called by God for his work is not beyond the Most High? The reality is that disappointment, confusion, hardship and trouble are part and parcel of this life to which we are called. The biblical example is that instead of sweeping the heart-pain under the rug, we come before our Father and express it. He is not shocked. He knows anyway. Coming to our Father when we are in pain, especially pain that we feel he could have prevented, is actually the highest form of trust and intimacy. Often my children will run to their rooms if I have hurt them by accident. What they really need is to come to me for comfort and a cuddle. Our heavenly Father has no accidents, but it is a similar principle. We need to run to him with our doubt, confusion and agony of heart, just as Jesus does on the cross. We know in our heads that he is good, but our hearts question it many times. It is healthy to be real about that and express it in the appropriate way: before him. We cannot stay in this place, lest unbelief settle in, but we deal with it best by expressing it rather than burying it. The psalmists model this beautifully because while they express the pain, they very often end with the truth. The three psalms we looked at above end in this way:

The LORD is king for ever and ever; the nations perish from his land. O LORD, you hear the desire of the afflicted; you will strengthen their heart; you will incline your ear to do justice to the fatherless and the oppressed, so that man who is of the earth may strike terror no more (Ps.10:16–18).

But I have trusted in your steadfast love; my heart shall rejoice in your salvation. I will sing to the LORD, because he has dealt bountifully with me (Ps. 13:5–6).

All the ends of the earth shall remember and turn to the LORD, and all the families of the nations shall worship before you. For kingship belongs to the LORD, and he rules over the nations . . . Posterity shall serve him; it shall be told of the LORD to the coming generation; they shall come and proclaim his righteousness to a people yet unborn, that he has done it (Ps. 22:27–31).

The psalmist has modelled the journey for us in each case. It starts with a situation that causes me pain; I come to my Father and express my pain and disappointment, and it ends with the truth of who he is and what he will do. Simply getting honest in this way, perhaps by telling a friend, praying a prayer or writing our own psalm, poem or song can be a powerful step towards freedom of the heart in this area.

I once prayed with a leader after God gave me a word of knowledge about someone in the room who was carrying disappointment. As we were praying, she remembered the disappointment she felt that her mother had died before seeing her grandchildren born. The Spirit fell on her and she wept her way to freedom as the buried disappointment, from many years before, was lifted from her heart.

2. Change Your Focus

A second key to this prison, or to go back to our original analogy, another explosive to shift the heart-rock of disappointment with God, is to train ourselves to change our focus. Author George MacDonald's definition of the 'careless soul' is helpful here:

It is a careless soul who receives good things as if they simply had a way of dropping into his hands, yet ever complaining, holds someone accountable for the setbacks he meets along the way. For the good that comes to him, he gives no thanks – who is there to thank? At the disappointments that befall him he grumbles – there must be someone to blame![3]

While most Christians don't go quite to this extreme, I've observed that we often focus not on the good that God has done but on the things he has not, or has not yet, done. I would often leave meetings disappointed and complaining to God that while we had seen a little finger slightly improved, the man who came in the wheelchair was left untouched. My post-match prayer times were frequently a sorry rendition on this theme. But as any good parent knows, gratitude attracts more gifts. The complaining child who finds issue with every meal soon faces the parental discipline of no dinner at all until she can express thanks for what she has. The birthday boy, in tears for the present that he did not get, is an ugly and unattractive sight, more likely to receive discipline than further goodies. It is not so different for us. Although we are called to pray 'Your kingdom come,' it must spring from hearts in gratitude for the kingdom we have already received in part. The writer to the Hebrews underlines this when he writes, 'Therefore let us be *grateful* for receiving a kingdom that cannot be shaken, and thus let us offer to God acceptable worship, with reverence and awe' (Heb. 12:28).

Have you noticed how bad news can be good news? I used to base my whole life on the foundation that God owed me something. It led to disappointment, disillusionment and near-suicidal thoughts. Then I had a revelation from the book of Romans: 'The wages of sin is death' (Rom. 6:23). I deserve to die! I am going to die and I deserve it, and God owes me nothing! I cannot tell you the freedom that I found from that truth. The apparently depressing news that I was going to die and that God owed me nothing led to life. Why? Because it meant that I could receive everything, even the smallest things, with a grateful heart. I deserve nothing but death. This truth clears the ground for the second half of Romans 6:23: 'But the free gift of God is eternal life in Christ Jesus our Lord.' I deserve nothing but I have a good Father who has brought me into his family and given me eternal life. This revelation changes the human heart to prepare us to receive the good gifts that our Father wants to give us.

Worship springs most easily from the grateful heart. When we first began to see people receive healing, we told the stories on Sunday mornings. Our response to the story was evidence of the state of our hearts. At worst there was a polite murmur, at best a very polite clap. I came to describe this as a 'golf clap' because it's best seen during a round of golf when the player hits an average but not great shot and the audience give the equivalent 'mediocre' clap. Given that we had waited so long and had been so desperate to see God move in power, it seemed wrong for his people to be giving such a lukewarm response. When I examined my own heart and asked those around what the problem was, I realized that it was largely either that God had not done the healing in the dramatic way that we wanted or that the person wasn't totally healed and we felt we couldn't celebrate an incomplete healing.

When Jesus encountered a lack of appropriate celebration in nine of the ten lepers that he healed, he was not best pleased. Clearly gratitude for all that God has done is the response that Jesus was looking for (Luke 17:17). I realized that any healing, whether dramatic or non-dramatic, a slight improvement to a poorly finger or a full-blown out-of-the-wheelchair experience, was something to praise God for. I decided to model something different. The next Sunday, the guy who had prayed on the train for the lady with the bad neck was scheduled to be interviewed.[4] As the story finished, I leapt to my feet and jumped and celebrated with whooping and shouts of 'Jesus!' It was most out of character for me. I looked around and saw that people were shocked that I was acting so extremely. But the point was made, and something began to change in our community as God weeded out the religious ingratitude of our hearts and replaced it with the fresh, childlike joy of the people of God. Now, if you come to King's Arms you will invariably hear a story on a Sunday of some kind of kingdom breakthrough. And when you do, as it finishes, and sometimes before it finishes, people will spontaneously jump to their feet and shout and cheer their great king Jesus, who does amazing things for his people.

Another powerful key we have learned is to celebrate other people's breakthrough while still waiting for our own. One lady, desperate to experience genuine joy in God because of the biblical promises, was part of a nine-month training programme that we run at our church.[5] She had been a Christian for more than twenty years and had known depression for many of them. She forced herself to celebrate as gradually, through the year, she observed others finding release and joy in God. Finally, after about five months, her turn came. The Spirit of God hit her and she laughed with joy for an extended period. She says that she has never been the same since. Celebrating others' breakthrough is very often the ground that prepares us for our own. It also models something of our Father's family in a unique way. Instead of becoming bitter over the blessings that others receive, we're truly able to 'rejoice with those who rejoice' (Rom. 12:15).

3. Laying Down the Right to Understand

Following on from the theme of finding the joy of God in every situation, the Apostle Paul writes from a stinking Roman prison, 'Rejoice in the Lord always; again I will say, Rejoice' (Phil. 4:4). As the Philippians already knew, he lived what he preached, and we read in Acts the earthquake-like applause that came from heaven when Silas and Paul worshipped in the Philippian prison some years earlier. However, this is not all he has to say on the matter. He continues, 'The Lord is at hand; do not be anxious about anything, but in everything by prayer and supplication with thanksgiving let your requests be made known to God. And the peace of God, which surpasses all understanding, will guard your hearts and your minds in Christ Jesus' (Phil. 4:5–7).

When I face unexpected difficulties, my response internally is very often, 'If only I understood, then I would have peace.' This phrase, or something similar, has been repeated by many Christians through the years. The problem is that while understanding can bring a level of peace, there is a greater peace on offer. Heaven's peace, Paul says, actually goes beyond understanding. It's a recognition of the fact that God has not promised us total understanding in this life. Instead he has promised us something greater: his peace. As Pastor James MacDonald once tweeted, 'You can't trust in the Lord with all your heart if you're trying to depend on your own understanding at the same time.'

Ultimately, although we feel as if understanding is our greater need, intuitively we know that this is not the case. Peace is a far greater need, as demonstrated by those who have phenomenal insight and influence but still lack the basic peace possessed by the average child.

Caroline and I have faced this many times. She has an ongoing back condition caused by a bulging disc. Yet back conditions are probably the number one thing that we see God touch and heal. A friend in our church tore his shoulder muscles in a nasty work-related incident. He endured surgery and nearly six months with his arm in a sling, with many people praying for him. The strange thing was, he related later, that during that time he prayed for at least five people with shoulder injuries who were all dramatically and instantaneously pain-free.

Smith Wigglesworth, who saw many dramatic healings, battled with painful kidney stones. His own daughter had profoundly impaired hearing. She used to travel with Smith and used a hearing 'horn' to hear him preach. In one meeting a man yelled out, 'If you are so anointed for healing, why does Alice use a hearing horn?' Wigglesworth replied, 'If you can tell me why Elisha was bald, I'll tell you why she uses a hearing horn!' Yet for all his bluster, his daughter's condition remained a painful mystery to Smith throughout his life.

The reality is that there is mystery in this kingdom-advance business. We just don't understand it. But perhaps that is how our Father wants it. We are too quick to turn fire into formulas and power into party tricks. Perhaps the mystery is designed by God to keep us humble and dependent on him, seeking him for greater revelation and pressing us into his Father's heart. He turns our mess into a message in the process. It's those who lay down their supposed 'right' to understand who are able to open their clenched fist and receive the gift of the peace that goes beyond understanding.

Many ask me questions about the healing ministry. I've found that 'I don't know' is sometimes the best and most truthful answer.

4. Untangling the Theological Ball of String

We have also found that sticking to a simple theology is the best way to keep the heart free from this unpleasant rock of disappointment. God is good. The devil is bad. God can use bad for good but he doesn't want bad. These three statements are a helpful summary. There are nuances, there are complications but fundamentally it was the devil who came to 'steal and kill and destroy' (John 10:10), while Jesus, on the other hand, came 'doing good and healing all who were oppressed by the devil' (Acts 10:38). We would do well not to forget it. The reality is that the reasons why kingdom breakthrough does not immediately happen are often hidden from us, for a shorter or longer time. Jesus' disciples ran into a particular 'stronghold' of the enemy when they tried to deliver the oppressed boy (Mark 9:14–29). Jesus does not blame their inability to do this on the will of God or even indicate that he was uniquely able to set the boy free. Either of these would be our natural conclusion. Instead Jesus indicates that this spirit was more powerful than any they had yet come across. 'This kind,' he says, 'cannot be driven out by anything but prayer.' Other kinds clearly did not need such prayer, but 'this kind' clearly did.

The fact that Jesus didn't pray in this incident indicates that he must have been talking about a lifestyle of prayer that he had built up but the disciples had not. Where we would turn to faulty theological conclusions about God's lack of willingness or Jesus' acting to demonstrate his uniqueness, Jesus seeks to lead and provoke his disciples into a greater lifestyle of power, pointing them to its source in intimacy with their Father. In fact Jesus' willingness to set free and manifest his Father's kingdom is the primary message that comes across throughout the gospels and the New Testament. While there are occasions when God seemingly uses or at least does not remove the enemy's tools, these are never held up as an example. Paul reports that he left his friend Trophimus sick in the port city of Miletus (2 Tim. 4:20) but he does not draw any theological conclusion from it, unlike many in the church today. It was clearly painful for Paul but it doesn't stop him pressing on.

5. Care for the Hurting

Finally, we've found that making sure we create a community whose primary motivation and 'end-game' is love is critical for this journey. Paul, writing to the Corinthians, protests against people whose end-game is simply power, revelation and great acts in the name of God. He calls these things a 'noisy gong or a clanging cymbal' (1 Cor. 13:1). Being sensitive to the pain of disappointment rather than marching across it with our faith jackboots is our primary call. As Randy Clark, a great man of faith and power, says, 'I cannot guarantee that people will be healed, but I can guarantee that we will love them.' It is hard to be prayed for again and again with no seeming improvement, and we must not pretend that it is not. Asking people if they want prayer rather than forcing it down their throats is key. Asking them what they want prayer for, as Jesus did when he asked the blind man what he wanted (Luke 18:41), shows them that we are interested in their heart, not just another 'healing scalp'. Making sure there are not crowds of people around the very sick and that they are comfortable as they receive prayer is also important. We run a group for the long-term sick where they can find support and care in an atmosphere of faith.

A dramatic lesson in this journey happened for us when, shortly after we had seen major breakthrough in healing, a lady in our church contracted breast cancer for the second time. I asked Angie if she wanted prayer, and she said that she wanted people to pray for her as long as they were willing. Many prayed and fasted for her. When she became too weak to go out, our worship leaders went to her house to lead worship for her. They wept as they sang and she just lay back smiling, loving her God even though she was too weak to join in. Two days before she died, she sent a message requesting that I come to visit her. As I sat beside her bed I asked her what message she would like to send back to the church. Her voice was so weak, I had to lean very close to hear her words. 'Tell the King's Arms,' she said, 'don't ever stop praying for cancer.'

Two days later she died. I spoke that Sunday of the courage of a woman who had faith to the end and was concerned that we would 'back off' because in her case we didn't get the breakthrough we wanted. Disappointment never kept its hold on her. It's time for the rest of the church to walk free too.

Notes

[1] When praying for people we often ask them to rate their pain 'out of ten'. While not a scientific measure, and of course one person's eight could be another person's four, we have found this helpful for us and the individual to measure any improvement.

[2] I am indebted to Bill Johnson for his teaching on dealing with disappointment.

[3] George MacDonald and C.S. Lewis, *George MacDonald – An Anthology* (Harper, 1946), p. 84.

[4] See Chapter 1.

[5] For more information on our training school, TSM, visit www.kingsarms.org/tsm.

9

TAKE A BREATHER

You may be slightly worried by the time you reach this part of the book. Do I really need to repent in all of those areas? It might take the rest of my life for me to change my thinking to that extent! I can relate to that. Before you despair, it's important to remember several things.

God does not require us to be fully transformed before he can use us. We met one young man because he was homeless and turned up at our night shelter. Over time he began to attend the church and came to faith in Christ, was filled with the Holy Spirit and became a passionate follower of Christ. He was keen to share his new-found faith with others. A team travelled to another church to teach the way that we go out onto the streets treasure hunting and seek to share the love of Christ with unbelievers. This young man, who only a short while ago was an unbeliever and homeless, was leading one of the small teams. They prayed together briefly and all wrote on a piece of paper 'clues' to where they felt the Lord would lead them. As he was the most experienced, the team were keen to follow his lead. He had two clues written down: 'black coat' and 'bus shelter'. One other team member had the name 'Susan'.

Faithfully they went off to the bus shelter, and sure enough right in the centre was a young lady wearing a long black coat.

The group walked up to her and our young man asked, 'Is your name Susan?' 'It is,' said the surprised girl. 'How did you know?' Not sure who was more shocked, the girl or himself, the team leader did not want to show that he had no clue what to do next. He had only been a Christian a few months! They began to share with the girl about the love of Christ and she blurted out, 'I just feel so broken.' One of the girls in the group excitedly grabbed the piece of paper on which she had written her clue. On the paper was a single word: 'broken'. Clearly they were in the midst of a God moment, and the Father was reaching out his arm of love for a young broken girl. Did this young man still have issues to work through? Absolutely. Did God still use him? Undoubtedly. Even when we are young in the faith or unprepared, or even when we have perhaps identified some areas of heart 'rock' but not fully dealt with them, God can use us. The Bible is overflowing with God's ability to use broken, fallen men and women in his grace. This does not excuse our need for repentance as the Spirit leads, but it should give us courage to partner with him to extend his kingdom even when we are a work in progress.

The previous chapters are only illustrative of some of the rocks of the heart. There are many others, but I have sought to outline these because they have been the ones that the Lord has particularly dealt with in me and in us as a community, and because I see them as most representative of the issues that Jesus dealt with in his own disciples. However, the key has to be listening to the Spirit for your life and your community. He knows each human heart and promises to lead us into all truth.

If, however, God is using you even though you haven't dealt with these issues, beware. Scripture and church history are littered with the stories of men and women who felt they had the divine stamp of approval because God was using them in power despite their continuing sin and rebellion. This must be a lesson for all of us. Sometimes the worst judgement is to get away with our sin again and again. Often the Father will warn us many times before allowing us to seemingly 'get away' with the issue until the consequence of our sin catches up with us. Frightening! A man once came to King's Arms with a healing ministry. An elder of another church had recommended him to me. I didn't have time to meet with him so asked a couple of guys from our welcome team to meet him for a coffee. They returned shaking their heads. I asked them what was wrong. 'He's moving in incredible power, if the stories he told today are true,' they both said. 'So what's the problem?' I asked. They looked at each other before replying. 'He's one of the most arrogant and self-righteous men I've ever met,' one of them quickly said. This is the tragedy of many powerful ministers in the church today. The gifts they have are sorely needed by the church, but their character issues and unwillingness to submit to authority keep them far away from the people they also need to minister to them.

Finally, if the Lord has pointed out an area of your heart that needs to change, what are you to do? You've seen the rock; it's big and it's been there for a long time. The river has been trying to flow round it, but you know breakthrough will only come when it finally gets detonated. Is a simple prayer at the end of a chapter enough? What steps do you need to take to ensure these boulders are blasted out of your life for good? How do you change a mindset, particularly one that's been present for a long time? Some people receive immediate deliverance with such a prayer. Praise God! For others, or in particular areas of the heart, the dismantling process seems to take for ever.

My own story may help. Several of these issues just seemed to drop off once I had the revelation of them. Disappointment was a case in point. Largely the freedom came in a single meeting or two as God exposed the sin and dealt with it to the heart level. I rarely find myself in those places now. Other areas have been more of a battle. Self-reliance has been one of the toughest rocks to shift from my own heart. To be truthful, I'm not sure it's totally gone even now, although I know that I am far freer than I ever have been. On the journey, I have discovered several stages to freedom.

STAGE 1: RECOGNIZE THE AREA

Until that moment on Diane's sofa (see Chapter 3), I was blissfully unaware of the sin of the pride of self-reliance. From that moment of revelation, everything has changed. It may be that this book has served up that revelation for you. If you recall, revelation is one of the two key ingredients, along with faith, that we need if we are to see the power of God. This applies in this area of heart change as much as any other. Once you 'know', there's no going back. My deliverance from the demonic stronghold that day was only the beginning. Demons invade, but there must be a door for them to gain access to our lives in the first place. The sin and responsibility were mine, even though they were making the most of my failing and magnifying its power in my life. But recognition that this was a major 'rock' in my heart was the first step. My response in accepting God's conviction was also critical. Notice that in the parable of the sower Jesus says that the first trick of the enemy is to remove the seed from those who 'don't understand' – or perhaps refuse to understand (Matt. 13:19). These are the people represented by the 'paths' that the seed cannot penetrate. What Jesus applies to unbelievers also applies in part to supposed 'believers'. I've seen many who have heard these things but refused to believe and accept the revelation, preferring to stay in their unbelief rather than walk into freedom.

Stage 2: Be Aware 'After the Moment'

I found that now my conscience was sensitized to this sin, I would begin to be aware of it, but only after I had already sinned. Often the Holy Spirit would convict me late at night as I recalled the day. Self-reliance most readily manifests in me when something goes wrong. Say, for example, I'm working on our finances and find we are overdrawn. My knee-jerk reaction is fear rather than faith, and I begin to despair and look for a way to fix the problem. I forget the times the Father has provided and immediately begin to sink into a pit of panic. Even my wife's calming words don't help. Later that night, when I've calmed down, the Holy Spirit will convict me of the real sin issues: fear and self-reliance! Instead of justifying or deflecting, it is at that point that we must respond to the Spirit's voice. Then, once we regularly are aware 'after the moment' and continue to walk out repentance, gradually we will move to stage 3.

Stage 3: Be Aware 'In the Moment'

I eventually found that I was aware as the event was happening that 'self-reliance' was at the door of my heart. Often it was the gentlest of nudges by the Holy Spirit, but like a man trapped in quicksand I seemed powerless to change my direction. However, it was a positive step forward, and later in the day I could repent and thank God that in his grace I was starting to see the sin at the point where behaviour could be changed, even if I didn't manage it that day.

Stage 4: Starting to Overcome It 'In the Moment'

Once I have become aware 'in the moment' of a certain area of sin, I've found that my next prayer needs to be to ask the Holy Spirit for his power to overcome 'in the moment'. He always provides if we will just trust that he will, and before long I found that in the moment I could see the issue and change my behaviour. What a wonderful feeling. When financial or other disasters strike I'm usually able to say, 'Let's see what the Father will do.' This is the case with the fear of public speaking for me. It's so rare that I feel it, and even when I do, the battle of the heart has been won to such an extent that I am able to quickly master it with the truth. In other areas I've wavered between stages 3 and 4 for many months. Sooner or later, though, stage four becomes the greater reality and occurs with greater frequency. Jesus is Lord!

STAGE 5: HELPING OTHERS

The final stage is when I am able to help others in the very area that was once an area of defeat for me. I remember an occasion when a man came to me and said, 'Simon, I know God has called me to lead but I'm terrified of public speaking.' I began to counsel him in the steps to freedom, beginning with my own testimony. Later I was able to reflect, 'Lord, it's so long since I felt like that that I can barely remember what it feels like.' When the Son sets you free, you will be free indeed. It might not always be instantaneous, but the journey always has an end, and for the follower of Christ the end is always victory.

I speak on these issues with many people at churches and conferences. Sometimes I only have a few minutes with someone at the end of a meeting or seminar. When that is the case, I am always trying to accomplish one thing. They have received the revelation through the teaching and the input of the Holy Spirit. That's why they are there talking to me. Now all they need is faith and perseverance. If, in these few minutes, I can see the flame of faith flicker and take hold of the combustible material of their hearts, I know that it's just a matter of time before they are free. Revelation plus faith always equals the power of God. Sometimes I tell people that I want them to look in the mirror every morning and say to themselves, 'Fear (or whatever the issues is), I am going to be free from your hold. You cannot bind me any more. Jesus Christ has set me free and will set me free.' This is critical, particularly the morning after they have failed in this area. It is not just positive speaking. Freedom will come if we just hold on to the one who sets people free.

From here, let's move on to the second part of our journey. Once the rubble has been removed, it's time to build.[1] In the remaining chapters I want to introduce several key revelations that were critical to this building phase. In some cases we are well on the way to seeing them established in our community. In others, it feels as though we have only just begun. I pray that in each one, God will lay a strong and healthy foundation as you marinade in these truths. Let's get pickling!

NOTES

[1] In truth, on our journey, the building and the destruction happened at the same time. I'm sure it will be true for you as well.

10

I WILL BE WITH YOU

Abide in me, and I in you. As the branch cannot bear fruit by itself, unless it abides in the vine, neither can you, unless you abide in me.

John 15:4

One afternoon early in our journey towards seeing the power of God break out of the church walls and onto the streets, a friend and I decided to go treasure hunting in the town centre. We took a few minutes to ask the Holy Spirit to fill us and guide us and then wrote down our clues on pieces of paper. After a fruitless twenty minutes we were led to approach a group of teenagers. Shortly after we began chatting to them, a guy who turned out to be an unofficial leader began to mock us and grabbed the piece of paper from my friend's hand. 'What's this?' he demanded. We told him that it was a list of clues, a bit like a treasure hunt. He scanned the list and then examined the clues. 'Bad back', he read, 'and basketball', he mocked. Then he stopped. 'Well, I've got a bad back and it did stop me playing basketball,' he suddenly puzzled. 'Where did you get this piece of paper?' We explained again and said that we felt we should pray for him, as maybe God had sent us there for him. He was very reluctant, as he said that he was a pagan, but ultimately agreed. He told us he had injured his back three years before and did not get it treated. As a result his coccyx had fused, leaving him in considerable pain and unable to play sport.

We laid hands on his lower back and rebuked the pain. In a second he began to swear, attracting the attention of the milling group of teenagers. 'What did you just do to me?' he cursed. We asked him what had happened, and he said he had felt a shot of heat go through his back. When we explained that this might have been God healing him, he bent over backwards and began to walk around on his feet and hands! As he did so he began swearing at the top of his voice and saying, 'These guys have just healed my back. I couldn't do this before.' We realized that swearing was his type of worship, which would just have to do for now. His female friend then asked us to pray for her, and then a young man approached my friend and asked for prayer. 'What's wrong with you?' my friend enquired. 'Nothing,' the guy said. 'Just pray.' My friend began to pray and prophesy over him the fact that God loved him. As he did so, the young man burst into tears, crying out as if in pain. Many stopped their conversations and turned to see what was happening. 'I'm nothing, I'm no one,' he sobbed. 'Why would God love me? Why would God love me?' He was crying out like a wounded animal, in great turmoil in his soul.

A girl approached me and asked for prayer for her broken arm. I wondered why she didn't have it in a cast, and she said that it was a fracture. She was supposed to have a sling but it 'wasn't cool'. Apparently she was going to hospital for a cast the next day. I asked her how much mobility she had and she moved it from tight against her chest to a few inches out, wincing as she did so. We quickly commanded the bone to set and the pain to go. We asked her to move the arm and check it out. She began to move it, and then a big smile appeared on her face as with increasing confidence she began to whirl the arm around her head. Swearing, she declared, 'It's completely healed. I have no pain.' As this happened I could feel a tangible shift in the spiritual atmosphere. I had never seen a broken arm healed, even in church! The hairs on the back of my neck stood on end, and I knew that something very significant was breaking out right in the town centre. I stood on tiptoes and shouted across the square, 'God is here and he's healing people and touching them right now. If you want to encounter him, come here now.' From the group of teenagers, which had now grown to a group of around thirty or forty milling around, some began to line up in front of my friend and me, waiting for prayer.

In total we saw at least seven dramatic healings or improvements that afternoon, and many others received prophetic words from God. One guy with three torn ligaments in his shoulder claimed to be pain-free; another with arthritis in his hands became pain-free. A girl with chronic migraines was having one as we prayed, but it left instantly. After about two and a half hours we gathered the crowd of teenagers together and explained to them the message of Jesus. We then spent time talking with a number and encouraging them to give their lives to following Christ. We walked home, thrilled with what God had done. As we did so, I felt the Lord speak very clearly to my spirit. 'This was not just for you, for your church or your town,' he said. 'This was to show that if I can do it in

Bedford, I can do it anywhere. What once was extraordinary will one day become ordinary.' I realized that God had shown us just a touch of what he was capable of. The secret was to be in his presence.

A Foundational Lesson

One of the foundational lessons that Jesus taught his disciples was that the presence of the Spirit of God was critical to everything they were to accomplish on earth. He modelled, taught and encouraged his disciples in this fresh understanding of God's immanent presence by his Spirit. Of course they understood that God is everywhere. But Jesus sought to bring them into the reality that the God who is everywhere loves to turn up somewhere. We see this in many different ways through the gospels.

Jesus emphasized the importance of intimacy with God's presence when he taught them to call God Father and modelled repeatedly that his first priority was always to spend time with his Father. Often in the gospels the writers record that Jesus withdrew to spend time alone with the Father (Matt. 26:36; Luke 11:1), and the disciples learned from him that even the pressing needs of the crowd would not divert him from this primary call (Mark 1:35–37). Jesus promised that this intimacy was not his alone but available for every follower of his when he said, 'The glory that you have given me I have given to them, that they may be one even as we are one, I in them and you in me, that they may become perfectly one, so that the world may know that you sent me and loved them even as you loved me' (John 17:22–23). What amazing intimacy we can have with God through the Holy Spirit!

Jesus taught them the power of God's presence when he showed them that he could do nothing by himself (John 5:30). He said that like branches removed from a grapevine, they were unable to do anything without ongoing connection with him (John 15:5). Jesus promised his disciples that this power would belong to them when he said, 'You will receive power when the Holy Spirit has come upon you' (Acts 1:8). We see throughout Acts that the disciples received again and again fresh filling by the very presence of the Holy Spirit. God was no longer remote; his presence had come to fill and to remain. Paul wrote to the church in Thessalonica that the message that he brought to them came with words 'but also in power and in the Holy Spirit' (1 Thess. 1:5).

Finally, Jesus taught them about the prophetic directional nature of God's presence when he told them that he only did what he saw his Father doing (John 5:19). We see that before major decisions he spent time seeking the Father's will and guidance. We see this directive prophecy throughout the New Testament with Peter, Philip, Paul, John and others. We see Paul being sent out for ministry when the Spirit commissions him and Barnabas at Antioch (Acts 13:1–3), and the apostle changing his missional focus under the Spirit's direction when in a vision a man appears to him to direct him into Europe (Acts 16:9). Paul is even rescued from death when an angel appears to him to encourage and strengthen him in the middle of a vicious storm (Acts 27:23).

The point is that this kingdom mission that we are called to cannot be accomplished without the presence of God. It was never God's intention to leave us alone to get on with the job: he planned that we should partner with him to accomplish his mission. I don't know about you, but I find that I tend to default to rules rather than relationship. Where, by nature, I would like rules, maps, lists and principles by which to work, I find that I am drawn into an adventure that is all about relationship with the Father, Jesus and the Holy Spirit. Where I naturally long for a textbook, I have the Bible: largely a collection of stories of the adventures of men and women with God. This self-reliant, rules-focused nature that I find in myself was the same spirit that Jesus found in the Pharisees when he said to them, 'You search the Scriptures because you think that in them you have eternal life; and it is they that bear witness about me' (John 5:39). How easy it is for me even today to look for these principles and miss the relationship that he is calling me into.

The Scripture cuts against this attitude though when it says, 'Not by might, nor by power, but by my Spirit, says the LORD of hosts' (Zech. 4:6). This is echoed again in the prophetic word given to Caroline and me all those years ago: 'I hear God say, "It's in his presence. It all comes from his presence."'

History has demonstrated time and time again that when God himself shows up, everything changes. Moody, Finney, Wesley and many others testify to the dramatic change that occurs with God's presence. Moody even said that he used to preach exactly the same sermons, almost word for word, but only a few would respond. Once the Holy Spirit came to indwell him, hundreds began to get saved while listening to the same messages.[1]

GOD'S PRESENCE IN THE UK

Even in the United Kingdom, little more than sixty years ago, we learned this lesson in the revival that hit the Hebrides in 1949. Duncan Campbell, the minister at the centre of the revival, tells the story of how it started one evening at the end of a church meeting:

When I went to the door of the church I saw a congregation of approximately 600 people. Six hundred people – where had they come from? What had happened? . . . Over 100 young people were at the dance in the parish hall and they weren't thinking of God or eternity. God was not in all of their thoughts. They were there to have a good night when suddenly the power of God fell upon the dance. The music ceased and in a matter of minutes, the hall was empty. They fled from the hall as a man fleeing from a plague. And they made for the church. They are now standing outside . . . Men and women who had gone to bed, rose, dressed, and made for the church. Nothing in the way of publicity, no mention of a special effort . . . but God took the situation in hand – oh, he became his own publicity agent. A hunger and a thirst gripped the people. 600 of them now are at the church standing outside.

. . . Now the church is crowded – a church to seat over 800 is now packed to capacity. It is now going on towards midnight. I managed to make my way through the crowd along the aisle toward the pulpit. I found a young woman, a teacher in the grammar school, lying prostrate on the floor of the pulpit praying, 'Oh, God, is there mercy for me? Oh, God, is there mercy for me?' She was one of those at the dance. But she is now lying on the floor of the pulpit crying to God for mercy.

That meeting continued until 4 o'clock in the morning. I couldn't tell you how many were saved that night but of this I am sure and certain that at least five young men who were saved in that church that night are today ministers in the Church of Scotland having gone through university and college.

At 4 o'clock . . . we left them there, and just as I was leaving the church, a young man came to me and said, 'Mr Campbell, I would like you to go to the police station.' I said, 'The police station? What's wrong?' 'Oh,' he said, 'There's nothing wrong but there must be at least 400 people gathered around the police station just now.'

. . . As I am walking along that country road – we had to walk about a mile – I heard someone praying by the roadside. I could hear this man crying to God for mercy. I went over and there were four young men on their knees at the roadside. Yes, they were at the dance but they are now there crying to God for mercy. One of them was under the influence of drink, but a young man he wasn't 20 years of age. But that night God saved him and he is today the parish minister, university trained, college trained, a man of God.

Now when I got to the police station, I saw something that will live with me as long as I live. I didn't preach, there was no need of preaching. We didn't even sing. The people are crying to God for mercy. Oh, the confessions that were made! There was one old man crying out, 'Oh, God, hell is too good for me! Hell is too good for me!' This is Holy Ghost conviction! Now mind you, that was on the very first night of a mighty demonstration that shook the island. Oh, let me say again, that wasn't the beginning of revival – revival began in a prayer meeting. Revival began in an awareness of God. Revival began when the Holy Ghost began to grip men and that was how it began. And, of course, after that we were at it night and day – churches crowded.[2]

These stories and other more recent ones convinced us of the need for his manifest presence in everything we do. We have learned about personal management from the best books. We have learned about speaking from the best preachers. We have learned about organization from the best organizers and we have learned about welcome from the best welcomers. We have learned so many good things about leading ourselves and leading a healthy growing church from some of the best in the world. There is still much to learn, and we are still learning. But without his manifest presence intimately empowering and guiding, it will all be worthless in his eyes. We have to have his presence!

Again we found that the Lord has led us on a journey to learn what we needed to learn in order to walk intimately with him and abide in his presence. I've found that there are two aspects to this: the personal and the corporate journey.

THE PERSONAL JOURNEY

By nature I don't like to spend time praying, because I like to get things done. I appreciate the irony of this statement. As you can imagine, it has been (and still is) quite a journey for me to learn the Jesus way. One breakthrough of mind occurred for me when I came across the definition of the Greek word *baptizo*, which is the source of our word 'baptism'. Both Jesus and John the Baptist promised that the disciples would be 'baptized' in the Holy Spirit (Matt. 3:11; Acts 1:5). In both verses the Greek word *baptizo* is used. There is another similar term in Greek, *bapto*, and it is helpful for us to understand the difference between these two words. Both mean to 'dip' or to 'immerse', but Matthew and Luke used the word *baptizo* rather than *bapto* for a very specific reason.[3] The best example of the difference in meaning comes from a Greek poet and doctor called Nicander who, in 200 BC, wrote a recipe about making pickles. He says that in order to make a pickle the vegetable should be first 'dipped' (*bapto*) into boiling water and then 'baptized' (*baptizo*) in a vinegar solution. Both verbs concern dipping, but we immediately understand the difference given this context. *Bapto* is a temporary, short dipping, but *baptizo* is an immersion for such a long time that it produces a complete change in the vegetable.[4] It goes in a cucumber and comes out a pickle![5]

CALLED TO PICKLE

When I first understood this I realized that I needed more pickling! This is not intended to be irreverent in any way; suddenly, spending time in God's presence took on a whole new meaning. No longer did I have to strive and strain to 'make something happen', as I realized that my first priority was pickling! Jesus summed it up when he declared that much fruit would be produced in our lives simply by 'remaining' or 'abiding' in him.[6] My prayer times changed dramatically and became far less 'driven' and far more 'pickling'! Our staff prayer times have changed considerably. Instead of praying through a list, they are much more frequently times simply of waiting on him, loving him and receiving from him.

One visiting speaker said that although she had been travelling and speaking for more than twenty years, she had never been in a prayer meeting like the one she attended with us. Another visitor came to join us for prayer before a meeting. At the end of this time, before we went into the meeting, he asked for prayer for his back. We quickly prayed and the pain that he had been living with for more than fifteen years was immediately gone. He told us later that he would often sleep poorly and it would take him a long time to get out of bed in the morning because of the pain. That night he slept well for the first time in many years and got out of bed pain-free the next day.

Just being in God's presence, praying quietly in tongues or listening to worship music, can often seem like a waste of time. I used to wonder what was being achieved. Even when his manifest presence comes and one spends time laughing or crying or shaking, the temptation is to wonder what the purpose of it is. Some, questioning this, have asked me why people laugh in church. Apart from the fact that we are meant to be joyful, because Scripture says that in his presence 'there is fullness of joy' (Ps. 16:11), the reality is that we often do not know what God is doing. Recently I was approached by a lady for whom I had prayed at a conference. She told me her story, saying, 'When you prayed, I immediately fell to the floor and began laughing. This had never happened to me before, and as I was at the front of the church I felt a bit silly. I was laughing and laughing and kicking my legs in the air. I said to myself, "This is crazy: I'm laughing and kicking my legs like a baby." Immediately God spoke to me and said, "And I am healing you of the wounds you received when you were a baby. Your mother did not want a girl, and you have lived your whole life with that rejection. This joy is healing you.'" The lady was in her mid-sixties, and God was doing heart surgery to heal her from decades of pain. One of our children's groups was learning about resting in God's presence in this way on one Sunday morning, and during that time three boys were healed, as far as I know without anyone praying for them.

PRESENCE TAKES PRIORITY

We long to be a people who are able to say, 'Come, Holy Spirit,' and see the Holy Spirit come to move in power. However, we first have to learn to come when he says 'come'. This is the relational way. There have been many times where I have been in my office and felt the Spirit fall. Immediately I will SMS various staff members with the words, 'Surf's up.'[7] Whoever is free will then make their way to my office to see what is going on. On numbers of occasions the power of God has fallen on virtually everyone present as he fills us with more of him. Often one person is weeping while the person next to them is laughing. The Holy Spirit does not seem to mind. Others receive freedom or empowering or walk into repentance. It can go on for some time. Sometimes I have felt that I had too much to do to take time for this! However, the Bible is filled with stories of ordinary men and women who did extraordinary things when filled with God's Spirit. We are learning to walk as they walked and take time to wait on him as our first priority. Interestingly, we have found that the work always gets done to an excellent standard, and when caught up with the wind of his Spirit I have written some of my best sermons in half the time it normally takes me.

The American revivalist Charles Finney said this after the Spirit fell on him:

> I immediately found myself endued with such power from on high that a few words dropped here and there to individuals were the means of their immediate conversion. My words seemed to fasten like barbed arrows in the souls of men. They cut like a sword. They broke the heart like a hammer. Multitudes can attest to this. Oftentimes a word dropped, without my remembering it, would fasten conviction, and often result in almost immediate conversion.

Interestingly, on the priority of the presence, Finney said that when he found himself losing power, 'I would then set apart a day for private fasting and prayer, fearing that this power had departed from me, and would inquire anxiously after the reason of this apparent emptiness. After humbling myself, and crying out for help, the power would return upon me with all its freshness. This has been the experience of my life.'[8]

This is still an area of growth for me, as I naturally like to do what I like to do and when I like to do it, ploughing on regardless! But the Holy Spirit is gently leading me further and further into the reality that he is the one in charge and that obedience to him is high on his agenda for my discipleship.

Some time ago I was preparing for two different meetings in the same week. I was concerned about the first because I felt that many of the people attending would not want to be there. I had little or no concern about the second, knowing the hunger for God that would be present in the room. However, things turned out very differently. At the first meeting the presence of God fell in a tangible way. Many fell to the floor in wonder and others were set free or heard God's voice speaking to them. I personally felt the power of God in a way that I have seldom felt before. The second was a good meeting and God did many things, but not in the same degree as the first. The day after the second meeting I was praying in the morning, asking God to show me why there was such a difference. I was surprised at the reversal from my expectations. That day we went for a walk with my small group, and one lady asked me what I had been doing that week. When I told her, she replied, 'I'm asking because I was woken one night this week and spent the night praying for you.' She was encouraged, and I was thunderstruck to learn that it was the night before the first meeting. It underlined again what I already knew: everything flows out of his presence.

DEAL WITH DISTRACTIONS

Apart from busyness, the biggest difficulty that has challenged me in the pursuit of more of his presence has been overcoming distractions. Laptops and mobile phones have been probably the biggest factor in distracting me from my pursuit. I dreamed once of massive breakthrough with unbelievers and believers, but the interesting part of the dream was that it started with me leaving my mobile phone behind. I know that God is saying to me that part of the breakthrough will only come as I overcome the tyranny of distractions. Jesus modelled frequently withdrawing to spend time in his Father's presence, and he was able to do so even though he was the only hope of the world. How much more do I need to. There is only one Saviour, by the way! Jesus also told his disciples to 'close the door' (Matt. 6:6) when they went to pray. Perhaps our challenge today is as much to close the 'electronic door' as it is to close the physical one.

John Piper once said:

> If all other variables are equal, your capacity to know God will probably diminish in direct proportion to how much TV you watch. There are several reasons for this. One is that TV reflects culture at its most trivial. A steady diet of triviality shrinks the soul. You get used to it. It starts to seem normal. It starts to satisfy your soul. And in the end the soul that is made for God has shrunk to fit snugly around triteness. [9]

MODEL PURSUIT OF HIS PRESENCE

Just as Jesus modelled the intimacy and dependence that he found in his Father's presence and the priority he placed on it, I've found as a leader that it is critical to do the same. Once at a conference I was attending there was a call for prayer for those who had never received the baptism in the Holy Spirit. I suspected that this might be my only chance to receive prayer in the whole conference, so I immediately went to the front. Two of our staff team noticed, and one said to the other, 'Simon's going to help pray for people.' The other, who perhaps knew me a little better, queried this conclusion: 'No, I bet he's going to receive prayer.' It was a little mischievous to go up for prayer when the ministry time was so specifically targeted to new Christians, but I was hungry for more of God!

Personal discipline, gifting and growth are critical for the follower of Jesus. But the most important thing is the conscious awareness of and dependence on God's presence. 'If you abide in me, and my words abide in you, ask whatever you wish, and it will be done for you,' said Jesus (John 15:7). We have found that this fresh focus on his presence has produced exactly the greater fruit that Jesus promised. It is not that we were fruitless before, but something of a different magnitude has happened. One young lady told me that although she had been a Christian most of her life, she was bound with fear before coming to the King's Arms and had never felt God's presence. Now, she says, 'I am so conscious of him being there.'

THE CORPORATE JOURNEY

As we began the personal journey of learning to prioritize God's presence we also began a corporate one. It needs to be said again that this came in parallel with learning about improving our welcome, preaching, structures and teams. Both the wine and the wineskin remain important. The fire does not exist in a healthy way without a fireplace. But fireplaces and wineskins are worth nothing without the fire and the wine! We must be people who are desperate for the fire and thirsty for the wine.

Prayer: Firstly, we found that our hunger for prayer increased dramatically. From one monthly prayer meeting which was reasonably well attended we have also added occasions of 100 hours of continuous prayer or sessions of 24-hour prayer for seven days a week. These have been significant times in which we slow down and make time to be with him. It is on these and other occasions that we have learned to hunger, pursue and encounter God together as a family. We have to have the presence of God! Stale, repetitive and boring meetings will not cut it for us any more. The wind of the Spirit must be felt and must be felt powerfully. What I have observed is that once people have tasted the life and power of the Spirit, brought together with a healthy and godly culture of hosting his presence, they never want to go back. The presence of God was always meant to be the thing that captivated and enthralled the people of God. Awe was meant to be in the house! I have longed for the sense of awe that you detect was present in the early church to be restored again to the church today. What has encouraged me is that as we have pursued his presence corporately – those moments of intense, awe-filled presence in our corporate times together have increased in frequency and power.

Discernment: We found that it was also critical to learn to discern what the Holy Spirit was doing in our corporate gatherings, both small and large. While God will often speak to me about what he is doing or is about to do, I live with the reality that I don't have the exclusive hotline to him, even if I am the one hosting the meeting. Very often he will speak to other people present, either before or after, to tell them his intentions. Recently during a Sunday meeting, one of our key prophets approached me and said that he felt God wanted to heal people that morning. I was not feeling anything particularly myself but I trusted his gift and so told those gathered that we were going to extend the worship time and finish with prayer for the sick. We saw a number healed, more than on a normal Sunday, and I was glad that I had listened.

This doesn't mean that people with a prophetic word have 'carte blanche' to direct the meeting wherever they desire. Sometimes the person hosting the meeting will have another idea of what God is doing and will go with that. Sometimes it is appropriate to let the prophetic person bring what they feel God is saying, and sometimes the host will share a summary of the word or words.

***Open to the Spirit, explanation for unbelievers*:** Sometimes things happen that are strange to the average unbeliever who may be present in the meeting. It is not that the Holy Spirit is unaware of the unbelievers present, but some of his church are! We wrestled hard with this issue and on occasions still revisit it to examine whether we feel that we are in the right place. I have been to many churches who would say that they are open to the Spirit, but the average unbeliever is totally freaked out by the goings-on. We took the decision many years ago that Sunday meetings are primarily for God's people to meet with God together. Having said that, they should be as accessible as possible for the unbeliever. We took this from Paul's letter to the Corinthians and other passages. It was clear that in the early church model, the main gathering meeting was primarily for believers. It was for their corporate worship, instruction, fellowship and communication. However, Paul was concerned that in this freedom, the Corinthians were not acting in a loving way to those Christians who were uninitiated in the things of the Spirit and to the unbelievers who were present. He writes:

> If, therefore, the whole church comes together and all speak in tongues, and outsiders or unbelievers enter, will they not say that you are out of your minds? But if all prophesy, and an unbeliever

or outsider enters, he is convicted by all, he is called to account by all, the secrets of his heart are disclosed, and so, falling on his face, he will worship God and declare that God is really among you (1 Cor. 14:23–25).

Paul was concerned not only that the Spirit should be allowed to move freely but also that the Corinthians should not abuse this freedom at the gospel-expense of those who were unbelievers or uninitiated. Rather, he wanted the power of the Spirit to be used to draw people to Christ. Several issues are key:

1. Heart issues: The team leading the meeting must examine their hearts. Where you find control, self-righteousness and uptightness, you will not often find the Holy Spirit moving freely. I have learned to look for these indicators in myself and to repent and free myself from them before I attempt to host a meeting.

2. Explanation: Early in Acts, Peter finds himself in a private meeting that bursts into the public sphere, with the power of the Spirit moving upon the disciples. Some have argued that the only manifestation was that the disciples spoke in different foreign languages. But this cannot have been the case, because people in the crowd thought that the disciples were drunk. When I see someone speaking French I do not think he is drunk; instead I assume he's French. If he then spoke in another language, I would assume he was a bilingual Frenchman. I would not assume that he was drunk. To be accused of being drunk, clearly the disciples must have been acting in a fashion that gave that impression, either staggering or perhaps shouting loudly, and in front of lots of unbelievers. That being the case, what was the Holy Spirit doing? Peter did not tell the believers, 'Stop being drunk in the Spirit: there are unbelievers who can see you.' Instead he *explained* what was going on, demonstrating that the behaviour that people were observing was not due to alcohol but by the Spirit. He *used the manifestation* to then point them to the prophet Joel and to the gospel. In a similar fashion, we have found that explanation is crucial in helping unbelievers and the uninitiated understand and engage with what is going on. The host of the meeting is key to this, at times commenting during the meeting to help people understand why others may raise their hands, shout out to Jesus, lie on the floor or shake under the power of the Spirit. Of course some unbelievers (and believers) struggle with it. However, many are happy enough once things are explained. After all, they have come wanting to encounter a God who is real and powerful.

3. Context: The context of the meeting is important. A carol service or baptism is different from a conference. There are some things that one does in one's own lounge that, while innocuous in themselves, you would not do when you had guests. The songs that we sing, the length and subject of the message, should all vary according to the context of the meeting. Recently we had a powerful tongue given on a Sunday morning. The lady bringing the tongue also brought the interpretation. The host explained what had just happened and encouraged people to keep focused on God and allow these words to fuel their worship. Afterwards, another lady who was there, who had been a missionary in Tajikistan, excitedly told the first, 'That tongue you brought was in fluent Tajik! And your interpret- ation was spot on.' I wouldn't miss these moments for the world, while recognizing that very 'guest-cen- tric' meetings such as carol services and baptisms need particular care in terms of how we handle the gifts of the Spirit.

4. *Addressing unbelievers*: We do everything with unbeliev- ers in mind during our meetings, from the welcome at the beginning to the ministry time at the end. In sermons, most times, there will be a section just for those who are seeking. This helps unbelievers feel part of what is going on and realize that this is appropriate to them. Additionally, we steer clear of using the terms 'non-Christian' or 'unbeliever' where possi- ble. We want people to feel part of things so that they can belong before they believe.

5. *Hosting*: Every meeting that we hold has someone to host it. This is a key role that helps maintain the values and culture that we love. We've found that this role, played correctly, helps to provide the appropriate stability and safety for the meeting. In times past, while being the host I have been overcome by the Holy Spirit. Instead of me trying to continue, immedi- ately one of our team has taken over, providing a safe context and explanation for the people gathered. The host needs to be aware of what is happening and deal with it appropriately. A noisy demonic issue needs a team to be quickly there, and the host can direct the ministry team if they are not moving fast enough!

6. *Follow-up conversations*: We encourage our church to speak with people if their behaviour seems strange. This provides a useful check of 'one-anothering', where the church, in good heart, can ask questions and offer to pray further if necessary. We must not be afraid to have these conversations, because the enemy would love to distort and damage the things that God is doing through fleshly shows or demonic activity that are not dealt with. Both of these will happen in our meetings (Jesus dealt with the latter in significant proportion) but they will not take over if we deal with them appropriately and in good heart, never allowing control or fear of the supernatural to affect our responses.

This journey of walking in his manifest presence is critical for the church today. For too long we have relied on techniques, man-made strategies and worldly learning to try to achieve the things of God. There is no substitute for the presence of God.

Notes

[1] For examples of these stories visit
http://tinyurl.com/mentransformed.
[2] Taken from a transcript of a taped message preached by Duncan Campbell in 1968, 'Revival in the Hebrides'
http://www.revival-library.org/pensketches/revivals/hebrides.
html.
[3] In fact none of the New Testament writers use the term *bapto* when referring to baptism in water or in the Holy Spirit. *Bapto*

is used only three times in the New Testament: in Luke 16:24, John 13:26 and Revelation 19:13. On each occasion it does not refer to baptism in the sense we are considering here.

4 In secular Greek *bapto* means (a) dip, (b) dip into a dye, and so dye, and (c) draw (water). *Baptizo* is an intensive form of *bapto* and means (a) dip, and (b) cause to perish (as by drowning a man or sinking a ship). Colin Brown (Gen. Ed.), *New International Dictionary of New Testament Theology* (Zondervan, 2008), Vol. 1, p. 144.

5 Some have argued that the words may have changed meaning between the time of Nicander and that of the New Testament. While this is possible, there must have been some difference between these words for the choice to have been made so explicitly by the New Testament authors. I believe the solution proposed is the most likely.

6 Psalm 1:3 is also helpful here as a reminder that fruit is borne by those who spend time meditating on God's word. Both are necessary.

7 I first heard Kris Vallotton of Bethel Church use this expression.

8 Charles Finney, 'Power from on High – What is it?' *The Independent,* New York, 18 January 1972, Gospel Truth Ministries, http://www.gospeltruth.net/1868_75Independent/720118_pfoh_what.htm.

9 John Piper, *Pierced by the Word: Thirty-One Meditations for Your Soul* (Multnomah, 2003), pp. 77–79.

11

WHAT IS IT?

Of the increase of his government and of peace there will be no end, on the throne of David and over his kingdom, to establish it and to uphold it with justice and with righteousness from this time forth and for evermore. The zeal of the LORD of hosts will do this.

Isaiah 9:7

I often sleep badly when travelling to speak, as the combination of a new bed, bags of travel sweets and late night meals rarely sits well with me. Maybe I should cut out the travel sweets, but as a father of three I find not having to share the bag of Haribo on a journey is just too good an opportunity to pass up. On the night before one conference I had a dream that seemed to last for the entire night. Over and over I dreamed of a man chasing a woman to abuse her. In the dream I somehow knew the man's first name. I had received words of knowledge in dreams before, but why did I have the same dream so many times? The next day, at the end of the meeting I gave the word that someone had either been abused or stalked by a man of this name. By the end of the morning a total of six people had responded to the same word: four women and two men. The ministry team fed back the details.

One lady had been stalked by a man bearing this name. Another lady had been raped by a guy with this first name. One lady had been locked in a room and was about to be abused when someone knocked on the door and saved her. A man of this name abused one gentleman when he was fifteen years old. He was now in his late fifties and had never told anyone before. The ministry team reported that each one had walked into massive freedom that morning. The kingdom of God had broken in.

A number of years ago there would be few in our church with any real understanding of the kingdom of God. To us it was a vague concept, a phrase that we had heard many times but with little clarity. Looking back now, it is not surprising that we could not 'proclaim that the kingdom is at hand' as Jesus told us to, as we had no idea what it was! Why is it that Jesus' hearers did not ask for greater clarity on exactly what the kingdom of God was? The answer, I believe, lies in the *piñata*.

For the uninitiated, a *piñata* is a large, hollow, papier-mâché container originally shaped like a donkey but now more likely to be shaped like Buzz Lightyear or some other popular character. The *piñata,* stuffed full of sweets, is hung up by a string from a tree or, if no tree is available, held by a willing but foolish adult. The kids then line up to take a stick and beat the living daylights out of it. It is supposed to be one hit each, but some of the kids cannot stop themselves and come in swinging the stick like a berserker intent on total *piñata* destruction. Now you understand why you do not want to be the adult holding it. When the *piñata* bursts open, the stick is cast aside and then there is a ruck of kids grabbing desperately for the largest handfuls of treats. There is usually crying, pain and despair as little Johnny gets less than a friend. As you can imagine, it is a real family event!

I believe that the phrase 'the kingdom of God' was like a *piñata* to first-century Jewish people. Not that they thought it was a donkey. What I mean is that although the term 'the kingdom of God' may have lost much of its meaning to us, it was stuffed full of meaning to them.

Firstly we need to understand that in English the word 'kingdom' usually means a geographical region or a place, for example the Kingdom of Morocco or the United Kingdom. However, to Jesus and the Jewish people the word used for kingdom was primarily one that described a reign rather than a region or place. A good working definition of the kingdom of God, therefore, is 'the rule of God over his people'. When Jesus spoke of the kingdom he was speaking about God ruling over people's lives.

Secondly, though, to understand fully what they took it to mean we need to look at what the people of Jesus' day were reading. A clue comes from one of Jesus' early sermons. Luke reports that at the beginning of his ministry, Jesus opened the scroll of Isaiah and read from it (Luke 4:17–19). Jesus read a paraphrased quotation from Isaiah 61, and in fact we find that Jesus, Paul and other New Testament writers all quote extensively from Isaiah. It is second only to Psalms as the most quoted book in the New Testament. Harold Willmington writes, 'Isaiah is universally looked upon as the greatest Old Testament manuscript, as written by the greatest Old Testament prophet. In unsurpassed eloquence Isaiah describes the greatness, grace, and glory of God, the virgin birth, dual nature, earthly life, sufferings, and resurrection of the promised Messiah. Isaiah 53 alone is quoted from or alluded to eighty-five times in the New Testament.'[1]

ISAIAH AND THE KINGDOM

If we want to understand what Jesus and his hearers understood the kingdom of God to be, it is no surprise, then, that it is to Isaiah that we need to turn. Even though Isaiah does not actually mention the term 'the kingdom of God', there are kingdom references everywhere you look.[2] In fact there are seventeen passages in the book of Isaiah that speak about the kingdom of God.[3] From these we can draw some very clear themes which indicate what people were expecting from God's kingdom. We shall now look at the seven themes which occur most frequently in these seventeen 'kingdom' passages.[4] (See also Appendix.)

1. Deliverance or salvation (occurs in all seventeen Isaiah 'kingdom' passages)

'The Spirit of the Lord GOD is upon me, because the LORD has anointed me to bring good news to the poor; he has sent me to bind up the broken-hearted, to proclaim liberty to the captives' (Isa. 61:1).

Isaiah prophesied seventeen times that when the kingdom came it would come with deliverance and salvation. The people of Jesus' day were desperate for deliverance from their Roman oppressors. Living in an occupied country, they scraped out an existence in constant fear. Yet the deliverance and salvation that Jesus brought was of a different nature.

We see over and over that Jesus' salvation was a salvation from our sin, and his deliverance was from the demonic strongholds of the enemy. In the gospels the word most frequently translated 'salvation' is *sozo*. At its heart it speaks of a liberty for people and a restoration to God's intent. In the beginning of Matthew's gospel, the angel tells Joseph that Mary will bear a son and they are to name him Jesus because 'he will save (*sozo*) his people from their sins' (Matt. 1:21). Here the salvation is spiritual. However, later in Matthew's gospel Jesus heals the woman with the issue of blood and declares, 'Take heart, daughter; your faith has made you well (*sozo*)' (Matt. 9:22). Here the same word refers to physical healing, and we see that Jesus' salvation is not simply salvation from sin but also invades the physical world. Finally, Luke applies the same word to a deliverance from demonic oppression: 'And those who had seen it told them how the demon-possessed man had been healed (*sozo*)' (Luke 8:36). In short, the salvation that Jesus was bringing from heaven to earth includes all aspects of humankind's brokenness and pain. The early church of course continued this, setting free the oppressed, releasing forgiveness of sin and seeing also the unjustly imprisoned freed (Acts 12:1–17).

We have seen as a church that as we have begun to expect more of God's kingdom to break onto the earth, salvation has increased in every one of these aspects. During one week, seven people gave their lives to Christ in different contexts. One lady was in her garden at home when the Spirit of God fell on her, convicting her of her sin. She found our number and called the church offices, saying 'Is there anyone who can pray with me? I must become a Christian and I can't wait until

Sunday.' At the end of the week, as I was praying about this the Lord spoke to me and said, 'Simon, this week has been extraordinary, but contend for it to become the ordinary. It is a picture of what I intend to do. This high-water mark will become a low-water mark.'

We have also seen an increase in deliverance from oppressive spiritual strongholds as we began to understand the full extent of what the kingdom is all about. One lady wrote:

Although I had a good and strong relationship with God, I had 'settled' in many areas of my life with things that at the time I thought were normal. I would wake up feeling the blackness of depression, and had to push it back each morning to leave the house. Some days I had intense battles just to get out of my front door. I was full of insecurity – managing not to act on impulses to self-harm or control my eating (as I had previously) but constantly plagued with negative thoughts about myself. As the church pressed into more of the Holy Spirit and the miraculous, I simultaneously believed the truth and couldn't overcome unbelief. I would feel both excitement and cynicism at the same time whenever I heard a testimony or saw someone encounter God.

Once I wrote down a list of 'things I believe', and 'things I shouldn't believe, but I do' . . . I shocked myself by filling three A4 typed sheets with examples like 'God can heal', but 'If someone is praying for healing and I join them, it will probably stop it from happening.' I signed up for healing prayer!

One night I experienced amazing deliverance from depression, pride (self-reliance) and unbelief. My life has never been the same again. Suddenly I was free to celebrate when I heard a testimony or saw someone meeting with God. I experienced some incredible encounters with the Holy Spirit. But more than that, there was no longer a dark undercurrent cutting under every time with God and every step of faith. I am free of depression and have never again felt controlled by it. I could clearly see and reject lies, and I experienced faith for God's power like I had never believed possible. Most surprising of all, I was comfortable and happy in my own skin, probably for the first time in my life.

From that point I grew continually in my hunger to see God move and I started to see others healed, set free and powerfully delivered when I prayed for them. I could teach and lead with authority and faith! I am so grateful for the utter transformation God has worked in my life.

This is a sign of the kingdom. But there is more!

2. Righteousness and justice (occurs in sixteen Isaiah 'kingdom' passages)

'To bring good news to the poor' (Isa. 61:1). 'Behold, a king will reign in righteousness, and princes will rule in justice (Isa. 32:1).

Isaiah 32, among other passages, speaks of the justice to come when the kingdom of God breaks in. Sixteen times Isaiah prophesied on this theme, the second most common theme of kingdom arrival. Jesus' hearers wanted justice. They were tired of corrupt governments. Although the justice that Jesus came to bring will eventually result in a completely just government, the more critical issue was the need for a righteousness of heart and a justice that flowed from the heart. Jesus brought the power of the kingdom to bear on the human heart, and from that victory all righteousness and justice will ultimately flow. The early church picked up this message of righteousness and justice, proclaiming what Christ had achieved on the cross and our new identity in him.[5]

Bishop Desmond Tutu grew up in the midst of one of the most oppressive and unjust political systems ever to be birthed onto the planet: apartheid. He tells the story that one day, when he was a child, he was standing in the street with his mother when a white man in priest's clothing walked past. As he did so, he took off his hat to young Desmond's mother. Tutu recounted, 'I couldn't believe my eyes: a white man who greeted a black working class woman!' The man was Father Trevor Huddleston, an English parish priest who became Tutu's greatest role model. Huddleston opposed the apartheid system by encouraging his poverty-stricken parishioners to stand up for themselves against oppression. When Tutu contracted tuberculosis, a sickness that nearly killed him, Huddleston took time to visit him every week for two years. He taught Tutu to adopt the daily prayer routine from which he has never wavered, and even brought him the schoolbooks he needed to graduate on schedule in 1950. When the kingdom comes, righteousness transforms hearts and justice starts to flow even into the darkest of situations. I have stood in the room where William Wilberforce and the 'Clapham Sect' prayed and planned the downfall of slave trading in the British Empire. It is not a large room, and it was humbling to think what a handful of men gripped by the desire for kingdom justice can do on the planet.

3. Peace (occurs in fourteen Isaiah 'kingdom' passages)

'To bind up the broken-hearted' (Isa. 61:1). 'For to us a child is born, to us a son is given . . . and his name shall be called

Wonderful Counsellor, Mighty God, Everlasting Father, Prince of Peace' (Isa. 9:6).

Isaiah's third cry was that when the kingdom comes we must expect peace. Often when we pray for people, the primary sign of God's presence is peace. Even when we're praying out on a street corner or in a workplace, it's amazing that unbelievers can detect this peace and vocalize it. In a troubled world, when God's kingdom breaks in, it brings peace.

Fourteen times Isaiah prophesied that when the Messiah came with his kingdom he would bring peace. This passage in Isaiah 9 is probably the best-known, where the prophet tells us that the Messiah's nature will be so intrinsically linked with this peace that he will be called the Prince of Peace. The Jews of Jesus' day wanted an end to physical war. Before this could happen, Jesus intended to bring about peace between people and God. When the angels declared at his birth, 'On earth peace among those with whom he is pleased' (Luke 2:14), they were announcing a new season of peace with God and a revelation of the pleasure of God for those who would receive it.

This concept of peace is larger than just the absence of war. It would have been based on the Jewish idea of *shalom*, which was found in Moses' blessing of the people of Israel (Num. 6:24). It is a heavenly peace that comes with God's presence and speaks of a completion or perfection of life and spirit. It carries a sense of wholeness both for people and for the world.[6]

Jesus frequently imparted this peace to those who were troubled. He spoke peace to an ostracized woman who would have lived with the stress of long-term sickness (Mark 5:34). He spoke peace to the sinful woman who had washed his feet with her tears (Luke 7:50). He spoke peace to his anxious disciples, lost in grief because of his death and now fearing for their own lives (John 20:21). He even spoke peace to a storm. Jesus lived in such a reality of peace that it poured out of him into a troubled world. When Jesus trained his disciples to go and do the things he was doing, he naturally trained them in this idea of bringing peace: 'Whatever house you enter, first say, "Peace be to this house!" And if a son of peace is there, your peace will rest upon him. But if not, it will return to you' (Luke 10:5–6).

Such was to be their awareness of heaven's peace that they could literally command it into a place or group of people. I have seen this reality in many ways. I've prayed for numbers of people who have insomnia, and very often their sleep pattern has returned to normal. One man experienced a massive deliverance as we prayed, and said to me months later that he had never again had a problem with sleeping. Often I have found that when people come to faith in Christ they experience a tremendous peace. It's the assurance of God's kingdom entering into their lives.

4. Joy (occurs in twelve Isaiah 'kingdom' passages)

'The oil of gladness' and 'everlasting joy' (Isa. 61:3,7). 'You have multiplied the nation; you have increased its joy; they rejoice before you as with joy at the harvest' (Isa. 9:3).

The Christian Indian mystic Sundar Singh was once thrown into a deep, dark pit filled with rotting dead bodies as a punishment for preaching the gospel in a village. He escaped with the help of a sympathetic villager and later wrote:

A wonderful peace filled my heart, so lovely that I cannot describe it. Never have I experienced greater blessedness in the peace of Jesus, received through prayer, than during those very days. Christ's peace turned that deep well into the Gate of Heaven. How was it possible to have the peace of God in the pitch-dark night, in the midst of corpses and dead men's bones? Joy like this, peace like this, comes from nothing in this world. God alone can give it.[7]

Isaiah prophesied twelve times that joy would come with God's kingdom. Many of us expect to find splendour and majesty when we finally see God. But David, the man who encountered God's presence almost more than any other, wrote that 'strength and joy are in his place' (1 Chron. 16:27) and again that in his presence 'there is fullness of joy' (Ps. 16:11). Even though it is not recorded in the gospels, Jesus would frequently have laughed. We can tell this because some of the stories that he told would have provoked immediate laughter (for example, the log sticking out of someone's eye, Matt. 7:5). We are also told that the crowds around Jesus rejoiced again and again. Interestingly, the only time Jesus' joy is recorded is when he rejoices that the disciples are healing the sick and driving out demons as he had done (Luke 10:21). I wonder what we think this looked like. Was it a gentle smile on Jesus' face? A slight chuckle?[8] Actually the word Luke uses means 'to jump for joy'.[9] If you've ever seen a Jewish party you will understand something of Jesus' abandoned celebration when he saw the reality of the first few change enough to enable them also to bring kingdom invasion. Of course this outbreak of heavenly joy does not mean that we will never experience difficulty. What marked out the early church, though, was their joy in the midst of difficulty, and especially when the Spirit was falling on them. We see that the disciples were filled with joy when the Spirit fell (Acts 13:52), and Paul says that the Thessalonians also experienced this manifestation of the Spirit (1 Thess. 1:6). Paul declares that joy is one of the three primary signs of the kingdom (Rom. 14:17) and lists it as the second fruit of the Spirit after love (Gal. 5:22). Peter, James, the writer to the Hebrews and Paul all talk of this kingdom joy experienced in great adversity. Peter, whose first letter is primarily to help those suffering extreme persecution, says that as they experienced Christ they experienced 'joy that is inexpressible and filled with glory' (1 Pet. 1:8). When God's kingdom comes it brings joy.

So why then are churches seldom places of great joy and Christians frequently depressed? If you ask the average unbeliever what they think about church, the most common word used would not be 'joy'. My informal surveys indicate it is a different word: 'boring'. Christians are seen not as joyful but as uptight, judgemental and boring. Something has to change! Before we can extend God's kingdom on earth we need to experience it ourselves.

As we have repented of control, cynicism and self-reliance, the uptightness has begun to drop away and our community has become a far more joyful place. We often have the delight of seeing whole rooms filled with joy. Worship, both corporate and private, has become a deeply joyful experience for many as we experience his kingdom breaking in.

I hope you're getting a clearer picture of what to expect when the kingdom comes.

5. God's presence as Spirit (or light) (occurs in nine Isaiah 'kingdom' passages)

'The Spirit of the Lord GOD is upon me' (Isa. 61:1). 'Arise, shine, for your light has come, and the glory of the LORD has risen upon you' (Isa. 60:1).

Isaiah prophesied nine times that God's presence and glory would extend to his people in an unprecedented way when the kingdom of God comes. We've devoted an entire chapter to this subject (Chapter 10), so there is no need to say any more here.

6. Healing (occurs in seven Isaiah 'kingdom' passages)

'Recovering of sight to the blind' (Luke 4:18).[10] 'Then the eyes of the blind shall be opened, and the ears of the deaf unstopped; then shall the lame man leap like a deer, and the tongue of the mute sing for joy' (Isa. 35:5–6).

Isaiah said repeatedly that when the kingdom came it would come with physical and emotional healing. The king would heal sick bodies and bind up broken and wounded hearts. A cursory glance through the gospels and the stories I have shared in this book should suffice to show that healing is part and parcel of what our King does. Every person that Jesus ministered to was healed. The early church did not see every person healed, but they saw many, many people healed. We do not see everyone healed but we do expect healing! We expect great healing, mass healings, extraordinary healings and shocking, city-changing healings. These are the things that the early church saw, and these should be the things that the church today will see, because the greatest days of the church are not in the past but in the future!

7. Comfort (occurs in six Isaiah 'kingdom' passages)

'To comfort all who mourn' (Isa. 61:2). 'For the LORD comforts Zion; he comforts all her waste places and makes her wilderness like Eden, her desert like the garden of the LORD' (Isa. 51:3).

Perhaps unexpectedly, the seventh most common theme that Isaiah spoke about is comfort. When we look at the life of Jesus it should actually be no surprise, because we see him bringing comfort wherever there are soft and broken hearts. We desperately need comfort, although sometimes we are too proud to admit it. I have personally traced the root of much sin in my life to getting false comfort when I am tired, upset or angry. How much sin in the church comes because we won't admit that we need comfort? The early church was not like this. In Acts it says that the early church received 'the comfort of the Holy Spirit' (Acts 9:31). The Apostle Paul was not ashamed to admit that he needed comfort, speaking of the 'God of all comfort, who comforts us in all our affliction, so that we may be able to comfort those who are in any affliction, with the comfort with which we ourselves are comforted by God' (2 Cor. 1:3–4).

As we began to admit our need, we saw his comforter arrive. I recall one man who had been beaten so badly by his dad when he was a child that he was hospitalized on more than one occasion. He shared how he had received freedom at one of our conferences three years earlier and had been able to call God 'Father' for the first time. Three years later he shared that in the subsequent years he had been reconciled with his father and they were now rebuilding their relationship. Throughout that time he had known the continual comfort and presence of his heavenly Father.

WORKING IT OUT

There are many other themes that Isaiah spoke of concerning the coming kingdom, but these primary seven will suffice to make the point. This kingdom is like a *piñata* packed full of goodness. Jesus and his hearers had no lack of understanding and expectation of what was coming with the kingdom of God.

It is not only Jesus who teaches us about the kingdom of God. Seventy times the writers of the New Testament mention preaching about the kingdom of God. All the major leaders of the New Testament era were said to have preached this message. John the Baptist and Jesus we might expect to do so, but the writer to the Hebrews, James, Peter, John and Philip all talk about the kingdom (Acts 8:12; Heb. 12:28; Jas 2:5; 2 Pet. 1:11). We also see that the entire book of Acts has this theme as Luke's giant 'bookends'. Right at the start of Acts he summarizes the close of Jesus' ministry as 'appearing to them during forty days and speaking about the kingdom of God', and he closes Acts with Paul under house arrest in Rome 'proclaiming the kingdom of God and teaching about the Lord Jesus Christ with all boldness and without hindrance' (Acts 1:3; 28:31). The importance of this theme of the kingdom cannot be overemphasized. David Devenish, a leader within the family of churches that we are part of, writes: 'The kingdom is to be our top priority. Jesus said, "Seek first his kingdom and his righteousness." The kingdom is to have far greater priority in our lives than concerns about material things or anything else. It has to be top priority for the church in its mission today.'[11]

Where our question is, 'What is the kingdom?' theirs was, 'When is it?' When Jesus came, saying, 'It's at hand,' the excitement must have been palpable. Do we have the expectation that we are meant to have when we declare 'The kingdom of heaven is here'? The application for us is significant.

THE IMPLICATIONS OF THE KINGDOM

This realization has a number of important implications, for us and for others:

For us

Once we understand what the arrival of God's kingdom looks like, we know something more of the fruit for which Christ died. No longer should we be content to live lives of fear, joylessness, hopelessness, sickness, injustice and a lack of God's presence. God's will is clear. Jesus taught us to pray, 'Your kingdom come, your will be done.' That is God's ultimate will. I can begin to contend, pray and believe God for more of the outbreak of the kingdom in my life. My role is to stand in the 'now' and join with the Spirit in seeking to draw the not yet into the now!

For others

Wherever I see something that is not of the kingdom, I can learn to operate on the basis of 'standing orders'. In UK banking, any individual can set up a standing order on their account to repeatedly pay a third party a certain amount.

Without further instruction, the bank will continue to pay out. In a similar way, when we understand the signs of the kingdom of God, we have 'standing orders' from heaven.

George Eldon Ladd, one of the greatest writers on the kingdom of God, wrote:

> While the Kingdom of God will not be realized as a state of perfect blessedness until Christ returns, God's Kingdom is at work in the world and is engaged in a mortal struggle with evil. The Church is the instrument of this struggle. Conflict therefore must ever be an essential element in the life of the Church so long as This Age lasts. Human history will realize something of the life and blessings of God's Kingdom because a new community has been formed in human society.[12]

Once I understand the signs of the kingdom, I know what God's will is. All I need to ask my Father is, 'What are you doing?' and 'What is my part in this?' More often than not our Father wants us to work off our 'standing orders'. My job becomes immediate and obvious: to do anything I can to be the answer to my own prayer 'Your kingdom come, your will be done.' It may take weeks, months, years or decades. We might not see everything that we want to see this side of eternity, but our job is to yearn for more and to die trying if necessary. A radical life has come into our church as we have grabbed hold of this reality. Instead of passively watching the world go by, people have begun to understand their role of partnering with the Holy Spirit to see God's kingdom come.

Now and not yet

One day there will be a full breaking in of 'heaven on earth', when Jesus returns. This view helps particularly in times of suffering or persecution. Peter reminds his readers that this full salvation is 'ready to be revealed in the last time' and that they are to rejoice in this even while experiencing many trials (1 Pet. 1:5). The emperor at this time was Nero, who would burn Christians on stakes in his garden to provide light in the evenings so that he could enjoy a late-night stroll. A healthy understanding of the kingdom 'not yet' helps us to persevere when we do not get the breakthrough right now or when we suffer for the sake of our King.

However, while we wait for the 'not yet' it is too easy for us to withdraw from the world. Instead of contending for greater breakthrough now, everything is shoved under the carpet of 'the kingdom is not yet'. Instead of grieving over our powerlessness to heal the sick, we declare that it's God's will that cancer is as prevalent as it is. Instead of weeping over the brokenness of marriages in our nation, we simply shrug our shoulders and think, 'That's just the way things are.' Instead of being moved to prayer and action over the poor, we think, 'What can we really do, anyway?'

While Jesus did teach a full future breaking in of the kingdom when he called us to pray 'Your kingdom come,' his major focus was on bringing the kingdom to people's doorsteps *now* and declaring to them that the kingdom is at hand *now* (Luke 11:20). One of our students, when asked what had changed most about her throughout the year of training, said, 'I realized that I didn't believe that things were going to happen now, even though I believed that they will happen one day. That's changed this year and I have a new level of expectancy.'

This error, that the kingdom is not-quite-yet or not-quite-for-me, is prevalent everywhere I travel. It destroys faith, because it robs the church of both the bold expectation that God will work and the courageous contention for more of the kingdom now. The warlike spirit that Jesus said extends the kingdom (Matt. 11:12) is removed from the church, and we remain passively waiting for God to do something. Of course God is sovereign and does have sovereign timing that we sometimes do not understand. But he also commanded us to 'heal the sick' (Matt. 10:8) and to say to them, 'The kingdom of God has come near to you' (Luke 10:9). Alexander Venter, an associate of John Wimber, writes:

The tension and mystery of the kingdom is critical to a proper theology and praxis of healing. We cannot dictate or control healing yet we cannot accept or surrender to sickness. We pray with confident authority and expectation of healing for everyone, yet we are humble and honest, trusting God with the results as only God can heal. We do both at the same time. We instinctively try to resolve tension by tending to 'either/or' because 'and/both' is messy. [But] too much 'kingdom now' leads to arrogance and presumption, demanding healing as if on tap. Too much 'kingdom then' leads to pessimism and fatalism, leaving healing to 'if it is God's will'. We too easily explain lack of healing by kingdom tension when we ought to push through in faith. This tension, embracing both the 'already' and 'not yet' of the kingdom, makes us living paradoxes. It is learning to live and minister in the overlapping of two ages: the power of the kingdom and the resistance of this age. It leads to persevering faith, optimistic realism, dependence on God, discerning the moment, honouring people's dignity, respecting the unknown, and leaving the results with God.[13]

In my experience, most Christians, and I include myself, struggle not from expecting too much from God but from expecting too little. We've seen on our journey as a church that a growing understanding of the size, scope and power of the kingdom has transformed our expectations of life. It is time to pray afresh, 'Your kingdom come.'

Notes

[1] See Harold L. Willmington, *What You Need to Know About the Book of Isaiah* (Liberty University, 2008)
   http://digitalcommons.liberty.edu/will_know/37.

[2] While there is some controversy, it seems that in Jesus' day readers were familiar with the Greek Septuagint, Hebrew translations and either written or oral versions of the Aramaic translations. In the fourth century AD these Aramaic translations became known as the Targum. Jesus uses phrases that are familiar to readers of all these versions. When it comes to the kingdom of God, the Aramaic translations of the Old Testament that would have been in use in Jesus' day are particularly helpful in identifying kingdom references, because they frequently use the term 'kingdom of God' or 'kingdom of your God' in a way that Greek and Hebrew Scriptures do not. In their book *Kingdom Ethics* (IVP USA, 2003), Stassen and Gushee make this point:

'Isaiah 40:9 says "Here is your God," and the Targum (Aramaic translation) says "The kingdom of your God is revealed." Isaiah 52:7 says "Your God reigns," and the Aramaic paraphrase says "The kingdom of your God is revealed." They go on to point out many other similar examples.

3 These are Isaiah 9:1–7; 11; 24:14 – 25:12; 26; 31:1 – 32:20; 33; 35; 40:1–11; 42:1 – 44:8; 49; 51:1 – 52:12; 52:13 – 53:12; 54; 56; 60; 61; 62.

4 Of course frequency is not necessarily a measure of importance, nor even the only measure, but it does serve as one indicator that can give us a helpful overview, particularly as we'll see they mirror so beautifully the things that we see Jesus doing.

5 Rom. 3:21, Eph. 4:24, etc.

6 Strong's: H7965 'šālom: peace, safety, prosperity, well-being; intactness, wholeness; peace can have a focus of security, safety which can bring feelings of satisfaction, well-being, and contentment.' *Kohlenberger/Mounce Concise Hebrew–Aramaic Dictionary of the Old Testament* (Oak Tree Software).

7 Sadhu Sundar Singh, *Parables and Insights of Sadhu Sundar Singh*.

8 If Luke had meant that, he would have used the word *chairo*, which means to be calmly happy. He uses this in the previous verse (20).

9 *Strong's Dictionary*: 'agalliao: properly, to jump for joy, i.e. exult: be (exceeding) glad, with exceeding joy, rejoice (greatly)'.

10 For a study on why Jesus reads 'recovery of sight to the blind', a phrase that is not in our version of Isaiah 61, see http://www.kjvtoday.com/home/reliable-hebrew-text/did-jesus-quote-luke-418-19-in-the-septuagint.

[11] David Devenish, *What on Earth is the Church For?* (Authentic Media, 2005).

[12] George Eldon Ladd, *The Presence of the Future* (William B. Eerdmans Publishing Co., 1996).

[13] Alexander Venter, *Doing Healing* (Vineyard International Publishing, 2009).

Who Am I?

'Wherever you go, there you are' is a phrase I have heard and used many times in my life. It is said mostly to people who are 'on the run' from situations or circumstances that are perhaps more self-induced than the individual would like to think. It is used to try to help them see that they will carry most of the issues with them, and these issues will ultimately resurface wherever they go. But I have started to see that while of course it does have a negative application (I carry my junk with me), it is also true positively. Everything that I am goes everywhere with me. Understanding who I am is key to understanding what I carry.

At the end of a recent training course, I asked the delegates to say briefly what God had done in them. The course was run over many months, so the work had enough time for testing. Here are some of the things that they said:

'I found freedom to love and to be loved. Freedom to be myself. Freedom to dream, even though I am old.'

'I broke free from the need to perform. I'm now comfortable with being outside my comfort zone.'

'I felt that God was going to abandon me. My deepest wound he has turned around to be my strongest foundation. I am the message now.'

'I have friends now. Before this I didn't have any friends. My mother is a very controlling woman and she didn't speak to me when I moved out. But now our relationship has been restored.'

'Understanding my identity. I have heard the audible laugh of God and I've known his joy and love. I didn't appreciate how much my parents' death affected me and I've now realized that instead of being alone I have a family.'

Notice how many of these things are related to identity. Freedom to be loved, to not perform and to dream while old are identity-centred issues. It is equally true that these people did not have their identity transformed during the course. The transformation happened when they accepted Christ; for many this was some years earlier. So what happened during this season? Identity was not transformed: it was realized. 'Realized' sums it up because it means 'to become fully aware of something'. That is what we need in this area of identity.

My sister-in-law and her husband have adopted a Chinese son. He was four when he was adopted and spoke no English. He also had Chinese features and colouring. Seeing him in family photos is a wonderful sign of the grace of God to rescue a little orphan and place him in a new family. His jet-black hair stands out against their blond, his dark skin against their pale. But he is loved and accepted just as if he were home-grown. When my wife visited the family after he had been with them for one year, she was curious to know whether he still remembered any of the Chinese language. She asked him gently, 'Do you still know any Chinese words?' He looked at her cautiously. 'How you know I China?' he remonstrated in broken English.

To him, his identity was caught up with his new family. He was so adopted on the inside that it shocked him to realize that anyone else would know that this was not his biological family. Identity realized! How the heart of God longs for the same response from his children who have been adopted into his family. How many of the church have realized and stepped fully into their new identity in the Father's house? On our journey we've found this realization to be critical in building up, once the Holy Spirit has torn down through repentance. The old lies need to be replaced by new truth. The darkness will return unless we learn to remain in this light. Whole books have been written on this subject, but three key revelations have been part of the identity realization process:

1. I Am Now in Christ

Because I am in Christ, I am now:

- *bought out of slavery*: 'Justified by his grace as a gift, through the redemption that is in Christ Jesus.' (Rom. 3:24)
- *dead to sin, alive to God*: 'So you also must consider yourselves dead to sin and alive to God in Christ Jesus.' (Rom. 6:11)

- *a recipient of eternal life*: 'For the wages of sin is death, but the free gift of God is eternal life in Christ Jesus our Lord.' (Rom. 6:23)

- *free from condemnation*: 'There is therefore now no condemnation for those who are in Christ Jesus. For the law of the Spirit of life has set you free in Christ Jesus from the law of sin and death.' (Rom. 8:1–2)

- *inseparable from the love of God*: 'Neither death nor life . . . height nor depth, nor anything else in all creation, will be able to separate us from the love of God in Christ Jesus our Lord.' (Rom. 8:38–39)

- *part of his body*: 'So we, though many, are one body in Christ, and individually members one of another.' (Rom. 12:5)

- *triumphing*: 'But thanks be to God, who in Christ always leads us in triumphal procession, and through us spreads the fragrance of the knowledge of him everywhere.' (2 Cor. 2:14)

- *a new creation*: 'Therefore, if anyone is in Christ, he is a new creation. The old has passed away; behold, the new has come.' (2 Cor. 5:17)

- *reconciled and a reconciler*: 'In Christ God was reconciling the world to himself, not counting their trespasses against them, and entrusting to us the message of reconciliation.' (2 Cor. 5:19)

- *a fruit-bearer*: 'Abide in me, and I in you. As the branch cannot bear fruit by itself, unless it abides in the vine, neither can you, unless you abide in me.' (John 15:4)

- *one with Jesus and the Father*: 'I in them and you in me, that they may become perfectly one, so that the world may know that you sent me and loved them even as you loved me.' (John 17:23)

The realization of these few truths alone is enough to turn any person upside down. What riches, what promises! Although we may not realize the truth of every one of these today, they are all true. We must pray, as the Apostle Paul did, that the eyes of our hearts are opened to know these things by experience (Eph. 2).

This is the truth. You have been bought out of slavery, you are alive to God. You have eternal life, you are free from condemnation. You are now inseparable from the love of God, you are a triumph and a reconciler and a fruit-bearer and one with the Father. We need to realize!

Much fruit grows out of the realization of who I am in Christ. Abiding replaces striving, enjoying replaces earning. Loving replaces longing and basking replaces bemoaning. Freedom kicks out slavery and warrior replaces subservient.

One thing that has been exciting for us is to see more and more of our children stepping into this revelation. Their boldness is leaving us staggered. A couple of teenagers were hugely impacted at a conference and together felt that their school had to hear the news. They asked a teacher if they could take a few moments of a lesson to share what God was doing. Having agreed to only a ten-minute slot, the teacher was impressed enough with their presentation of the gospel's impact on their lives that she gave over the whole lesson. Two 13-year-olds then bravely answered questions for the next fifty minutes.

This identity journey also builds upon the freedom we have found from self-reliance (see Chapter 3). The two are intrinsically linked together. The Apostle Paul went on his own journey of being set free from self-reliance, while again not using that exact term. (It's OK, the word Trinity isn't in the Bible either.) He writes to the Philippians:

> For we are the circumcision, who worship by the Spirit of God and glory in Christ Jesus and put no confidence in the flesh – though I myself have reason for confidence in the flesh also. If anyone else thinks he has reason for confidence in the flesh, I have more: circumcised on the eighth day, of the people of Israel, of the tribe of Benjamin, a Hebrew of Hebrews; as to the law, a Pharisee; as to zeal, a persecutor of the church; as to righteousness under the law, blameless. But whatever gain I had, I counted as loss for the sake of Christ. Indeed, I count everything as loss because of the surpassing worth of knowing Christ Jesus my Lord. For his sake I have suffered the loss of all things and count them as rubbish, in order that I may gain Christ and be found in him, not having a righteousness of my own that comes from the law, but that which comes through faith in Christ, the righteousness from God that depends on faith – that I may know him and the power of his resurrection, and may share his sufferings, becoming like him in his death, that by any means possible I may attain the resurrection from the dead (Phil. 3:3–11).

Paul here picks out some significant areas of his life where, naturally, he could have found confidence and fallen into self-reliance. His religious purity, his reputation, his clear passion and energy (he calls it zeal), his family status. These were all hugely important to the people of Paul's day and the obvious things on which to build a life or a ministry. But he says he 'counted everything as loss'. The word he uses here for 'count' can also be translated 'consider' and it means to 'reflect upon'. He also puts it in the perfect tense, which is different from the English tense of the same name. Where the English perfect is used for things that happened in the past, the Greek perfect is only used for things that happened in the past but have ongoing effects that are still being felt at the time of writing. The perfect tense is used sparingly in the New Testament and always for effect. For example, when Paul writes, 'I have been crucified with Christ,' he uses the same Greek perfect for massive impact: he literally means, 'I am in the present state of having been crucified with Christ.' In the same way, and from the details on Paul's list, it is clear that he had taken time to reflect on everything in which he could naturally find confidence and had made a conscious decision to do so no more. We do not know when this happened, but it is still impacting him some years later as he is writing.

Why does he consider this process important? He tells us it is 'because of the surpassing worth of knowing Christ Jesus': he sees these things as they really are now, in comparison with Jesus. He says this is in order that:

- I may gain Christ and be found in him. The word 'gain' is linked to the sense of gaining a profit or advantage. There's something uniquely profitable for the human soul in Christ, and Paul wants it. This is actually the ultimate worship or 'worthship'. It is saying that Jesus is worth more than everything. Until we have realized that Christ is worth more than anything else we can rely on, we will not profit as much as we could.

- I may not have a righteousness (or right standing before God) of my own but one that is from God. Again, until I have let go of self-reliance I am still in part clinging to a worthless righteousness compared to the one that God wants to give me in Christ.

- I may know him and the power of his resurrection. The intimate knowledge of Jesus comes to those who have been through this process. Power flows more powerfully to them and through them.

- I may share in his sufferings. Such value did Paul place on knowing Jesus that he wanted to pay any price to know him more. Where can I find him? he asked himself. By following him into suffering. Not a popular message today, but one that echoes what Christ himself said: 'If anyone wants to be close to me, let him take up his cross and follow me' (Matt. 16:24, my paraphrase).

- I may become like him in his death. The ultimate promise for those who have walked this journey is the transformation into the image of Christ.

So this is the road set before us. Are we willing to lay down self-reliance to gain these things? Are we willing, like Paul, to step into our new identity in Christ? There is a clear cost. But like Paul we will see that the payoff is incomparable. If we wonder at how Paul was able to withstand such abuse, this is clearly the secret. Once the unstable identity based on performance, family or reputation had been rejected, his identity was now rock-solid and secured in Christ. The Jews could persecute and stone him, but still he pressed on. The church could argue and criticize him, but Paul kept going.

His previous churches could say he was a terrible speaker, but Paul didn't stop. His friends abandoned him; it hurt but didn't stop him. He went through immense difficulties, even shipwrecks and bandits, which would cause any of us to reflect on whether this was our calling; Paul soldiered on. How? One secret surely was found here: his identity had been realized and nothing could move it from the rock of Christ.

2. I Am Now a Heavenly Citizen

'But our citizenship is in heaven, and from it we await a Saviour, the Lord Jesus Christ' (Phil. 3:20). 'So then you are no longer strangers and aliens, but you are fellow citizens with the saints and members of the household of God' (Eph. 2:19).

My understanding of citizenship is really quite paltry compared to that of the Apostle Paul. His understanding of it, drawn from his culture, was the bedrock of this revelation. On more than one occasion Paul called upon the fact that he was a Roman citizen to save his skin (Acts 16:37; 22:25).

To be a Roman citizen, Paul knew, carried with it great protection and rights. He used his confidence in his citizenship to secure those rights of protection and provision. If all this comes from Roman citizenship, he must have reasoned, how much more comes with having a heavenly one. Paul, like Jesus, knew that his life was secure until it was his time to die. He knew he had access to resources that others did not. He knew that he had access and privilege because of it.

Ram Babu, an Indian evangelist, has tapped into something of the same reality. He often speaks in very dangerous places

– places that worry some of his supporters. His response is simple. 'If it's my time to die,' he reasons, 'no one can save me. But if it's my time to live, no one can kill me!' Confidence like this flows most naturally from the realization that you are a heavenly citizen.

The story of the rich young ruler illustrates a similar reality. When Jesus asks him to sell all he has and give it to the poor, the man goes away sad, thinking that Jesus wants to make him poorer. But he missed the point. Look what Jesus offers: 'When Jesus heard this, he said to him, "One thing you still lack. Sell all that you have and distribute to the poor, and you will have treasure in heaven; and come, follow me"' (Luke 18:22).

Like the young man, we most naturally equate heaven with 'the place where we go when we die'. Given this lens, it seems as though Jesus is saying, 'Live a life of poverty now, and afterwards, when you're dead, you'll be better off.' But I don't believe that this is what Jesus meant. When he refers to heaven, Jesus never uses it in the context of 'the place where you go when you die'. Just two examples from Matthew should suffice:

'In the same way, let your light shine before others, so that they may see your good works and give glory to your Father who is in heaven' (Matt. 5:16).

'But I say to you, Do not take an oath at all, either by heaven, for it is the throne of God . . .' (Matt. 5:34).

In Luke, even just a few verses before, Jesus refers to heaven when he says, 'But the tax collector, standing far off, would not even lift up his eyes to heaven' (Luke 18:13).

The rest of the gospels reveal the same conclusion. To Jesus, heaven was a present reality and the location of the throne of

God his Father. When he wanted to refer to the place you go when you die he used a different word – paradise: 'And he said to him, "Truly, I say to you, today you will be with me in Paradise"' (Luke 23:43).

We can see from other Scriptures that Paul had the same understanding of heaven as a present reality (Eph. 6:9; Phil. 3:20). This has massive implications for our understanding of the story of the rich young ruler and also what it means to be a heavenly citizen. Firstly, Jesus was not promising him pie in the sky when you die, but steak on the plate while you wait! If heaven is *now*, not *future*, it means that when Jesus promised the young man 'treasure in heaven' he was not actually making him poorer. Which has greater wealth, earth or heaven? Jesus was giving the rich young man the opportunity of a lifetime: to access heaven's resources for kingdom work. This is not an 'every Christian should drive a Porsche and never get sick' gospel. This is living life as Jesus did with access to his Father's resources.

When the disciples come to Jesus to tell him that the people had nothing to eat, he first tries to train them to look for heaven's resources. 'You give them something to eat,' he says. The disciples scratch their heads and look clueless, so Jesus takes the job back from them. What does he do? Matthew tells us, 'He looked up to heaven and said a blessing' (Matt. 14:19). Why look to heaven? To see what's in the cupboard. Jesus drew what he needed out of heaven's resources. How? Because he knew he was a heavenly citizen.

We've been learning to step into this realization in many ways.

A guy was involved in a 'hit and run' accident and was knocked off his bicycle. As he made contact with the ground, he bit off a considerable portion of his tongue, about an inch. Surgeons were unable to do anything for him in this regard (and advised him that unfortunately tongues do not grow back) and just patched up the rest of his face with some fifty stitches. Two days after the accident, he met a group from King's Arms. The swelling meant he looked terrible, and because of his shortened tongue, his speech was difficult and fairly incomprehensible. The team prayed for him, one lady surprising herself as she prayed for the tongue to grow back. A few days later, he phoned to say that the swelling in his face had improved dramatically and that he was grateful to God for it. Three weeks later the lady met him again. She was thrilled as, with a cheeky smile, he stuck out his tongue to show her that it had grown back fully.

Another team was giving out Christmas presents to a group of homeless or ex-homeless people at an organized Christmas party. They had carefully wrapped the presents before the evening and knew exactly how many were in the bag. After dinner everyone was waiting for the presents to be distributed. Normally some people would leave early, but on this occasion no one moved, because of the expected gifts. The problem was that a count of the people in the room revealed that they were significantly short of presents. The team leader counted the people and stopped counting at sixty: there were more than sixty people there. The news was not good, as they had only forty-five presents. They prayed together over the bag of presents and decided that there was nothing for it but to give out the presents and see what God would do. Remarkably, even though nobody left the room, not only did they have enough presents, but there were a number left over.

It's time for the church to realize that we are heavenly citizens and we operate from our Father's resources. What he orders, he pays for!

3. I Am Now a Member of a Royal Priesthood

'But you are a chosen race, a royal priesthood, a holy nation, a people for his own possession, that you may proclaim the excellencies of him who called you out of darkness into his marvellous light' (1 Pet. 2:9).

This is extraordinary when you think about the richness of it. I was once worthless and cast out, unholy and unclean. Then Jesus came and paid for my sin, cleaned me up, brought me into his family and made me a king and a priest like him. The implications are best seen in light of the Old Testament priesthood. They are many, but there are four key areas: significance, influence, authority and access.

Significance
Priesthood: Priests in the Old Testament received no land or inheritance of their own: 'You shall have no inheritance in their land, neither shall you have any portion among them. I am your portion and your inheritance among the people of Israel' (Num. 18:20). The priests were set apart for God, to administer sacrifices on behalf of the people. Ultimately the priests got their significance from what they were set apart to do, ministering to God himself and declaring who he is.

Royal priesthood: As Peter tells us, we have been made a royal priesthood in order to 'proclaim the excellencies of him who called you out of darkness into his marvellous light' (1 Pet. 2:9). When we understand that we are significant and that we are royalty, people around us will see just how amazing our God is. Our significance comes from showing and telling the world who our God is.

However, there is more. As a royal priesthood we get our significance not just from what we do (although that is wonderful enough) but from who God has made us to be: 'But to all who did receive him, who believed in his name, he gave the right to become children of God' (John 1:12).

We have incredible significance, not just because we are priests (what we do) but because we are children of the great King and so are kings ourselves. Our significance now comes not just from what we do but from who we *are*.

A man came up to me once to thank me for the impact I had made on his life. I was confused because I was sure I had never met him before, even though he was speaking as though he knew me. After a while he said, 'I didn't even come on the training course: it was my wife. But she has come back so changed, it has changed me.' Thrilling! A realization of identity so profound that others are changed by it at second hand. This is the destiny of the whole bride of Christ.

Influence

Priesthood: Priests in the Old Testament had influence with God on behalf of his people. 'Then Moses said to Aaron, "Draw near to the Altar and offer your sin offering and your burnt offering and make atonement for yourself and for the people, and bring the offering of the people and make atonement for them, as the LORD has commanded"' (Lev. 9:7).

Royal priesthood: The influence we're now to have on people is seeing them become all that they can be in Christ, seeing them be all that God has called them to be.

We have all been called to do great exploits for God. When disciples asked, 'Who is the greatest in the kingdom of heaven?' (Matt. 18:1), they had completely missed the point. Interestingly, there must have been something about being with Jesus which led these very ordinary men to believe they weren't just destined to a life of mediocrity. But they drew the wrong conclusions. Their influence should have brought them security, not feelings of jealousy. Then they could have focused on serving others and celebrating others' success.

We need to recognize the influence we have as priests. As Paul says, we are 'ambassadors for Christ, God making his appeal through us' (2 Cor. 5:20).

An ambassador carries the influence of his country far beyond its borders. When you meet an ambassador on foreign territory, the influence, weight, power and authority of that perhaps far removed country are found in the ambassador. God's kingdom, as it were, goes with you!

A teacher was in a football lesson when a key player was injured. The boy was rolling about on the ground while the other young people gathered round. One of the lads, knowing the teacher was a Christian, began to provoke him. 'It's not like you're Jesus, sir, is it?' he said. The teacher was provoked in his spirit, because although he knew he was not Jesus, he also knew that Christ was in him. 'Right, lads, let's pray for him now.' He showed them how to lay hands on their injured team mate and command sickness to leave. Immediately the lad jumped up, saying that he now had no pain. Kingdom influence goes with you, even into hostile or indifferent territory.

Authority

Priesthood: Jesus said to a man with leprosy, 'See that you say nothing to anyone, but go, show yourself to the priest and offer the gift that Moses commanded, for a proof to them' (Matt. 8:4). He instructed him to go and show himself to the priest so that he could confirm that he was now clean. Priests had the authority to say whether or not someone had been healed.

Royal priesthood: As sons and daughters of the King, we now have the authority to command healing and forgiveness and to order evil spirits to obey.

'Heal the sick, raise the dead, cleanse lepers, cast out demons. You received without paying; give without pay' (Matt. 10:8). Wherever we see evidence of the enemy's kingdom at work, we need to start believing that God has given us a mandate to contend for his kingdom to come in that place or situation.

Access

Priesthood: In the Old Testament, only the High Priest had access to the Holy of Holies, the place where the very presence of God dwelt in the temple. He could only go in once a year.

Royal priesthood: When Jesus died on the cross and rose again, 'The curtain of the temple was torn in two, from top to bottom' (Matt. 27:51). Now that we are sons and daughters of the King, we have unlimited access to his presence and his resources, with no restrictions. This is all such good news. The question is, will we believe it and start to live in the good of it?

Bob Woodruff, a former president of Coca-Cola, once said, 'It is my desire that everyone in the world have a taste of Coca-Cola.' This goal has almost been achieved. I was speaking once to a man who had travelled to some of the most remote parts of the world. He said that in some places the people have never seen a white person before or even heard that there are white people. The people do not wear shoes and have very little clothing – but they have cans of Coca-Cola. Oh for the church to have the same attitude concerning the kingdom of God – that everyone will have at least a taste of it. Once they taste the real thing, they'll join us in being hungry for more.

John Wesley said we should 'do all the good we can, by all the means we can, in all the ways we can, in all the places we can, at all the times we can, to all the people we can, as long as we can'. This is the spirit of those who have realized their new identity!

13

I Can Grow

By faith Sarah herself received power to conceive, even when she was past the age, since she considered him faithful who had promised.

Hebrews 11:11

Some time ago we were calling out to God as a church for the blind to see in our town. I then heard a story from another church in town where a lady who was 94 per cent blind had been healed. She had been suffering from retinal cone dystrophy, a rare condition of the eye. During a family meeting based on the story of the blind man that Jesus healed by putting mud in his eyes, several people suggested putting mud on this lady's eyes. A children's story time suddenly became very practical. The lady was very keen, and a small amount of mud was placed on each eyelid, at which point she declared, 'Well, if I'm healed I ought to be able to read.' She grabbed a nearby prayer sheet and immediately began to read – much to the shock of the church. Her life was transformed and she subsequently booked an advanced eye-test, in which both retinas were X-rayed and declared perfectly normal. When we heard this story, I knew we had to celebrate with them. I invited the lady and her pastor to come and tell us the story. They did so, and I think were surprised when the whole church jumped to their feet and began to celebrate wildly.[1]

Great Power – Great Faith

How do people move from unbelief to walking in great faith? This of course is the road that Jesus' disciples travelled. On more than one occasion Jesus rebuked the disciples for their lack of faith. The reason is obvious when we understand that faith and power are intrinsically linked.[2]

The story of Abraham's wife Sarah, who was unable to conceive a child, makes this abundantly clear: 'By faith Sarah herself received power to conceive, even when she was past the age, since she *considered him faithful* who had promised' (Heb. 11:11).

In the original story, when Sarah is first told the news that she will become pregnant in her old age, she is cynical. So cynical, in fact, that she laughs mockingly at the thought (Gen. 18:12). Something clearly happened to Sarah on the journey, and as she began to believe in the faithfulness of the God who had made the promise, power flowed into her womb and healed her of her barrenness. After giving birth to Isaac, she said, 'God has made laughter for me; everyone who hears will laugh over me' (Gen 21:6). In a beautifully ironic twist Sarah, the woman who laughed at God, becomes the woman who laughs with God. She even named her son Isaac, meaning 'laughter', as a constant reminder of the joy that God had brought her.

This link between faith and power is made again and again in the Bible (1 Cor. 2:4; 2 Thess. 1:11; Rom. 1:16). Jesus

wanted his disciples to move in the same power in which he
was moving (John 14:12). He also wanted them to be able
to train others (Matt. 28:19). The material that he had to
work with was less than promising. This group of unlikely
future church leaders could not possibly train others or move
in power themselves without a dramatic change in this mys-
terious thing called faith.

LEVELS OF FAITH

From as far back as I could remember I had battled with the
idea of faith. While I had clearly enough faith to be saved
(at least I hoped I did), faith for anything else seemed to
slip through my fingers like sand. Was saving faith the same
as faith for God's power? Was faith a gift that some had
and others didn't? It wasn't for want of desire, as I desperately wanted to have great faith. But I seemed relegated to
the division of those whose faith was worse than that of an
English football fan before a World Cup: outwardly hopeful
but inwardly preparing for another humiliation. I existed in
this state for years, wallowing in my own faithless stew with
seemingly no hope of escape.

One summer I went to a conference and heard a message
that gave me a lifeline. The speaker was looking through
the New Testament and describing the levels of faith that
we see there. First there was *no* faith, which Jesus said his
disciples had on more than one occasion (Mark 4:40). Then
there was *little* faith, which Jesus said you had if you sank
mid-way through walking on water (gulp!) (Matt. 14:31).
Then there was *weak* faith, which Paul declared we would

find even among believers (Rom. 14:1). Then there was *strong* faith, which Paul said Abraham had but also 'grew' into as he gave glory to God (Rom. 4:20). Finally there is *great* faith, which Jesus saw in only two people, who were both from despised backgrounds as far as the Jews were concerned: a Gentile woman who pressed him for the deliverance of her demonized daughter, and a Roman centurion (Matt. 15:28 and Luke 7:9).

Now one could perhaps quibble over the exact scale and whether great faith is better than strong faith, or whether weak faith is of less effect than little faith, but this would be to miss the point. The revelation that hit me that day like a spiritual tidal wave was simple: if Abraham and Sarah can grow in faith, others can grow in faith. Maybe Jesus pointed out that he saw great faith in a Gentile woman and a Roman centurion in order to make it clear that great faith can be found anywhere. Perhaps when he chose his disciples Jesus stacked the decks against himself to make this very point. If the likes of Peter, Thomas and Nathanael could grow in faith, *anyone* can grow in faith. If that is true, it means . . .

I can grow in faith!

I know that this might not seem the most profound of insights, but to me it has had the same effect as when my small son first discovered that he could climb over the stair gate: escape. The sudden realization that I no longer had to stare through the bars of my own limitations while others explored the great world beyond, and that I could actually *do* something to grow in faith, was a mind-blowing, fuse-popping break-through.

Of course, this naturally led on to another question . . .

Growing in Faith

How do you grow in faith? Through the years of my Christian life I had listened to many sermons and read many books on faith. I'd been encouraged to have great faith, inspired by stories of people with great faith, jealous of others who seemed to have great faith, but never had I heard a sermon on how you grow in faith. The best that I had heard was on the famous Hebrews passage which proclaims, 'Faith comes by hearing.' Growing in faith is as simple as reading the Bible more, many seemed to conclude. But I had read the Bible for years, and still my faith was paltry. Even the recent repentance from my unbelief was only part of the journey. It was as if the soil was clear from debris but now faith had to grow. I began to study this subject, learning from anyone and everyone that I saw operating in faith. God began to show me how to grow in faith, to the point where, miraculously, faith began to grow! I began to expect people to be touched by God. When we gave the call for prayer for healing, no longer was there the sick feeling in my stomach of looming disappointment. Two breakthrough moments stand out. The first was when I received a word of knowledge at church for someone with a neck condition. Before the meeting, the Lord had spoken to my spirit and told me to stand the person up and tell them that they were healed already. I had never done this before, but I had learned a little about obedience and so decided to try it. I gave the word at the end of the meeting and waited. After a few minutes a lady stood. I asked her to move her neck and check it out as it was probably healed already. As she moved her neck, the shock was clearly seen on her face. 'All the pain has gone,' she declared, with a beaming smile on her face. The second was when I gave a word of knowledge about pain in the lower jaw on the left side. No one responded in the meeting, but the next day we heard that when it ended one person had sent an SMS to a friend, saying, 'You should have been here tonight, as I know you have jaw pain and there was a word about it.' The friend immediately texted back, 'You won't believe it: as I received your text, all the pain left!' Another person went home and sent an MSN message to their friend saying the same thing. Their friend also responded, 'You won't believe it: as I read your message, all my dental pain left.'

These stories, among many others, showed us that growing in faith is possible. What was most exciting was that this wasn't just one or two individuals but a whole community that was growing. In the years that have followed we have learned a few more keys and had the joy of teaching Christians from many different backgrounds how they can also grow in faith. Five faith-builders and two faith-busters form the basis of this teaching.

FAITH-BUILDERS

1. You can grow

The first key to growth is to go through a mind-transformation similar to the one that I experienced when I realized that great faith was not exclusive to the Christian superstars but instead is the destiny of every child of God. The fact is that no matter where you start from or how pitiful your faith is right now, you can grow in faith. Believing this and repenting (changing your mind) about any thought that disagrees with this is your launch pad. You can have great faith. This is not the empty promise of a TV diet-show host. If Abraham can grow in faith, so can you. When Jesus commended great faith, I believe he was not trying to make us feel depressed but to fill us with encouragement: 'If these guys can do it, then anyone can do it.' Taking some time out with God to ask if our mind has truly been changed on this is a critical starting place.

2. Your Father is the source

The second key is the realization that faith is not faith in itself. You are not trying to pull yourself up by your own bootstraps. Faith is by nature faith 'in' something or someone, and for us it is rooted and grounded in the character of the Father. The writer to the Hebrews makes the point that faith is made up of two components: 'Without faith it is impossible to please him, for whoever would draw near to God must believe that he exists and that he rewards those who seek him' (Heb. 11:6).

Two things are necessary if we are to draw near to God in faith: belief that God exists, and belief that he rewards those who seek him. Faith is the continual expectation of ongoing encounter with a good, loving and generous Father.

Notice that belief in the existence of any type of God is not enough: for it to be genuine biblical faith, we must also believe that he is a good Father who loves to reward his children. When asked to help the disciples to grow in faith, Jesus points out that a tiny mustard seed-sized faith is enough to do incredible things in God (Luke 17:5–6). The point, I believe, is this: they were seeing the size of faith all wrong. Great big faith is not like a great big muscle, able to lift things by itself. The strength of great faith comes not from its size but from what, or rather who, it is connected to – our Father!

When Jesus uses the example of having faith as small as a 'seed', he was using an illustration from the predominant agricultural culture of his day. For Western culture, perhaps he would use something like a fuse. A fuse is small, but it stands between the gigawatt-generating potential of the power station and your TV set. Without a working fuse, no matter how much power is being pumped from down the road, your TV will remain silent. In the same way, faith simply conducts the power from God into our lives and the lives of those around us. The lower our 'resistance', the greater the power that can flow.

The key to a life lived close (drawn near) to God is thus to live with the awareness of a good heavenly Father who is always blessing (rewarding) his children. It's living with this expectation of good things from my Father that lowers my resistance and allows his power to flow. It is to continually bring him my issues and concerns and to expect that there will ultimately be a good outcome from them all. It does not mean that bad things will not happen to me. It does not mean that there will not be times of loss and difficulty. All the great heroes of faith experienced these challenges. In the midst of them, though, great faith is able to run to the fortress (as Spurgeon described it) of Romans 8:28, which says that 'for those who love God all things work together for good, for those who are called according to his purpose'.

This is why it is so critical to have repented of self-reliance. If I am my only source, all I can expect is what I can do. But if the Father becomes my source, all that he asks me to do becomes possible, because he provides the resources or power to do it. Understanding the kingdom is also critical, because it teaches me what my good Father wants to do. Instead of passively waiting, I am actively engaged with the Father's plan.

A couple of young people from King's Arms were in the town centre when they saw a man on crutches. After taking some time to pluck up the courage required, they went over to him and explained that they were Christians. At first he was fairly hostile, because he'd had a negative experience when he was prayed for once before. So instead of praying they agreed that they would attend a quiz night that he was hosting if he would come to church. Subsequently he came, and at an Alpha course he received some healing in his legs and gave his life to Christ. A kingdom awareness and consciousness of a good Father who loves to welcome each one home made this life change possible. Practically, this key works best as we spend time in God's presence and reading his word. Learning to talk to him 'as a man speaks to his friend' (Exod. 33:11) and reading his word to know him, not just to know about him, become key lifelines.

Understanding that my Father is the source does not mean that he will answer every prayer in the positive. Let's face it: we would not want God to say yes to every one of our prayers! My Father is not a vending machine, and I can't thump him if the prayer-coins do not yield the correct goods. What it does mean is that I have the expectation of good from him no matter what his answer is. 'No' or 'wait' will be seen as good when I realize that my Father only gives good answers and ultimately works all things for good.

3. No more ransom notes

Thirdly, to operate in great faith we have to stop holding God hostage to our experience. Taking this stance enables us to pursue the breakthrough that God has promised, without giving up. This does not mean that I am in denial of my experience, as some have taught. When I am clearly sick but declare that I am healed and that these are 'lying symptoms', I stray away from the earthy reality of both Scripture and genuine faith. If I am sick, I am sick. God is still the healer, and until I am dead in a box, healing is still a possibility. Of course, even if I do not receive healing in this life, he is still the healer, because I will certainly get the ultimate healing of a brand new body when I receive eternal life. It is a win–win situation. If I need provision, my Father is still the provider, no matter how long I have to wait for the provision or what means he uses to provide. A big change happened in my heart when I realized that no one arriving in eternity would be able to say to God, 'You let me down.' It's just not possible for him to make a mistake or let anyone down. This revelation dealt a massive head-wound to my natural self-pity. Instead of shaking my fist at a reluctant deity, I could begin to dialogue with a loving Father about what the problem might be. If you want to grow in faith, you have to let go of previous experiences that set themselves up in your mind and hold God's word to ransom.

4. Spiritual malabsorption

Fourthly, the principle of spiritual malabsorption must be understood if we are to grow in faith. Intestinal malabsorption is a disease that means that food is not absorbed properly in the intestine and the body becomes weak. Compare this to the psalmist's view of ancient Israel: 'How often they rebelled against him in the wilderness and grieved him in the desert! They tested God again and again and provoked the Holy One of Israel' (Ps. 78:40–41).

What was the cause of this grief and testing? 'They did not remember his power or the day when he redeemed them from the foe' (Ps. 78:42).

This is spiritual malabsorption. If I fail to remember what God has done, it ultimately causes me to rebel against and grieve him. It breeds an ungrateful heart that does not expect him to do the things he has done in the past again. I have found that I can pray like crazy for God to break into my situation. He does; I thank him and move on. A few months later I can be in a similar or even the same situation and have the same response. The point, of course, is that I did not learn the lesson the first time. I came out of the first miracle unchanged inside. This reality applies not only to the things God has done in my life but also to what he has done in the life of others. Proverbs says, 'The memory of the righteous is a blessing' (Prov. 10:7).

This is why in Scripture we see God repeatedly instructing the people of Israel to teach the stories of old to their children. He does not want the next generation to have to start again (Ps. 145:11–12).

In practical terms we have found that we must become far better recorders and tellers of stories. I have pages and pages of stories of the things God has done. In this book I have selected only a few – maybe less than 5 per cent – to tell you. We've also changed our Sunday meetings to reflect this. A few years ago I asked one of our staff team to begin weekly Sunday interviews with people who had been healed or had seen kingdom breakthrough. She agreed and asked me how many stories I could give her to start with. I gave her two. 'What happens when they run out?' she asked. 'Just tell them again until we get some more,' was my advice. By the grace of God, over the next nine months we had a three-minute interview every week. Not once did we have to repeat a story. This section of our meetings accomplishes so many things, sending messages from 'The front is not just for the leaders' to 'Kingdom life is best expressed outside this meeting.' Often when people talk to others on the streets, in shops or in workplaces they start by saying, 'I've heard of your condition being healed before.' What they mean is that they've heard someone give testimony on a Sunday. This builds their faith and creates an openness in the unbeliever for them to pray. Stories help to mobilize and disciple the whole church. One church member sitting at a bus shelter saw another lady hobble up and sit down. Immediately she felt God impress on her that she should offer to pray. 'But Lord,' she complained, 'I haven't had any training!' The reply came: 'Offer to pray, and I will train you on the job.' So she did, copying exactly what she had heard people describe when they told their stories on Sundays. The lady received immediate pain relief and was very grateful, walking around limp- and pain-free!

5. Set goals

Lastly, we found that setting goals was a critical faith-builder as it enabled us to focus as a community on the breakthroughs we needed next. When I told you that we set the goal of thirty miracles on the streets, I did not mention that our prayer meetings and private prayer times became filled with cries of 'God, we're asking you for the first one.' We prayed together again and again for this.

Later I was provoked when I spoke to yet another member of the church who was taking anti-depressants. Clearly we don't see everyone healed this side of heaven, and there are always times when medical assistance is necessary. Nor did I see this as a failure for the individuals concerned. But it challenged me that it seemed that the church was popping as many anti-depressant pills as the world around. If we've truly met the Prince of Peace, at least our statistics should look better!

We began to pray as a church for breakthrough. Month after month we cried out to God that this Goliath would come down. Then finally we 'got one'. A lady who had been taking anti-depressants for her entire adult life had a dramatic encounter with God during a church weekend away. Another lady suffering with suicidal thoughts after the birth of a child received prayer and immediate relief. Under the guidance of her doctor she stopped taking the prescribed tablets and enjoyed a new sense of peace and joy. Something of the power of depression is being broken off the church!

Using these faith-builders in a systematic way through-out our community has produced a huge amount of fruit. Looking across the church and in the lives of those close to me, I can see a massive shift in the level of faith, expressed in what people expect that God can and will do.

FAITH-BUSTERS

We have also learned that there are some key faith-busters that have to be dealt with if a community is to build a healthy and sustainable measure of great faith.

1. Dig out poor teaching

I realized that many in the church had previously received poor teaching by well-meaning but misguided Christians on this subject of faith. We had to teach on this area and destroy the unhelpful teachings one by one, usually with follow-up conversations. The major ones are as follows:

'You are not healed because of your lack of faith': Jesus never said this to a sick person and neither did his disciples. While faith is critical, telling someone that their lack of faith is the reason they are not healed is tantamount to spiritual abuse: you leave them unhealed and now it's their fault. Even if I suspected that this was a major concern and a possible reason for lack of healing power, I would never say this to a person as it simply will not help them grow in faith. Helping someone to grow in faith is not best started by pointing out their lack. Jesus did say to the people ministering healing that it was their lack of faith that people were not healed. But even this must be understood in the context of the loving relationship he had with his disciples. In the area of breakthrough, blame is best avoided. I personally am happy to concede that I need to grow in expectation of what my Father can and will do in every situation. When someone I minister to doesn't get the required breakthrough, I prefer to bring it to my Father, asking him to work in me, rather than start throwing the blame around on others.

'If you had faith you'd stop taking your medicine': We believe that when you are healed, the doctor will tell you to stop taking your medicine. If the medicine itself may be preventing the person from testing out their healing, just ask the doctor to reduce the dose for a while in a simple test. Daniel did this when he wanted to be removed from the king's prescribed diet and his 'minder' was not keen. The results brought glory to God, as God's power was seen in his and his friends' lives (Dan. 1:8–16).

'If you visit a doctor it shows lack of faith': A healthy faith is rooted first in God, as he is the source of healing. But it also recognizes that the same God who is the power behind supernatural healing also provides the power for the body to naturally heal itself and the wisdom for medical professionals to do their job. While much of the church's prayers have been reduced to 'God guide the hand of the surgeon,' which clearly demonstrates a profound lack, the equal and opposite error of shunning medical help must be avoided. We have a number of doctors in our community, and it is my joy that they are people of great medical wisdom and great faith. The two are not mutually exclusive, and I believe the best results occur when the two disciplines of supernatural and natural healing work together in mutual honour.

One example of this came from a lady in our church who was having a surgical procedure while she was awake. The surgeon was a Muslim but was happy for her to have worship music playing throughout. She began to pray in tongues, and the surgeon asked her what it was that she was saying. She explained, and he asked her to speak up so that he could hear. After the surgery, the surgeon confessed that he had been able to understand what she had been saying. 'You were saying, "Lord, you are my sustainer. You will sustain me. It is to you I will return,"' he said. A wonderful example of evangelism under the knife!

'God sent this to teach me something': This one is more complex than the other faith-busters. While God clearly is sovereign over all and can teach us through anything, I would suggest it is not the primary teaching of the New Testament that God sends sickness to teach us truth. Jesus says that it is the Holy Spirit who will lead us 'into all truth' (John 16:13). He never says this about sickness. There are some caveats to this. Clearly God does occasionally use sickness and even death as a tool to teach his people and others a lesson that they will not learn another way. The plagues of Exodus, the temporary blinding of Elymas (Acts 13:11) and the deaths of Ananias and Sapphira (Acts 5:1–11) have to remind us that in judgement God can do anything he likes. However, this is by far the exception rather than the rule, especially in the New Testament, where a far better covenant has been given to us. Even under the old covenant God uses 'I am the Lord your healer' as one of his seven covenant names (Exod. 15:26). We are not now facing a situation where the Father is sending sickness, Jesus is healing people and we are caught on the sidelines, unsure of which team to join. Can we learn through suffering and sickness? Absolutely. Do we still pray for healing because our Father loves to heal? Absolutely.

We've found it critical to take the teaching and beliefs that we have had regarding healing and kingdom breakthrough and bring them again to the light of Scripture. This is critical to a culture of sustainable power, otherwise these unhelpful practices and beliefs begin to undermine the very culture that is trying to be established.

2. Persevere

One huge faith-buster that we have had to battle is a lack of perseverance. Some have been taught explicitly that to pray more than once shows a lack of faith. Jesus, however, trained his disciples to pray without losing heart by telling them the story of a poor widow who gets what she wants from a reluctant judge purely by never giving up (Luke 18:1–8). The point, of course, is not that our Father is like the judge but that if perseverance can eventually persuade an evil and unwilling judge, how much more will it persuade a good and willing Father? John G. Lake, the great American missionary to Africa, used to say that many told him God was not willing to heal after they had prayed for someone once or twice. 'We sometimes pray for twenty days straight for the most difficult cases,' he declared. This perhaps was why he saw countless cancers and other incurable diseases healed by the power of God.[3]

Cameron Peddie, a less well-known Scottish minister who lived in the early twentieth century, tells this story of a lady he ministered to:

When in good health she was a great church worker and revelled in every form of service . . . But then osteoarthritis laid hold upon her and gradually its ruthless onslaught made her give up all the work she enjoyed – even housework. For 12 years she was scarcely able to walk. Every possible form of medical treatment was applied in vain. Finally . . . she was brought to [me].

I gave her weekly [prayer] for three months before the pain began to lessen. She had faith and patience and she persisted in coming. Within one year her suffering was greatly relieved; within two she was completely healed.

To show her gratitude and to prove the reality of her cure, every Thursday she travels by bus . . . bringing fruit and flowers to lonely widows . . . climbing sometimes fourteen flights of stairs . . . She has been doing this for four years . . .

My experience with rheumatic cases is that every type yields but it requires time and patience. Rheumatoid arthritis, fibrositis, sciatica and lumbago respond fairly quickly but osteoarthritis and neuritis are very stubborn. Two to four months pass before the pain and restrictive movement . . . begin to disappear. The removal of the dense encrustations around the joint is a gradual process. Weekly [prayer] is required. Some sufferers come expecting us to perform instantaneous cures as Jesus did and they lose patience and give up hope when a cure is delayed. But with faith and patience, especially patience, every rheumatic condition yields. [4]

This story provokes me because of the expectancy and perseverance shown. We must rediscover this spirit if we are to see the breakthrough that we dream of. While we don't always know why we must persevere, one thing is clear from Scripture: we must! It's critical to have as much faith after you have prayed as before. I've found that understanding the difference between a healing and a miracle is helpful here. Miracles are instantaneous, and while we like to see them they are not always the way that God works. Jesus said, 'They will lay their hands on the sick, and they will recover' (Mark 16:18). It is just as significant if God brings about the healing slowly: they are still healed! We can easily miss the fact that this sometimes happened when Jesus ministered. John records, 'Jesus said to him, "Go; your son will live." The man believed the word that Jesus spoke to him and went on his way. As he was going down, his servants met him and told him that his son was *recovering*. So he asked them the hour when he *began to get better*' (John 4:50–52).

If Jesus experienced the situation where people recovered slowly rather than quickly, then so will we. Understanding these things will help us to walk faithfully and to persevere. One young man really got hold of this principle of perseverance when he saw another guy in the church in agony with a bad back. He found out that the man had to wear 'patches' of painkillers to help him deal with the pain, and determined to pray for him every week. For four weeks he prayed with him each Sunday evening, with no change. On the fifth Sunday he noticed that the guy was not present. He decided to go out into the car park to look for him and, when he strolled out there, found the man holding onto his car with his back locked in a spasm. Immediately he prayed and the power of God fell, freeing him completely from pain.

We have found that while our faith is not perfect by any means, the more we live out these faith-builders and uproot these faith-busters, the more faith has grown in our community. Of course, there is always more that we can do and more that we can receive. Jesus wondered whether when he returned he would find faith on the earth (Luke 18:8). We're hoping to be part of the answer to his heart's cry. May he find faith here.

NOTES

[1] You can listen to this story at http://www.kingsarms.org/cm/content/view/151/78/.

[2] I am grateful to Bill Johnson for the inspiration for much of our journey that has produced this chapter.

[3] Kenneth Copeland, *John G. Lake: His Life, His Sermons, His Boldness of Faith* (Kenneth Copeland Publications, 1995).

[4] J. Cameron Peddie, *The Forgotten Talent* (Arthur James Ltd, 1985), pp. 54–55.

That Wall is Coming Down

Whenever I visit other churches I try to spend time helping people open their hearts to allow the Holy Spirit to remove the rocks. I have found, though, that it is equally important to equip people with some practical tools to help them in administering the gifts of the Spirit that will begin to flow. Breaking free from fear and stepping into courage is critical, because you cannot steer a stationary ship. Once the ship is moving, though, steering becomes a highly required function!

In one church we spent a number of sessions helping people step into freedom. In the next session I spent fifteen minutes teaching them how to recognize the voice of God speaking to them, followed by two minutes waiting on God to hear his voice. Then came the shock. I asked only those who had never given a word of knowledge before to come to the front, limiting it to the first twenty people. They faithfully came, slowly at first. Each gave their word or sense of what God was saying, and then I asked people to respond if it applied to them. At the end of the meeting we took a note of those who had been healed or 'remarkably improved' during that session. The cases reported were as follows:

- Tinnitus that had been present for more than a year and was starting in the second ear had completely left.
- A girl with a hernia (not a Christian), who said she had been in excruciating pain, said that she was saying to herself, 'He won't heal me, he can't heal me,' but she was now completely pain-free.
- Someone with pain in the left knee which was possibly due to arthritis was pain-free and had mobility.
- Someone who came with a splitting headache was now headache-free.
- A mouth ulcer disappeared.
- A back condition was touched and the individual became pain-free.
- Someone with shoulder pain had no pain and complete mobility.
- Someone with a throat problem that had meant that they were struggling to swallow or speak was pain-free (and spoke).
- A bubble under the skin associated with a knee injury had disappeared and all the pain had left.

This came from just a ten- to fifteen-minute teaching time, two minutes of waiting on our Father to speak and then ten minutes of prayer. All done in thirty minutes, and most of those healed had responded to words of knowledge given by people in the church who had never given words before. When I travel to speak, we nearly always do this exercise and when we do, we always see at least four or five healings.

SEEING WHAT THE FATHER IS DOING

The reality is that God is always speaking. Jesus made it clear when he said, 'My sheep hear my voice' (John 10:27). After all, he is the word of God, so he can hardly help but speak. Jesus himself was guided by the voice of his Father and he declared, 'the Son can do nothing of his own accord, but only what he sees the Father doing' (John 5:19). We see the same continual direction operating in the lives of the followers of Christ. By looking at their lives and drawing from our own experience we can observe a number of ways in which God speaks to his children to spur them into kingdom-advancing activity. How did Jesus and the disciples 'see' what the Father was doing to be guided to join him? There are many books on this subject far more comprehensive than I can be here, but as a primer for those unfamiliar, here are seven ways that I have found, both biblically and through my experience, in which God speaks to guide us into kingdom breakthrough:

1. Dreams

In Acts, Luke records, 'And a vision appeared to Paul in the night: a man of Macedonia was standing there, urging him and saying, "Come over to Macedonia and help us"' (Acts 16:9). This may have been a vision given while Paul was awake, or it may have been a dream.[1] Either way, Paul clearly receives direction from the Holy Spirit.

God speaks through dreams; biblically there is no doubt, as there are so many examples. I personally gave dreams no weight until my wife began to explore this area. On many occasions her dreams have opened up ministry opportunities or exposed the enemy's schemes against our church or our family. On one occasion my wife dreamt that my hairdresser had been praying and crying out to God. The next time I visited, I almost told her about the dream but at the last minute lost my courage. A month later, when I was due to go again, Caroline reminded me of the dream and told me to be sure to tell her. I asked the Lord to make it really easy for me, and a few moments after I sat down in the chair my hairdresser said, 'So, how's your wife?' I told her that a strange thing had happened and Caroline had dreamed that she had been praying and crying out to God. 'That's strange,' she said, 'I never pray, but this week probably for the first time in my life I have prayed about a situation.' There followed a fruitful conversation that has resulted in many other conversations about Jesus and the church.

We have found that opening ourselves to the fact that God might be speaking to us through dreams and making it a priority to record the dream as soon as we wake up (and to then take time to pray about it) has been critical to hearing God clearly in this way.

2. Visions or pictures (moving or stationary)

Secondly, we see that God speaks through visions which can be static or moving, words or pictures.[2] Ananias has a vision where the Lord instructs him to go to Saul, lay hands on him to heal him of his blindness and give him instruction in the faith (Acts 9:10). Peter has an open vision on the roof of a friend's house, which propels him into a mission with a Gentile family (Acts 10:9–17). Paul has a vision (again in the night, which meant he was either up and praying or dreaming while asleep) while he was in Corinth, encouraging him to press on in the mission to which God had called him there (Acts 18:9–10). We have learned that staying awake to what is going on in the supernatural realm is very helpful for kingdom breakthrough.

I was ministering at an Alpha course one evening when I saw the word 'death' written across the forehead of a young man in the front row. I did not see the words literally, but in a way that's hard to describe, I knew that this word was written there. The Lord gave me nothing else for the young man and, for obvious reasons, I felt very nervous in saying, 'I see death written on you.' I wrestled for a few minutes and then decided how I would approach it. 'Does the word "death" mean anything to you?' I started.[3] As soon as I opened my mouth I knew the significance of the word myself. 'Someone close to you has died,' I said, 'and they were only close to you at the end of their life. And God says that he loves you in the same way, and more so than that person did. That relationship was a picture to you of his love.' The young man's face remained entirely expressionless throughout. At the end of the evening he ran from the room, quickly followed by an Alpha Team member wanting to find out the problem. They found him outside, weeping, and he quickly told them the whole story. He had been estranged from his grandfather for most of his life but had been powerfully reconciled when he found out that his grandfather had not disliked him as he had supposed. The grandfather had died a few months after that reconciliation. He knew exactly what the words meant to him; he had always felt that if there were a God, that God would hate him. He now realized that that was a lie and quickly came through to faith in Christ.

If you want to open yourself to receive more visions or pictures in this way, all you need to do is ask. He is a good Father who loves to speak to his children. You must have intentionality and expectancy when you ask, though, or you will receive nothing (Jas 1:6–7). Then in every situation ask the Holy Spirit to show you what he is doing. As with everything, there are different degrees of gifting, and some will have greater frequency or clarity than others. However, all God's children will hear his voice.

On one occasion Jesus says to Nathanael, 'Because I said to you, "I saw you under the fig tree", do you believe? You will see greater things than these' (John 1:50).

Clearly Jesus heard his Father in this way on many occasions, because he says, the son only does what he sees the Father doing (John 5:19). This seems a strange expression to describe hearing God's voice, until you realize that hearing sometimes involved seeing!

In this story, we see that Nathanael's faith came from this encounter with Jesus. Are we expecting the same in our day?

3. An impression, a knowing or a sense
The third way in which we have found that God speaks is through impressions. Less clear than a vision or picture, these are a gut sense that helps us to know what the Father is up to. We can only imagine that Jesus had this 'gut sense' when, while walking along the street, he stopped under the tree into which Zacchaeus had climbed. As far as we are aware, Jesus had never met Zacchaeus before and had no way of knowing his name. However, he confidently declared, 'Zacchaeus, hurry and come down, for I must stay at your house today' (Luke 19:5).

I'm surmising here that Jesus received Zacchaeus' name by an impression, though he may well have heard the audible voice of his Father. We are not told. What we do know is that the result was wonderful and a kingdom breakthrough came to Zacchaeus' household that day. We have learned that we can often sense what the Father is doing in this way. Once while in a restaurant in a Muslim nation I looked over at the waiter. I asked the Father what he was doing and sensed that the man had a shoulder or neck problem. Nothing from his movement gave this away: I just had a sense. At the end of the meal I asked my host to come with me to speak with the man. I explained that I felt that God had told me there might be something wrong with his shoulder. Was it the case? No, he replied, it is fine. I was a little bit puzzled but just assumed that I had got it wrong. (Get used to that feeling, by the way.) However, another waiter overheard us and said that he had a problem with his shoulder. When I looked at him I realized that this was actually the man that I had been looking at when I received the word; I had mistaken him for the other guy! We asked if we could pray and he agreed. We laid hands on his shoulder and prayed, and he told us that he was instantly pain-free and had full mobility. The first waiter then said that he had a knee problem and asked if we would pray for him.

We've found that learning to tune in to these impressions is a key way to hear what the Holy Spirit is telling us about our Father's business. There is nothing like telling someone what is wrong with them, or better still, their name *and* what is wrong with them, to open them up to the things of God!

As far as growing in my ability to receive impressions is concerned, I've found that before meetings it's helpful to close my eyes and picture a skeleton. I then ask the Lord to light up the parts of the skeleton that need healing. I will then sense several areas light up and I will write these down. These form the basis of words of knowledge that I will bring in the meeting. It might seem a trivial thing, but when inspired by the Holy Spirit it can be powerful. We have seen many healed as a result.

4. Compassion and annoyance

Another way in which Jesus 'saw what his Father was doing' was through his own internal compassion for an individual or group. This compassion guided him for a ministry change. Matthew tells us:

> When he saw the crowds, he had compassion for them, because they were harassed and helpless, like sheep without a shepherd. Then he said to his disciples, 'The harvest is plentiful, but the labourers are few; therefore pray earnestly to the Lord of the harvest to send out labourers into his harvest.' And he called to him his twelve disciples and gave them authority over unclean spirits, to cast them out, and to heal every disease and every affliction (Matt. 9:36 – 10:1).

We see here that Jesus was propelled to equip and send out his disciples for the mission because of the compassion that he felt for the size and number of needs in the crowd. His compassion guided him to what his Father was doing, and he knew it was time for him no longer just to minister alone but also to equip and send out others. He also used compassion to guide him in whom he should minister to personally. On one occasion, at a funeral, Luke records, 'When the Lord saw her [the deceased's mother], he had compassion on her and said to her, "Do not weep." Then he came up and touched the bier, and the bearers stood still. And he said, "Young man, I say to you, arise." And the dead man sat up and began to speak, and Jesus gave him to his mother' (Luke 7:13–15).

This gives us a beautiful picture of a Saviour who was not indifferent to sickness and death but was frequently moved with compassion. In the same way, once we have repented of orphan thinking, judgements and pride, we will find that our compassion will begin to flow as the Father fills our heart with his. Frequently I find myself weeping as I pray for people and feel the love or compassion of God for them. On one occasion I was praying for a pastor and began to be overcome with weeping. His hard exterior soon melted as I wept for him, and he began to weep himself. Much kingdom break-through flows out of compassion for the broken.

In stark contrast we also find that Jesus and the disciples at times saw the Father's works through Spirit-inspired annoyance! Our sense of frustration and annoyance is probably one of the major areas that need sanctifying. However, once the Lord has his hands on it, it can be something that he uses to guide us into his ways. Jesus was once really aggravated with the Pharisees' hardness of heart when he sensed that their religious baggage was causing them to use a broken man for their own political ends:

> Again he entered the synagogue, and a man was there with a withered hand. And they watched Jesus, to see whether he would heal him on the Sabbath, so that they might accuse him. And he said to the man with the withered hand, "Come here." And he

said to them, "Is it lawful on the Sabbath to do good or to do harm, to save life or to kill?" But they were silent. And he looked round at them with anger, grieved at their hardness of heart, and said to the man, "Stretch out your hand." He stretched it out, and his hand was restored (Mark 3:1–5).

Notice that rather than deal with this quietly, Jesus, provoked by their hardness of heart, actually inflames the situation by bringing the man in front of them and healing him before their eyes. You get the idea that he was tuned in to his Father's righteous anger and it was that which showed him what the Father was doing. I love, too, the way that Jesus is angry with the Pharisees yet feels compassion for the man: a true sign of an emotionally whole heart.

We see the same with the Apostle Paul when a demonized slave girl was bothering him. After being annoyed by her cries for many days, he rebuked the demon in her, and she was immediately delivered. It seems strange to us that this holy frustration leads to kingdom breakthrough, but it's clear that when sanctified, it does! On this occasion Paul did not act out of compassion for the girl but because he had 'become greatly annoyed', presumably by the enemy's bothersome use of the girl (Acts 16:18).

One lady in our church was grieved and enraged in her heart over the stories of paedophile rings in the UK. She felt that there was little she could do as, with children at home, her time was fleeting. She knew, though, that she did have time to pray. She felt the Lord laid on her heart two towns in the UK and she began to pray for God to break up secret rings and free children who were being subjected to the worst atrocities. After a few weeks of praying she excitedly relayed to us the news that she had seen in the national press. In one of the towns the police had broken up a large paedophile ring, with many people being brought to justice. It gave her faith to continue to pray, and a few months later she was encouraged to see a similar breakthrough in the other town. It was as anger and compassion flowed from the heart of her King and as she allowed herself to be moved by it that breakthrough began. Again we see that sanctified annoyance led to kingdom breakthrough.

5. Seeing faith in others

The fifth way that both Jesus and Paul 'saw what the Father was doing' was that they observed faith in other people and responded accordingly. On one occasion Paul was looking around after preaching and saw a lame man. 'He listened to Paul speaking. And Paul, looking intently at him and seeing that he had *faith* to be made well, said in a loud voice, "Stand upright on your feet." And he sprang up and began walking' (Acts 14:9–10).

How do you 'see faith'? Paul, it says, looked at him intently. Whether it was a natural expression of interest or excitement he saw in the man, or a supernatural revelation that came to Paul as he looked, we do not know. What we do know is that Paul took the time to look at an individual and saw something that he knew was a sign that the Father was instilling faith into them. There are two lessons here for us. For those of us who preach, how often does the gospel that we preach inspire faith for healing like this? Ouch! Secondly, for all of us, how often do we miss kingdom breakthrough because we don't take the time to look intently in order to see what the Father is doing by his Spirit?

Jesus, by contrast, saw not the faith of the individual who needed healing but that of the friends who brought him. 'And when he saw their faith, he said, "Man, your sins are forgiven you"' (Luke 5:20). The same principle stands: faith can be seen if we will look for it and learn to recognize it, and kingdom breakthrough is sure to follow if we partner with it.

I personally find it easier to see cynicism than I do faith, but I'm learning to train myself to see faith as well! I once noticed a lady whose face was almost shining as I preached. I immediately recognized that she had faith for something, but didn't know what for. I saw that she responded to the invitation for prayer at the end, and I was delighted to see that she came forward to give testimony. 'Jesus has just healed me of fifteen years of neck pain,' she said. She then began to move her neck around to demonstrate the freedom from pain and the full mobility that she had received. It was one of those occasions when I could understand what Jesus meant when he said to people, 'Your faith has made you well.' I had seen it!

God also often speaks through the requests of others for help. Jesus responded to these with expectation: 'I will come and heal him,' he boldly declares to the centurion or his delegates who needed help. He obviously saw what the Father was doing simply through the request. Whenever someone expresses a need, I now feel prompted to offer to pray.

On a broader scale, it's often obvious where God is working if we have eyes to see. The apostles realized that God was up to something in Antioch, from the reports coming back of a great number of people believing and turning to the Lord. They sent Barnabas to check these reports out, and he, joined by the Apostle Paul, helped found one of the most influential churches in history (Acts 11:22). Have we got the same 'eyes to see'? We've been aware that God is touching particular families when a mum then a sister and a brother all come to faith. Zecheriah writes, 'Ask rain from the LORD in the season of the spring rain' (Zech. 10:1 which suggests that there's something significant about partnering with God's seasons. But this starts with us understanding and seeing what they are.

6. Sympathetic pain or remembering a healing or miracle

I don't have any strong biblical examples to cite, but I have experienced the Father showing me what he is doing through a sympathetic pain or a memory of a kingdom breakthrough that I have previously seen. Sympathetic pains come out of the blue and disappear in the same way. I've only had God speak to me in this way on one occasion, and it was while I was closing a meeting. My neck was suddenly in agony and I began to think that I needed to finish quickly and go home. Then I remembered that I had asked the Lord to speak to me through sympathetic pain, so I asked if there was anyone in the room with a chronic neck pain. A guy immediately responded; the Lord touched him, and he became pain-free.

I also occasionally find that God reminds me of a healing or kingdom breakthrough when he wants to repeat the same thing. I have no direct evidence for this, but I do wonder whether Jesus operated on this basis to a greater degree than we can tell from the narrative. In the case of most of the miracles recorded in the gospels, the things Jesus was doing had been done before by the prophets or saints of old, albeit not on the same scale or with the same frequency as those that he did. I wonder whether Jesus, with his great knowledge of Scripture, was reminded by the Father of things that he had read before. The need for bread for his followers could have reminded him of Elisha's similar bread-multiplication miracle with his disciples (2 Kgs 4:42–44). The widow who had lost her only son could have reminded him of the similar resurrection story of the widow that Elisha knew (2 Kgs 4:32–37). Pure speculation, I know, but a pet theory that I'm fond of!

I have certainly seen this 'holy' reminding operate on a number of occasions. In one meeting I was reminded of a back injury that I had seen. I told the group about it, and sure enough, a number of backs were healed. One minister I know has a set of cards on which he has written some of the things that he has seen God do. Before a meeting, he will go through the stories to remind himself and build his faith. A sanctified memory is a great tool in the hands of Jesus!

7. An audible voice (externally or internally audible) or an angelic visitation

I have not experienced the audible voice of God, but a number of my friends have. When God wants to speak, he speaks!

One fun story came from a 5-year-old in our church. At lunch after the morning meeting, his parents asked him how his group had been. 'I saw God!' he confidently declared. Thinking that there must have been someone dressed up for a fun re-enactment, his parents quizzed him further, asking what God had looked like. 'He was really tall and all white,' he said, describing clothes that glowed white. 'I didn't want to touch him because I thought the glow might burn my hand.' His parents were confused. This did not sound like normal fancy dress! They asked him what God had been doing. 'He walked around the room, putting his hand on the head of each child,' he said. 'Then he shot up through the ceiling.' His parents realized then that he had seen an angel moving around the room. 'Did he say anything to you before he left?' they asked him excitedly. 'Yes,' said the little boy. 'What did he say?' they pressed for more. 'I can't remember,' he said. This fact alone was what made the story so authentic to me. Beautiful!

God is always speaking in these ways and others. The main thing that I have found is important in learning to hear and respond to God's voice is to break free from fear, in particular the fear of failure. This is why it's critical to walk through the repentance steps first. For many weeks a friend and I stood at the front of our church and gave out the words that we felt we were hearing from God. Usually no one responded. It was so bad that some weeks I felt I could have said, 'There's someone here with a head,' and no one would have come forward. However, one week my friend stood up and picked out a lady in the group. She asked her to stand and said, 'I see you writing. Do you have anything to do with writing?' 'I do,' replied the lady: 'I'm a journalist.' Faith instantly rose in the room as the lady burst into tears, knowing that God himself had revealed this and was speaking to her. The interesting thing was the effect that this had on the church. They usually saw people come with mature gifts. They were wowed, but it didn't leave them feeling that they could do it. This, though, was different. They had seen someone 'bomb out' and get it wrong on many occasions, battling through the fear of failure. Something happened in a number of people as they realized that they too could grow in seeing what their Father is doing and joining him in it.

PARTNERING WITH GOD

Along with learning to see what the Father is doing, we have found it is critical to teach people what to do in the situation of kingdom breakthrough. We've found that there are six things to bear in mind when ministering to someone, whether Christian or not:

1. Ask the person what is wrong and if they are currently in pain

You don't need a detailed diagnosis, but it is often helpful to find out whether the person knows exactly what is wrong. It is also helpful to know whether the person is in pain at that moment and, if so, to ask them to grade the pain out of ten. This will help later to determine whether the pain has decreased. If the situation is not for physical healing, we would ask them some details that will help us as we minister.

2. Tell stories to build faith

We have found it helpful to tell people if we have seen someone else in the situation that they are facing touched by God. If not, other stories that are similar or even seemingly more difficult can be helpful. Where the person is caught in addictions, stories of friends who found freedom either over a period of time or instantaneously will help to bring hope. Often I only have a few minutes to speak to someone, but I know that if I can leave them in a place of faith, it is very often just a matter of time before they are free.

3. Ask if you can pray and lay on a hand

It is notable that Jesus did not instruct his disciples to pray for the sick but to heal the sick. The primary model of healing that we see in the New Testament is not prayer but the laying-on of hands. Jesus actually used many different approaches to healing, but it seems clear that this was the most common (Mark 6:5; 8:23; Luke 4:40; 13:13).

The prophet Habakkuk writes, 'Rays flashed from his hand; and there he veiled his power' (Hab. 3:4). I believe this was a prophetic sign of the coming Messiah and his usual mode of ministry. In a similar way we have found that huge benefit comes as we lay hands on people. Firstly there is the spiritual and healing benefit. Often people will feel warmth that goes beyond the normal heat generated by the body. Sometimes people will actually exclaim, 'Your hands feel like they are on fire!' On other occasions they feel a soothing icy coldness. This is very encouraging for both the one being ministered to and the minister. When this happens, I try to keep my hand on the spot for as long as the heat or cold remains, to allow the Holy Spirit to do his work. There is also the emotional benefit, as there is something hugely comforting about human touch.

We've found the best way to work with those who are not yet Christians is to ask them if we can pray. Most will say yes, the only issue being that they expect you to pray at home, not there and then! Once it is agreed that we mean to pray now, we simply ask if they feel happy for us to lay hands on the area. Most are happy with this.

It is important not to make this a superstition, and it's important not to press it upon the unwilling. I always ask whether people would be happy for me to place a hand on the afflicted spot – only if this is appropriate, of course. Apart from the shoulder or upper back, if I'm praying for a lady I will always ask her to place her hand on the spot first and put my hand on top of hers. This maintains an appropriate boundary.

Even if the person does not need a physical healing, I will ask if I can put a hand on their shoulder. It's such a powerful, connecting and human thing to do, and I believe we transmit power in this way.

4. Heal the sick (or oppressed or hurting)

The fact that Jesus told his disciples to heal the sick does not mean that praying for the sick is wrong: all prayer is good, and in fact James reports that the elders will 'pray over' a sick person (Jas 5:14). However, I don't see this as being the norm in Jesus' own ministry. Matthew writes that Jesus commanded them to 'heal the sick' (Matt. 10:8; compare also Luke 9:2; 10:9). Following this, we do as Jesus did and command sickness to leave, the pain to go and strength and healing to come. In Christ, the authority is ours to do so. We also command spiritual oppression to leave, because we have an invading kingdom!

The benefits of this model are twofold. Firstly, it is what Jesus told us to do. That has got to help. It forces us into the reality that we have authority over the sickness in Christ's name and also that the healing power is flowing from us.

There is also a second incidental, but important, benefit. If I pray for the sick and they are not healed, it is easy for the person (Christian or not) to be left with the impression that the God that I just appealed to is reluctant, indifferent or impotent. I can end up leaving them with a greater barrier to God than they had when I arrived. If, in contrast, I speak to the sickness and tell it to leave and it does not leave, the conclusion is much easier to frame. I say to people, after two or three prayers (or more if they are open), 'Look, see how it goes: sometimes people recover later on. But if not, you need to know that if Jesus were here you would be healed. He healed everyone that he prayed for! I am just a follower of his and am still learning. I'd love to pray again if you'd like, or you can come to church and we can pray for you.' This way I leave them with far fewer barriers to God than if I were to pray in the traditional way.

It is also true that many people recover later on. Caroline was once speaking to a friend who was not a Christian about her own back condition that had flared up. 'Have you tried prayer?' he asked. She was slightly surprised at his response. 'Yes,' she said. 'No, I don't mean praying for yourself,' he said, 'but actually getting someone to put their hand on you and pray for you.' Caroline was dumfounded. 'You mean praying for healing in Jesus' name?' she asked. 'Yes,' he explained. 'You remember the back condition that I had and you prayed for me? I've never had any pain since, and that must have been eighteen months ago.' Caroline was left open-mouthed. Not only had he never told her that he had been healed from this long-standing condition, he had also never mentioned that it had changed his perspective on God!

Of course if the area that you are praying for is not a sickness, this is less relevant. But you can still model speaking to situations, commanding them to change or shift in Jesus' name.

5. For physical healing, ask the person to start moving the part that's injured

If the issue is that the person needs physical healing, we have found it important, at some point early in the 'prayer', to ask them to start moving the afflicted part if it is possible for them to do so. There's something about the step of faith that is important. Our natural tendency is to run away before they have tested it, but this fear must be overcome. It is often as the person begins to move that the healing begins to flow. Jesus often got people to take a step of faith in this way, washing in a river, coming outside the town, getting up, etc. We also ask how the pain is feeling, again out of a possible maximum of ten. Often it has decreased or mobility has increased, which is an encouragement to ask, 'Can we pray again?'

6. If they are not healed, give wise follow-up counsel

If breakthrough does not immediately come I will still make much of God! I will tell stories of others who were prayed for multiple times and help them understand the principle of perseverance. I will also make much of the fact that God loves them. In this way, we have found frequently that people have been hugely blessed and encouraged even though they were not healed at that moment.

OPPORTUNITIES EVERYWHERE

The reality is, if we open our eyes there are opportunities everywhere for kingdom breakthrough. When Jesus pulled a kingdom opportunity out of seemingly nowhere while his disciples were fetching lunch, he said to them, 'Do you not say, "There are yet four months, then comes the harvest"? Look, I tell you, lift up your eyes, and see that the fields are white for harvest' (John 4:35).

The disciples' issue was not the skills for the role but the expectation of God's activity and pace in kingdom break-through. Similarly, I've found that I've had to change my expectation. I once visited London with my wife for a day out together. We had a lovely time, and on the way back she asked if I had enjoyed it.

'I did,' I said. 'The only disappointment was that we didn't have any opportunity to minister to anyone. I was looking out all day but nothing seemed to be happening.'

She looked blank. 'You're kidding,' she said. 'There were loads today. I didn't take them because I wanted to just be with you!'

'When?' I exclaimed. 'I didn't see one.'

'There was the couple on the train on the way to London. They smiled at us and we said a few words, but that would have been so easy to open up. Then there was the couple on the park bench over lunch. They said they were from another country – we could easily have opened that one up. Then there was the man in the park smiling at us; no problem there. Then there was the guy in the market. We bumped into the same guy twice in a market crowded with thousands of people in the middle of London. He thought it was weird, and you even said to him, "This is a weird coincidence." That was an open door!'

I was astonished. How could I have missed them all? Two people went through the same situations for an entire day. One, wanting and praying for opportunities, could not see even one. The other, not wanting any opportunities, saw at least five. I realized that as with the disciples, the issue was not that God needed to give me more opportunities. I had to learn to lift up my eyes and see the fields already white for harvest. Let's lift up our eyes and see what the Lord is already doing.

Notes

1 Typically a vision is said to be something you see while you are awake, while a dream is something you experience while asleep.

2 All visions occur while you are awake, but they can be open or closed: open visions are something you see with your eyes open and closed visions happen when your eyes are, well, closed!

3 If the reasons are not obvious to you, just don't do it!

Culture Eats Strategy for Breakfast

Now the eleven disciples went to Galilee, to the mountain to which Jesus had directed them. And when they saw him they worshipped him, but some doubted. And Jesus came and said to them, 'All authority in heaven and on earth has been given to me. Go therefore and make disciples of all nations, baptizing them in the name of the Father and of the Son and of the Holy Spirit, teaching them to observe all that I have commanded you. And behold, I am with you always, to the end of the age.'

Matthew 28:16–20

In his final instructions to the disciples, Jesus calls them to train future followers to 'observe' all that he has commanded them. The word used, *tēreō*,[1] has a stronger sense than the English word 'observe' that is commonly used to translate it; it means to keep watch over, to guard, to keep strictly.[2] He wants them to guard over the ways of thinking and acting, the revelation of how the world is, the truths about God and humankind that he has revealed to them and commanded them to live by. He is not asking them to do this alone; he promises to be there with them. What we see in the book of Acts is the church doing just that. They 'guard' and pass on the way of life that Jesus had taught them. They love Scripture as he did; they are courageous in the face of opposition as he was; they relate to the Father as he did; they preach and teach the people as he did; they have a focus on prayer as he did; they move in signs and wonders as he did; and they found it all on love and community as he did. This is guarding at its best. Rarely has the church seen it done as well. We've found that it's critical to reintroduce this theme of guarding, using a different word that means a similar thing: 'culture'.

WHAT IS CULTURE?

Culture is the characteristics of a particular group of people, defined by everything from language and religion to cuisine, social habits, music and arts.[3] It actually derives from the Latin word *cultura*, which means to guard or to till (as in to prepare land for crops). When we till[4] or cultivate an area we set a boundary and within that area we remove everything that is harmful to the growth of the things we want. We eradicate weeds and thereby encourage the good crops to grow. The boundary is particularly important, because it is the first point that the wild plants will seek to overrun.

I think cultivating or defining a culture has a sense similar to what Jesus was driving at when he called the disciples to 'teach them to observe all that I have commanded you'.[5] I like the image of cultivating, because I think it describes what Jesus intended: to create an area, or in this case a type of community, where good plants can grow because you have guarded them by eradicating all the plants that you do not want to grow. It picks up nicely Jesus' parable of the sower, where it was the weeds, rocks and shallow soil that made the difference to the fruit produced by the kingdom seed. The seed was the same in every instance, but it was the preparation (or lack of preparation) of the soil that made one seed fruitful and the others unfruitful. It also aligns nicely with the prophetic word that the Lord spoke to us and that I referred to in Chapter 2: 'The kingdom is like a seed; it has life within itself. Remove everything that is stopping it growing and it will grow.'

We've been excited to see the application of this principle. Recently we took our leaders and their families away to a retreat centre. Our children love this venue and, because it is completely secure, parents relax as the kids hare around the building. Some other guests also joined us for the weekend, and as they arrived a group of children were charging around in their usual fashion. One of the guests was wearing a neck brace to support her neck after a whiplash injury. As she walked through the door, one of the children, a 4-year-old, screeched to a halt. Pointing at her, he said, 'What's that thing on your neck?' in a way that only 4-year-olds or people with no social skills can.

'It's a neck brace,' she said. 'I've hurt my neck.'

'That's not right,' he said. 'We need to pray.' He prayed briefly and then charged off on his game. This story encouraged me because this is not the response or expectation we would have had even a few years ago; culture had begun to change, and the children were catching hold of it!

The reality is that every group or organization has a culture. Unless you define it, it will be defined for you. It's critical to define your culture, for as Peter Drucker, the business guru, once said, 'Culture eats strategy for breakfast.'[6] It's important to focus, agree and understand our strategy. But establishing a culture is far more important and far more effective. As we draw this book to a close, I hope you'll agree that the things we have spoken of are critical not just for every individual but for every church, Christian community or business to get hold of. If we could see the whole church living like this, free from the rocks that block the flow of the Spirit, free from control, judgement, fear, unbelief and the other Spirit-river inhibitors, we could be on the brink of a worldwide revival. In fact, some of the revivals that have already happened would probably have taken over the whole world and still be going if they had not been polluted and resisted by the things that block the Spirit's flow. There's been no shortage of power in the church, but there have been many blocks to the healthy flow of the Spirit's life.

The things that we have learned and that I've tried to demonstrate in this book are critical, I believe, to the future success of the church's health and mission. We simply must get back to doing the job that Jesus told us to do, and in the way he told us to do it. The issue is not, however, just one of individual transformation, but the transformation of entire churches to live this way. It must also not be for a few short weeks or months but for a sustained period of years and decades. It's going to take a culture change.

I've been excited to watch the culture of our church change over the last five or six years. Interestingly, some of the things that we have learned are important in bringing about such a change are also the things that Paul instructed the young church leader Titus to do as he went to work on Crete, an island where Paul had preached the gospel and established a number of churches some years before. Rather than a detailed exposition, a broad-brush look at Paul's letter to Titus will help us to see the key guidance he gives Titus on establishing a new culture in the churches that he was working with. Whatever our particular sphere of influence, whether a family, small group, church or movement of churches, there are some phenomenally important lessons to be learned here:

ESTABLISHING A CULTURE IS A WORK IN PROGRESS

'This is why I left you in Crete, so that you might put what remained into order' (Titus 1:5). Paul had been in Crete for a short time with Titus and had then left Titus there to finish off the work of establishing the churches in correct kingdom culture.[7] Although we do not know how long Paul was in Crete, the first thing that we notice should encourage us. Even the great Apostle Paul knew that culture transformation was a work in progress. If he knew this, how much more should we? Culture transformation is a process that takes time, much as individual transformation does. That is not to say that the Lord doesn't sometimes work very quickly across a whole community: he has done and still does. But very often for a complete way of thinking to change, not just in an individual but across a whole community, to the point where it never reverts to what it was before, takes some time. It's critical that we remember this so that we don't become discouraged.

We found that as we repented of, say, the rock of unbelief, we would find many came through to breakthrough, and faith began to grow. But then we would drift, disappointments would come in, and unbelief would settle again. The

Lord in his grace would call us to repentance again and a deeper work would begin.

The thing is, we cannot rest on this. Just like agriculture, the nature of this fallen planet and the nature of the human heart are such that we will forever be fighting the weeds! But fight we must, and keep digging them up and rooting them out.

I heard a story of an American visitor who was visiting the grounds of a college in Cambridge. Enjoying the beautiful lush grass, he asked the groundsman how it had been achieved.

'Simple,' the man replied. 'Just water it, roll it, weed it.'

'But I'm doing that,' replied the visitor, 'and my grass doesn't look like this.'

'Ah,' replied the gardener, 'just keep doing it for 100 years and it will.'

The journey of cultural change is a similar work in progress. We must not give up, for fruit will surely come.

WE MUST START WITH LEADERSHIP

'Appoint elders in every town as I directed you' (Titus 1:5b). 'Show yourself in all respects to be a model of good works, and in your teaching show integrity, dignity, and sound speech that cannot be condemned' (Titus 2:7–8).

Paul first tells Titus to deal with the leadership in this area of cultural transformation. Titus' own character and conduct was critical, and he was also to work closely with the next tier of leadership, the elders in every community. The principle, of course, is straightforward: leaders will generally set the high-water mark in every area that they are trying to establish. 'Don't do what I do: do what I tell you' just doesn't cut it when it comes to seeing people genuinely change for the long haul. As I've described in earlier chapters, the fact that our leaders have been authentic with their own battles and struggles to grow in faith and pursue this journey of growing in God has been one of the most releasing things for our people.

I remember one Sunday morning when I stood on the left side of the area at the front of the church and said, 'Guys, this is where we are. We don't expect any breakthrough or pray for much breakthrough, but there is no disappointment. Our expectations are so low that it's impossible to be disappointed!' I then walked to the right-hand side and said, 'Guys, this is heaven. There'll be no more tears and no more pain, and every prayer will be answered.' I then stood in the middle. 'Guys, this is the ground in between. This is where I want to live my life. I can't go back to that other place; it's not what I'm called to. This is the ground, the ground of disappointment and mystery and apparent failure. But it's also the ground of great joy and great breakthrough. It's the ground of seeing things that we never dreamed possible before. This is the ground that I want to stand on.' It was one of those moments when I found myself prophesying and preaching at the same time, caught up with what the Spirit of God was saying to us. It was a holy invitation. I knew that I could not call the church to stand on ground that I wasn't willing to stand on myself. From that point they have watched me step out and fail, watched me cry over loss, watched me live with mystery. But they have also seen me grow in boldness and accuracy and anointing. I remember one meeting in which I called out a word of knowledge for someone with a pain in their side. A lady responded and we prayed, but there was no apparent improvement. The next morning she woke up in worse pain. 'Lord,' she prayed, 'Simon gave this word yesterday. I believe it was from you. Will you heal me now?' Immediately the pain left and did not return. Stories like this encouraged me because I saw that it was no longer just my faith but the faith of a whole community that was growing and strengthening.

Again and again as leaders we have had to deal with our own hearts as the Lord has called us to repentance. Peter writes that judgement starts first with the household of God (1 Pet. 4:17), before it extends to the world. If first with God's house, then first with the leaders in God's house!

We Must Deal with Rebelliousness

'There are many who are insubordinate . . . They must be silenced, since they are upsetting whole families by teaching for shameful gain what they ought not to teach' (Titus 1:10–11).

Interestingly, Paul spends as long telling Titus to deal with the rebellious as he does telling him to deal with the leaders. Whenever there is change, some people will rebel against it either through brokenness, fear or sheer pride. If they are promoting their alternative culture to others in the community it is especially important to deal with it quickly, for their own sake and the sake of the whole community. Too many Christian leaders shy away from this important stage, hoping that the rebellion will simply die down of its own accord. It will not. Rebellion, left unchecked, will become a full-on revolt.

Notice that Paul says that Titus should rebuke them sharply (Titus 1:13 in the ESV translation). I am not sure that this gives the right sense, because the word actually means 'abruptly' rather than 'harshly'. I believe that what Paul is saying is that we must deal with it quickly and not let it linger.

There have been times in our community when I have not dealt with gossip and rebellion quickly enough, either out of the fear of other people or simply because I wanted to put my head in the sand. But I have learned, and am still learning, that when there is a sniff of it, it is time to move fast. Engaging people in dialogue quickly is the easiest way to distinguish the misguided sheep from the wolves.

Of course, there is also a warning for all of us. We will all be tempted to rebel. 'Therefore, as the Holy Spirit says, "Today, if you hear his voice, do not harden your hearts as in the rebellion" . . . But *exhort* one another every day, as long as it is called "today", that none of you may be hardened by the deceitfulness of sin' (Heb. 3:7–13).

To exhort means to summon, to encourage and to implore. Cultural shift comes as we refuse to keep each other at arm's length but instead have enough trust to challenge one another's actions and exposed motives. I was recently complaining about a senior politician to a couple from our church. They said, 'We used to complain like that, but you preached an excellent sermon once on honouring those in leadership over our country, as Peter honoured the crazed Emperor Nero' (1 Pet. 2:17). Gulp! My own sermon came back to bite me and to deal with my own rebellion.

We Must Apply the Culture to Different Groups

Older men, older women, young women, young men, workers and employers (Titus 2:1–9).

Paul instructs Titus to apply this new culture to different groups represented in the communities that he was dealing with. We have learned a similar principle: it's not just a one-off sermon that creates culture change but a sustained message delivered at every level. We have learned to see even unbelievers live with a greater understanding of how they are meant to be. In fact, like Jesus, we come into contact with some 'unbelievers' who have more faith than the believers! Right through the church, our teams have sought to apply these truths and help people to deal with unbelief, grow in identity, walk in boldness and grow in their understanding of God as Father.

I love the fact that the next generation in particular are getting it. One young mum was recently visited by a health visitor who revealed that she herself had not been able to carry a baby to full term. In fact she had lost four babies. The mum lacked the courage to ask to pray for her, but afterwards, as she confessed her fear to friends, she told them to hold her accountable. 'I will pray for her next time she visits,' she told them. On the next visit she noticed that the health visitor was wearing sickness wristbands (often worn to overcome morning sickness). She tentatively asked if she was pregnant again, and the health visitor said she was, sharing how anxious she was that she would lose this baby too. At the end of the visit, the mum offered to pray, surprised at how thankful the health visitor was to receive the offer.

The mum explained to her young daughter that they were going to pray for the health visitor so that she could join in. The pre-school child asked Jesus to look after the baby in the lady's tummy and help it grow and then whispered something in the health visitor's ear. The lady looked shocked and asked how the daughter knew. 'What did she say?' asked the little girl's mum. 'She asked me what I bought in Tesco. I just stopped in Tesco's to buy lunch, but how would she know that?' she wondered, having not mentioned it and having no Tesco bag. The mum had to explain that sometimes God gives people a word of knowledge simply to show us that he knows us and loves us. For the next eight months, every night before bed, when asked who she wanted to pray for, the little girl replied that she wanted to pray for this health visitor. Less than a year later they were overjoyed to meet her new baby! The health visitor personally thanked the little girl for her prayers, saying that she knew that they had made a difference.

WE MUST ROOT CULTURE SHIFT IN IDENTITY, NOT PERFORMANCE

For we ourselves were once foolish, disobedient, led astray, slaves to various passions and pleasures, passing our days in malice and envy, hated by others and hating one another. But when the goodness and loving kindness of God our Saviour appeared, he saved us, not because of works done by us in righteousness, but according to his own mercy, by the washing of regeneration and renewal of the Holy Spirit, whom he poured out on us richly through Jesus Christ our Saviour, so that being justified by his grace we might become heirs according to the hope of eternal life (Titus 3:3–7).

After writing these words, Paul reminds Titus that in bringing these changes to people, he must not come as one who has always 'got it sorted'. He must remember that his identity was no different from theirs but has now been radically changed.

As we exhort and encourage one another, we must appeal to identity, not law. Why? If you appeal to law you help to develop a legalist; if you appeal to identity you help to develop a child of God.

Throughout its history the church has reverted to the law in its desire to achieve the things that it feels, often rightly, that God wants to achieve. But ungodly approaches will not bring about godly fruit.

WE MUST NOT BE AFRAID OF REPETITION

'Remind them' (Titus 3:1); 'insist on these things' (Titus 3:8).

We grow bored easily and we continually want the latest thing. But Paul warns Titus not to be like that. People need to hear the same things again and again. We have found this principle to be true. Someone who was reading a draft of this book came across a familiar story. She told her husband, weeping once again, 'I must have heard that story a hundred times, but God does something new in me every time I hear it!' If you think about it, Jesus' teaching, given over three years, must have been highly repetitive. Even reading all the teaching from the four gospels would scarcely take a day. Yet he taught for three years solidly. Clearly he told the same stories and parables in numerous places on numerous occasions. Two things were achieved: the disciples were personally changed and they really knew the teaching, so were able to record it later!

THE END RESULT MUST BE CULTURAL TRANSFORMATION

'So that in everything they may adorn the doctrine of God our Saviour' (Titus 2:10).

The whole point of this culture shift in the church is cultural transformation of the region around. Paul Manwaring, a British church leader living in America, says, 'Apostolic bases will always result in cultural transformation.' This we see all the way from the pages of the New Testament to the church today.

We can have an amazing impact on communities as we start to touch one life at a time.

We didn't hear what had happened to the group of twenty or so teenagers that I mentioned in a previous chapter until about a year later. A different group were out treasure hunting in the town centre and had the word 'library' on their maps, and two people had the words 'long black coat'. So they went to the library and saw a guy with a long black coat who was part of a group of Gothic-looking young people hanging about.

They went over to the teenagers and started talking about the treasure map, and one of the lads said, 'Oh, are you Christian healers? We know all about you! Some other guys came and prayed for us earlier on in the year and my girlfriend got her wrist healed, and someone else got prayed for and was crying, and someone else got their back healed. We know all about this!'

So the team asked if anybody wanted prayer today. The teenagers pulled over one of the guys and told them, 'Pray for him!' They asked him what he would like them to pray for. He replied that he had pain in his back, and they started to pray for him. As they prayed, they could feel a lot of power. They asked him if he could touch his toes. He could, and declared that he was pain-free.

We've had many incidents like this in which different groups or individuals encounter the same people and are able to move them on a notch further in their journey to knowing Christ. This is the power of cultural transformation inside the church: sooner or later it begins to leak out!

Arnold Dallimore wrote of an army of God in the introduction to his book about the life of George Whitefield:

> And what manner of men will they be? Men mighty in the Scriptures, their lives dominated by a sense of the greatness, the majesty and holiness of God, and their minds and hearts aglow with the great truths of the doctrines of grace. They will be men who have learned what it is to die to self, to human aims and personal ambitions; men who are willing to be 'fools for Christ's sake', who will bear reproach and falsehood, who will labour and suffer, and whose supreme desire will be, not to gain earth's accolades, but to win the Master's approbation when they appear before his awesome judgement seat. They will be men who will preach with broken hearts and tear-filled eyes, and upon whose ministries God will grant an extraordinary effusion of the Holy Spirit, and who will witness 'signs and wonders following' in the transformation of multitudes of human lives.[8]

Whoever you are, and for whatever reason you picked up this book, I want to urge you to join us on this adventure of seeing the church transformed into what it was always designed to be. We are expectant for salvation and fruit beyond anything we have ever seen before. Before it comes, and even for it to come, the church itself must be prepared for the harvest. As someone once said, hurt people hurt people, but free people free people. Let us become free and go out to free some people. The kingdom of God is at hand!

NOTES

[1] *Tēreō*: to keep watch upon, to watch over protectively, guard, to mark attentively, to heed, to observe practically, keep strictly. William D. Mounce, *Mounce Concise Greek–English Dictionary of the New Testament* (Oak Tree Software).

[2] In fact Matthew 28:4 uses the same root word *tēreō* for the guards who guarded Jesus' tomb.

[3] Culture: Douglas Harpur, *Online Etymology Dictionary*, http://www.etymonline.com/index.php?term=culture.

[4] Till: *Chambers 21st Century Dictionary Online* http://www.chambers.co.uk/search.php?query=till&title=21st.

[5] We are not talking here of eradicating the distinct national or societal culture of a local church. Nor are we talking about styles of worship or preaching. We're talking about the parts of a culture that directly affect the move of the Holy Spirit within any community. If you think that the Holy Spirit will move in just any culture, look at Nazareth and think again!

[6] Luther Johnson, 'Culture Eats Strategy for Breakfast' http://www.relationaldynamicsinstitute.com/?p=48.

[7] Scholars do not agree on exactly when Paul was in Crete or for how long.

[8] Arnold Dallimore, *George Whitefield* (Banner of Truth Trust, 1970), I:16.

APPENDIX

The table on the following page gives a summary of the seven primary themes foreseen by Isaiah of the coming kingdom of God, and how Jesus and the early church saw them come into fruition.

Kingdom Theme	Luke 4/Isaiah 61 Reference	Number of Isaiah Passages	Jesus' Ministry	Church's Ministry
Deliverance or salvation	'liberty to the captives'	17 (e.g. Isa. 61:1)	Demonic deliverance; forgiveness of sin	Demonic deliverance; forgiveness of sin; unjustly imprisoned; being released (Peter, Paul, etc.)
Righteousness and justice	'liberty to the oppressed, good news to the poor'	16 (e.g. Isa. 32:1)	Jesus' judgements (healing on Sabbath; woman in adultery, taxes, etc.). The Cross!	Declaration of what was achieved on the cross (Rom. 3:21) and the identity of the new man (Eph. 4:24)
Peace	'bind up the broken-hearted' (Isa. 61:1)	14 (e.g. Isa. 9:6)	Calming of the storm (Mark 4:39); emotional healing (Mark 5:34 'go in peace'); peace to the disciples (Luke 24:36); peace on the mission (John 20:21)	Release of peace to worthy household (Matt. 10:13); proclamation of peace with God (Acts 10:36); pursuit of living in peace (2 Cor. 13:11)
Joy	'the oil of gladness' (Isa. 61:3)	12 (e.g. Isa. 9:3)	Joy at his birth (Matt. 2:10); joy in reception of the kingdom (Mark 4:16); joy in persecution (Luke 6:23); joy in ministry success (Luke 10:17); joy in prayer (John 16:24); joy at the resurrection (Matt. 28:8)	79 mentions in the non-gospel letters; mass joy in Samaria (Acts 8:8); joy after persecution (Acts 13:52); joy in gospel reports (Acts 15:3,31); joy in salvation (Acts 16:34); Paul's normative description of the kingdom (Rom. 14:17); joy in the state of the church (2 Cor. 7:16); joy in a stinking jail (Philippians)
God's presence	'the Spirit of the Lord is upon me/has anointed me'	9 (e.g. Isa. 60:1)	Jesus' baptism (Matt. 3:16); on return from wilderness (Luke 4:1); on ministry success (Luke 10:21); etc.	Pentecost (Acts 2:4); prayer meetings (Acts 4:31); deacons (Acts 6:3); mass fillings (Acts 10:44), etc.
Healing	'recovery of sight to the blind' (Isa. 35:5)	7 (e.g. Isa. 35:5)	Every person Jesus ministered to was healed	Many, many that the church ministered to were healed
Comfort	'to comfort all who mourn' (Isa. 61:2)	6 (e.g. Isa. 51:3)	The promise of the comforter (John 14:26); Jesus' comforting words (John 14); the promise of future comfort for Lazarus (Luke 16:25)	Comfort in affliction (2 Cor. 1:3); comfort from one another (2 Cor. 13:11)

Authentic

We trust you enjoyed reading this book
from Authentic Media. If you want to be
informed of any new titles from this author
and other exciting releases you can sign up
to the Authentic newsletter online:

www.authenticmedia.co.uk

Contact us

By Post:
Authentic Media
52 Presley Way
Crownhill
Milton Keynes
MK8 0ES

E-mail:
info@authenticmedia.co.uk

Follow us:

Contents

Contents

Foreword

Although it is many years since I took the exams which led to my becoming a chartered accountant, certain things linger in the mind, and my initial encounter with double-entry book-keeping is one of them.

This book has re-awoken the memory of trying to make sense of debits and credits and the basics of accounting. It presents a new approach to arming a student with an understanding of the principles of double-entry book-keeping.

I have been very impressed by the techniques created by the author, and by the jargon free explanations. I feel sure that this book will save many people a great deal of time in understanding basic principles, and it is a book that I would have welcomed had it been available when I started my accounting studies.

John Talbot F.C.A.

This book is dedicated to
anyone who has had to come to terms
with double-entry book-keeping.

Introduction

Welcome to the wonderful world of accounting.

There are many ways of keeping your accounts (including a shoe-box!), but the preferred method, used by every trained book-keeper and accountant throughout the world, is **double-entry**.

Many books and courses are already available. However, most are taught from an academic view point. They tend to throw you in at the deep end and assume you will not be overcome by the tidal wave of jargon.

This book takes an entirely different approach. By using just a few transactions and some simple **guidelines** you will understand the **logic** of double-entry, and by the use of a few **key** words the jargon will fall into place.

Words like **nominal ledger** and **trial balance** will become second nature. You will have no problem with your **debits** and **credits**. In short, you will be able to **post a journal** just as easily as you can now post a letter!

By the end, you will be able to talk, **and understand**, the same language as your bank manager, accountant, and tax inspector.

If you intend to keep your accounts on a computer, the last chapter will help you decide which package to buy.

This is followed by a list of useful contacts, a glossary of accounting terms, and an index.

Finally, may we wish you many happy accounting years.

Notes to the book

This book is arranged in two parts. The first takes you through the basics, from your very first entry, right up to the main financial statement of a business: the balance sheet.

The second part goes into detail with regard to all the different types of transaction you are likely to come across.

If you are using this book in conjunction with a formal accounting course or with a view to becoming a certified or chartered accountant, you should pay particular attention to chapter 9. This outlines the differences between the logical approach of this book and the traditional methods taught at a college or university.

All the illustrations have been numbered according to their chapters so a reference like *figure 10.5* means chapter 10 illustration number 5.

Some accounting terms vary from country to country. The glossary will point you in the right direction.

Part 1

The principles of double-entry.

1 • Accounting for everything

When we buy something there are **two** things to consider: the account which is paying for it (eg. bank or cash) and the item itself (eg. petrol, stationery, insurance).

In a **single-entry** accounting system **transactions** are recorded one after another in a book which typically has columns for the account used and the analysis of what was bought (*figure 1.1 shows £10 worth of cash being spent on petrol*).

Payments Book		Accounts		Analysis Headings		
Date	Reference	Bank	Cash	Petrol	Stationery	Insurance
27th June	TSD Services		10.00	10.00		

figure 1.1

Whilst we have no problem looking at the bank and cash columns as **accounts**, we rarely think of the analysis headings as **accounts** in their own right.

In a **double-entry** system all of the above are referred to as **accounts** (eg. a cash account, a petrol account etc.), and more importantly, **separate** entries are made for each **account** involved in a **transaction**.

In the above example, **two** entries are required: one to show where the money came **from** (cash), and the other to show where it went **to** (petrol). This **from** & **to** aspect of each transaction is known as **crediting** and **debiting**. It is what the term **double-entry** means.

In order to record these entries we need somewhere to write them down: these are called 'original books of entry' or more commonly, **Journals**.

2 • The Journal

The journal is simply a book with various columns where we record our day to day business transactions.

The minimum number of columns required is five: the **date**, the **account**, a **reference**, a **debit** and a **credit** column (*figure 2.1*).

Journal				
Date	Account	Reference	Debit	Credit

figure 2.1

All your transactions are entered one after another in **date order** in the journal, therefore the journal contains a complete history of your transactions as they occur.

In practice, a business will use more than one journal, each of which will be devoted to a certain aspect of the business and each will be given a name to reflect this (eg. 'general journal', 'cash book journal'). However, the principle of entering your transactions in a journal in the first place remains the same.

For the following examples we will enter all our transactions in just one book which from now on we shall refer to as 'the journal'.

Lets start with the transaction outlined on the previous page: purchasing £10 of **petrol** by **cash** on 27th June.

Two accounts are involved in this transaction (petrol and cash) so we will need to make **two entries** in the journal.

The point of the entries is to show how the money **flows** from one account to another.

To achieve this the first entry will credit one of the accounts and the second will debit the other. However, deciding which account to debit and which to credit is not particularly obvious.

This is where our first **guide** to accounting comes in: Every transaction must come **from** somewhere and go **to** somewhere else. The **from** side is the **credit** side and the **to** side is the **debit** side (*figure 2.2*).

figure 2.2

The problem is remembering that **from=credit** and **to=debit**.

The other thing that doesn't help is that traditionally the debit column is shown to the left of the credit column (*see figure 2.1*).

Therefore if we add a third term to our formula:

from=credit=**right**

to=debit=**left**

we can remember it as **from right to left** (*figure 2.3*).

figure 2.3

If you apply this **from** and **to** principle to our first transaction you will know which account to debit and which to credit: the money is coming **from** cash and going **to** petrol so we **credit cash** and **debit petrol** (*figure 2.4* - the arrow shows the flow of money).

Journal			(to) Debit	(from) Credit
Date	Account	Reference	Debit	Credit
27th June	Cash	J1		10.00
27th June	Petrol	J1	10.00	

figure 2.4

Lets take a look at the cash account to understand exactly why we **credit** it when we are taking money **from** it.

The cash account should be thought of as a real cash box. When you remove some money to buy some goods, you should replace it with a receipt or petty cash slip to say what the money was used for. A receipt or petty cash slip is a form of **credit note**, so the cash box now contains a credit note instead of the cash, hence we show the entry as a credit. (Logically, if you returned the goods because they were faulty, the receipt would be given back in exchange for the cash).

Looking at the debit side, the petrol account now has the money (albeit in the form of half a tank of petrol!), it got the money from cash so it is in **debt** to cash - hence it is entered as a **debit**.

This is the fundamental principle of double-entry, we are keeping track of where the money came **from** (a **credit**) and where the money went **to** (a **debit**).

Furthermore the first **rule** of accounting states that all the debits **must** equal the credits. Therefore, provided all your entries are correct, no money can ever escape the system or be introduced into it without a complete record of it being shown in the journal.

We will now enter a second transaction: a £50 cash sale on the 29th June. If we apply the from/to guide again we can see that the money has come **from** sales and is going **to** cash so we **credit** sales and **debit** cash (*figure 2.5*).

Journal			(to)	(from)
Date	Account	Reference	Debit	Credit
27th June	Cash	J1		10.00
27th June	Petrol	J1	10.00	
29th June	Sales	J2		50.00
29th June	Cash	J2	50.00	

figure 2.5

You will notice that as well as introducing a new account called 'Sales' we have also used a new reference number 'J2'.

The reference number ties together the two sides of each transaction. The reference used can be anything you like as long as it is unique for each transaction. The reference we have used begins with a 'J' to show that it has been entered in the Journal.

Most transactions have a piece of paper associated with them (ie. a receipt from the garage where you bought the petrol or an invoice for your cash sale), therefore it is a good idea to number each receipt or invoice sequentially with a unique reference (eg. J1, J2 etc.) rather than use the original number on the receipt.

It then becomes easy in the future to check your entries against the original paperwork to verify that the accounts are correct.

As we enter more and more transactions it will become increasingly difficult to calculate our current cash balance (or for that matter our total sales).

Therefore we need a way of looking at each account separately.

This is achieved by making **exact** copies of the entries in the journal to another book called the **ledger**. This is called **posting**.

When posting you are not **moving** an entry, but making a **copy** of it somewhere else. Your original entries will therefore always exist in the order you entered them in the journal.

Posting is traditionally done at the end of each month but is entirely at your discretion - if you need to know what your sales figures are, then you will need to make sure all your transactions are entered in the journal and posted to all the relevant accounts in the ledger.

3 • The Ledger

A ledger is just another book but with each page devoted to a single account. It is simply an alternative view of your journal entries - the journal entries are in **date** order, the ledger is a re-arrangement of the journal in **account** order.

The important thing to remember is that **all** your transactions are entered in the journal **first**. The ledger merely contains **copies** of them re-arranged by account.

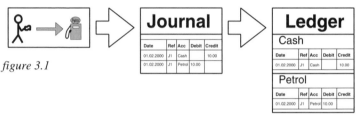

figure 3.1

Just like the journal, most businesses will use more than one ledger, each devoted to a certain aspect of the business and each given a different name to reflect this (eg. 'Sales Ledger' and 'Purchase Ledger'), but whatever the case, a single general ledger will **always** be opened. This is called the **Nominal Ledger**.

This is the only ledger we shall be using for the rest of the examples in the first part of this book.

Although it is termed 'nominal' for reasons which will become clear later, it is nevertheless important to realise that it is the main ledger of a business (ie. where other ledgers are also in use, the final balance of those ledgers will also be held in the nominal ledger). Therefore, the nominal ledger will hold the full picture of a business however many other ledgers are used.

In order to post (ie. make copies of) the entries from the journal we must draw up a list of the accounts used so far and give each one its own page in the ledger.

We need three accounts at this stage: a **cash** account, a **petrol** account and a **sales** account.

The layout of each account in the ledger is identical to the journal with the exception that the 'account' column is no longer required - we are looking at the entries of just one account so it can be included as the title of the page instead (*figure 3.1*).

Nominal Ledger	Cash Account		
Date	Reference	Debit	Credit

figure 3.1

Once we have posted our entries into the ledger we can then begin to see how the business is doing.

Posted entries are **exact** copies of the original. If the entry was a **debit** entry in the **journal** then it is also a **debit** entry in the **ledger**.

This is how the cash account looks after posting the entries made so far (*figure 3.2*):

Nominal Ledger	Cash Account		
Date	Reference	Debit	Credit
27th June	J1		10.00
29th June	J2	50.00	

figure 3.2

Although we can now see the relevant entries we don't yet know what the balance is; furthermore we don't know whether that balance means we have a surplus or a deficit of cash.

Working out the balance is straightforward: we start by adding up the debit and credit columns and show the totals on a new line (*figure 3.3*).

Nominal Ledger	Cash Account		
Date	Reference	Debit	Credit
27th June	J1		10.00
29th June	J2	50.00	
Totals		50.00	10.00

figure 3.3

We then subtract one from the other to get the balance using the following rules:

If the **debit** total is greater: the **balance=debits-credits** and the result is put in the **debit** column.

If the **credit** total is greater: the **balance=credits-debits** and the result is put in the **credit** column.

In other words, we are always going to get a **positive** balance, and it will always be placed under the **highest** total (this is the reason the columns were totalled first).

In this example the debits exceed the credits so the balance=£50-£10 and the result of £40 is placed under the debits column (*figure 3.4*).

Nominal Ledger	Cash Account		
Date	Reference	Debit	Credit
27th June	J1		10.00
29th June	J2	50.00	
Totals		50.00	10.00
30th June	Balance b/d	40.00	

figure 3.4

The term 'Balance b/d' is an abbreviation of 'balance **brought down**' - we have literally brought down the balance to the next line.

We have assumed that we balanced the account on the 30th June therefore we have used that date for the 'Balance b/d' line.

Because the balance of every account is always expressed as a positive value it doesn't tell us where we stand in relation to it (eg. do we have a surplus of cash or is it overdrawn?).

We can overcome this by applying our **from/to** guide again (**from=credit** and **to=debit**):

In this example we know we have a surplus of cash because the balance is in the **debit** column (more money has gone **to** the cash account than from it - see figure 3.4 on the previous page).

An account is balanced for two reasons: firstly to tell us the balance on a particular date, and secondly to save us having to add up all the previous entries again if further entries are posted (ie. we only need to add the new entries to the previous balance).

We can now apply our formula to the petrol and sales accounts to get their balances (*figures 3.5 & 3.6*):

Nominal Ledger	Petrol Account		
Date	**Reference**	**Debit**	**Credit**
27th June	J1	10.00	
Totals		**10.00**	**0.00**
30th June	Balance b/d	**10.00**	

figure 3.5

Nominal Ledger	Sales Account		
Date	**Reference**	**Debit**	**Credit**
29th June	J2		50.00
Totals		**0.00**	**50.00**
30th June	Balance b/d		**50.00**

figure 3.6

We have spent £10 on petrol because the balance is in the **debit** column (more money has gone **to** petrol).

We have earned £50 from sales because the balance is in the **credit** column (more money has come **from** sales).

Having entered our transactions in the journal and then re-arranged them into separate accounts (by posting them into the ledger) we then draw a double line under the last entry in the journal (*figure 3.7*):

Journal				
Date	Account	Reference	Debit	Credit
27th June	Cash	J1		10.00
27th June	Petrol	J1	10.00	
29th June	Sales	J2		50.00
29th June	Cash	J2	50.00	

figure 3.7

The double line is to remind you that the previous entries have already been posted to the ledger (in other words you don't want to post them again should you make further entries).

If you look at figures 3.4, 3.5 & 3.6 which show the ledger accounts you will see we have also drawn a double line, but this time it is under the **totals**. This is there to remind you that the previous entries have already been added up and the 'Balance b/d' is the place to start from the next time you balance the account.

We will enter one more transaction in the journal: a payment of £30 from cash to a new account called **drawings** (*figure 3.8*). This transaction represents the owner of the business 'drawing' out money for his or her own wages (this only applies to the self-employed and partnerships, the owners of limited companies are treated differently and this is covered in chapter 15).

Journal				
Date	Account	Reference	Debit	Credit
27th June	Cash	J1		10.00
27th June	Petrol	J1	10.00	
29th June	Sales	J2		50.00
29th June	Cash	J2	50.00	
30th June	Cash	(to Drawings)		30.00
30th June	Drawings	(from Cash)	30.00	

figure 3.8

Figures 3.9 & 3.10 show the effect on the ledger accounts once the new entries are posted.

Nominal Ledger	Cash Account		
Date	Reference	Debit	Credit
27th June	J1		10.00
29th June	J2	50.00	
Totals		50.00	10.00
30th June	Balance b/d	40.00	
30th June	(to Drawings)		30.00
Totals		40.00	30.00
30th June	Balance b/d	10.00	

figure 3.9

Nominal Ledger	Drawings		
Date	Reference	Debit	Credit
30th June	Cash	30.00	
Totals		30.00	0.00
30th June	Balance b/d	30.00	

figure 3.10

The reference used is different in this case because an invoice or receipt has not been issued for the transaction. Instead we have entered a suitable description. This description is called a **narrative** in accounting terms.

A narrative is essential if no source document is available. Without one we would never know what the money was used for (or where it came from) if we were looking at just a single account.

The next step is to check that all the journal entries have been posted correctly to the ledger. This is called a **trial balance**.

4 • The Trial Balance

The trial balance is a complete list of your account balances from the **nominal ledger**. The layout is similar to the ledger except that only three columns are required: the **account name** and a **debit** and **credit** column.

Just the final balance line of each account is copied into the trial balance using the **debit** column if the account has a **debit** balance, or the **credit** column if the account has a **credit** balance (*figure 4.1*).

Trial Balance as at 30th June		
Account	**Debit**	**Credit**
Cash	10.00	
Petrol	10.00	
Sales		50.00
Drawings	30.00	
Totals	**50.00**	**50.00**

figure 4.1

The debit and credit columns are then totalled and checked that they match each other to satisfy the first rule of accounting (**all the debits must equal the credits** - see page 10).

If they are not equal to each other it is proof that a mistake has been made. An **audit** is then carried out to find the error.

An **audit** simply means going through each entry in the **journal** to check that it matches the original paperwork (this is called an **audit trail**). If no error is found then it must be due to a mistake when posting the entries to the ledger. The audit then continues by checking each journal entry against the ledger entries.

Having said this, all larger businesses will carry out an audit even if the trial balance balances because mistakes may still be present.

For example an original transaction of £10 from cash to petrol may have been entered as £100 from cash to petrol in the journal, or one side of a journal entry may have been posted to the wrong ledger account.

If a mistake is discovered a **reversing entry** is made in the journal to nullify that part of the transaction which was wrong, followed by a **correcting entry** to put it right.

A **reversing entry** is a duplicate of the original but with the amount put in the opposite debit or credit column (ie. if the original was a debit, the new entry will be a credit).

A **correcting entry** is also a duplicate of the original but this time to the correct account or for the correct amount.

We will illustrate this with an example. Suppose our original transaction for petrol was in fact for repairs. The reversing entry would credit the petrol account £10 and the correcting entry would debit the repairs account instead *(figure 4.2)*.

Journal				
Date	**Account**	**Reference**	**Debit**	**Credit**
27th June	Cash	J1		10.00
27th June	Petrol	J1	10.00	
29th June	Sales	J2		50.00
29th June	Cash	J2	50.00	
30th June	Cash	(to Drawings)		30.00
30th June	Drawings	(from Cash)	30.00	
30th June	Petrol	J1 (reversed)		10.00
30th June	Repairs	J1 (corrected)	10.00	

figure 4.2

Having corrected any mistakes and posted the new entries to the ledger the trial balance will need to be drawn up again to check that no further mistakes have been made.

The trial balance is termed a **report**. This is because it is not held in a ledger, but merely produced when required as a way of checking the books.

As far as this example is concerned we will assume that the original entries were correct in the first place and move on to the next chapter to discover if the business is making a **profit** or a **loss**.

5 • The Profit & Loss Account

The **Profit & Loss account**, as its name implies, tells us whether we are making a profit or a loss: are we earning more money than we are spending? (a profit), or vice-versa (a loss).

The layout of the profit & loss account is just like any other account; the only difference is that it consists of the balances from other **accounts** rather than original transactions.

The accounts involved are those to do with **revenue** and **expenses**.

Before we go any further we must clarify what constitutes revenue and expense accounts:

Revenue accounts are used to record the sales and any other taxable income of a business.

Expense accounts are for goods or services you have bought in order to run your business.

(Note: some revenue and expense accounts should not be included **directly** in the profit & loss account. Instead, they are combined in one or two interim accounts which are then posted to the profit & loss account. They are of no concern to us yet and are outlined in chapter 8 and covered in detail in chapters 13, 14 & 16).

To compile a **profit & loss account** we must open one in the **nominal ledger** and **transfer** the balances of our **revenue** and **expense** accounts into it. We can then use our **from/to** guide on the resulting balance to determine if a profit or loss has been made.

Transferring a balance from one account to another means zeroing one account by crediting it if it has a debit balance (or vice-versa) then debiting the other account (or vice-versa). In other words if the balance of a sales account is £50 **credit**, then we **debit** it £50 and **credit** the profit & loss account £50. All we are really doing is **moving** the balance from one account to another (the sales account's balance is now zero because the profit & loss account holds it).

We need to do this because all the accounts are being held in the **same** ledger.

So far we have used only one revenue (sales) and one expense (petrol) account (*figures 5.1 & 5.2*):

Nominal Ledger	Sales Account		
Date	Reference	Debit	Credit
29th June	J2		50.00
Totals			**50.00**
30th June	Balance b/d		**50.00**

figure 5.1

Nominal Ledger	Petrol Account		
Date	Reference	Debit	Credit
27th June	J1	10.00	
Totals		**10.00**	
30th June	Balance b/d	**10.00**	

figure 5.2

Like all transactions, **transferring** a balance from a revenue or expense account to the profit and loss account is achieved by making entries in the **journal**.

We have two balances to transfer so we need to make a debit and a credit entry for each of the balances.

Figure 5.3 shows the journal complete with our new entries:

Journal				
Date	Account	Reference	Debit	Credit
27th June	Cash	J1		10.00
27th June	Petrol	J1	10.00	
29th June	Sales	J2		50.00
29th June	Cash	J2	50.00	
30th June	Cash	(to Drawings)		30.00
30th June	Drawings	(from Cash)	30.00	
30th June	Petrol	(to P&L)		10.00
30th June	Profit & Loss	(from Petrol)	10.00	
30th June	Sales	(to P&L)	50.00	
30th June	Profit & Loss	(from Sales)		50.00

figure 5.3

Notice that like the 'drawings' transaction we have used a narrative to explain the transfers. The fact that the narrative uses an account name as a reference is irrelevant - all that matters is that it is clear and to the point.

We can now post the new journal entries to the **three** accounts affected by it in the ledger, namely **sales**, **petrol** and the **profit & loss account**. Figures 5.4 & 5.5 show the sales and petrol accounts.

Nominal Ledger	Sales Account		
Date	Reference	Debit	Credit
29th June	J2		50.00
Totals			50.00
30th June	Balance b/d		50.00
30th June	(to P&L)	50.00	
Totals		50.00	50.00
30th June	Closed		

figure 5.4

Nominal Ledger	Petrol Account		
Date	Reference	Debit	Credit
27th June	J1	10.00	
Totals		10.00	
30th June	Balance b/d	10.00	
30th June	(to P&L)		10.00
Totals		**10.00**	**10.00**
30th June	Closed		

figure 5.5

We have used the term 'closed' instead of 'balance b/d' for the sales and petrol accounts because the profit & loss account is usually compiled at the end of an accounting year and this signifies that no more trading will take place in that year.

The sales account balance showed £50 credit so the journal entries debited the sales account £50 and credited the profit & loss account £50.

The petrol account showed £10 debit so the journal entries credited petrol £10 and debited profit & loss £10.

Nominal Ledger	Profit & Loss Account		
Date	Reference	Debit	Credit
30th June	Sales		50.00
30th June	Petrol	10.00	
Totals		**10.00**	**50.00**
30th June	Balance b/d (net profit)		**40.00**

figure 5.6

The net result is that the balances in sales and petrol have been zeroed and are now included in the profit & loss account. This account has then been totalled and balanced and now shows the net profit (*figure 5.6*).

We knew which column to use for the balance because the credits are greater than the debits so we subtracted the debits from the credits and put the result in the credit column; **remember the guide to balances**:

If the **debit** total is greater: the **balance=debits-credits** and the result is put in the **debit** column.

If the **credit** total is greater: the **balance=credits-debits** and the result is put in the **credit** column.

We can now apply the **from/to** guide and ascertain that there is a profit because the balance is on the **credit** side. In other words more money has been made **from** revenue than has gone **to** expenses.

It may help if we re-arrange the profit & loss account horizontally rather than vertically (*figure 5.7*).

Profit & Loss Account				
Expenses	**Debit**		**Revenue**	**Credit**
Petrol Account	10.00		Sales Account	50.00
Total Expenses	**10.00**		**Total Revenue**	**50.00**
Balance on 30th June				**40.00**

figure 5.7

It is now obvious that more money has come from revenue than has gone to expenses (this type of layout is known as a 'T' account - see 'Notes for Students' in chapter 9).

Suppose the sales total was £10 and the petrol £50, a horizontal profit & loss account would look like this (*figure 5.8*):

Profit & Loss Account			
Expenses	**Debit**	**Revenue**	**Credit**
Petrol Account	50.00	Sales Account	10.00
Total Expenses	**50.00**	**Total Revenue**	**10.00**
Balance on 30th June	**40.00**		

figure 5.8

The balance is now on the expenses side which means more money has gone **to** expenses than **from** revenue, therefore a loss is shown.

This transferring of account balances to create a profit & loss account should only be done once at your year end otherwise (if you do it say, every month) you will end up with multiple postings for many of the accounts (eg. if you transfer your petrol balance to the profit & loss account every three months, you will need to add all four posting's together to see your total petrol expenses for the year).

Having said this, a profit & loss **report** can still be produced whenever you want simply by **copying** the balances of your revenue and expense accounts on to a separate sheet of paper (just like a trial balance). In other words you can still **balance** each account whenever you like provided you don't zero the balance by transferring it to the profit & loss account until year end.

The profit & loss account is an amalgamation of your revenue and expense accounts for the **current year**. It reflects just one aspect of your business. Ultimately it too will be closed (like the sales and petrol accounts) and a new profit & loss account will be started for the following year.

A quick resume of everything we have done since the first chapter may be useful at this point:

1. Open the **journal** and enter our day to day business transactions.

2. Open the **nominal ledger** and make exact copies of the journal entries into the ledger accounts (this is called **posting**). Draw a line under the journal entries to remind us that they have been posted.

3. Total and **balance** each ledger account, draw a line under the total and bring the balance down to a new line (ready to be added to the next batch of postings).

4. Produce a **trial balance** to ensure all the credits equal the debits.

5. If any errors are found, make **reversing** and **correcting** entries in the journal, post these to the ledger accounts and redo the trial balance.

6. Make some new entries in the journal to **transfer the balances** (ie. move them) from the revenue and expense accounts to the **profit & loss account** and post these to the ledger.

It is stage 6 that has been dealt with in this chapter.

Having established the profit & loss account (and before we close the books for the year) we must do one more thing: take a look at the business as a whole. For this we need to prepare the **balance sheet**.

6 • The Balance Sheet

We can now look at the main equation of a double-entry system which will show that the first rule of accounting (the debits must equal the credits) not only applies to each transaction but continues right up to the main financial statement of the business; the **balance sheet**.

The **profit & loss account** reflects the balance of a specific area of your business over a **particular period of time**. The **balance sheet** reflects the current balance of everything **since the business began**.

The **nominal ledger** holds this information, so like the trial balance we can compile the balance sheet by copying all the account balances into a report. The only difference is that the accounts are re-arranged to show what the business **owns** and what it **owes**.

In accounting terms these are called **assets** and **liabilities**.

Assets

These are the things the business **owns**. They are usually broken down into two groups: **Fixed Assets** and **Current Assets**.

Fixed assets include capital items like the business's premises (assuming they are not rented), company cars and office equipment.

Current assets include money in the bank, petty cash, and money owed to the business by its customers. (See chapter 16 for a more detailed description).

Liabilities

These are the things the business **owes**. They too are usually broken down into two groups: **Liabilities** and **Equity**.

Liabilities include overdrafts at the bank, loans to the business by people other than yourself and any money owed by the business to its suppliers.

Equity represents what the business owes to the owner of the business. To understand this you need to look at the business as an item in its own right: there is **you** the **owner**, and there is also **your** business.

The reason we need to separate the business from the owner becomes obvious once you realise that the owner may have other liabilities and assets which are not connected with the business (eg. the owner's home).

Another way of looking at equity is that you may have loaned the business some money or the business may have made a profit which you have decided to leave in the business: the business therefore **owes you** some money - this is a **liability** to the business and therefore represents (and is shown as) your **equity** in the business.

Although the equity section is only a part of a business's liability, it is a major part. We can therefore look at the balance sheet as being composed of three groups: **assets**, **liabilities** and **equity**.

These three groups make up what is known as the **accounting equation**:

Assets = Liabilities + Equity

A balance sheet (just like an account) has two sides, furthermore the two sides must equal each other (this is why it is called a balance sheet).

By looking at the equation you can see that we have **Assets** on one side and **Liabilities** & **Equity** on the other.

Just like any mathematical equation a balance sheet can be re-arranged in any order you like:

Equity = Assets - Liabilities
Liabilities = Assets - Equity

For the purposes of this book we shall use the first version (**Assets = Liabilities + Equity**) since we can use a new guideline to decide which accounts go in which section:

All accounts with **debit** balances go on the **assets** side.

All accounts with **credit** balances go on the **equity** and **liabilities** side.

To decide whether an account with a **credit** balance goes under **equity** or **liabilities** you need to make sure you understand the relationship between the business and the owner of the business as outlined on the previous page.

The important thing to realise is that both equity and liabilities are the same thing as far as the business is concerned: they represent the creditors of the business (ie. people to whom the business owes money).

All we are doing is splitting the creditors into two sections; **equity** represents what the business owes you, **liabilities** represents what the business owes its suppliers.

This is all fairly straightforward. We can follow the guideline by copying each accounts balance into the left or right side of the balance sheet depending on its debit or credit status (*figure 6.1*).

Balance Sheet as at 30th June			
Assets	(Debit balances)	**Liabilities**	(Credit balances)
Cash Account	10.00		
Drawings	30.00	**Equity**	
		Profit & Loss	40.00
Balance	**40.00**		**40.00**

figure 6.1

However the point of a balance sheet is to tell you as plainly as possible about the overall state of the business.

The balance sheet in figure 6.1 is fine but ideally the drawings account should be included as part of your equity whatever its balance (because it represents money you have taken from your business).

We can show this by placing brackets round its balance and putting it under equity (*figure 6.2*). The brackets tell us to treat the balance as negative so the equity can be totalled as £40 profit less £30 drawings = £10 Equity.

Balance Sheet as at 30th June			
Assets		**Liabilities**	
Cash Account	10.00		
		Equity	
		Profit & Loss	40.00
		Drawings	(30.00)
Balance	**10.00**		**10.00**

figure 6.2

Another complication (as far as clarity is concerned) is if the business made a loss. If we reversed the figures to show £50 spent on petrol and £10 received from sales this would result in a **debit** balance in the profit & loss account and a **credit** balance in Cash (which in effect means it is overdrawn!).

We can happily place brackets round the profit & loss account but what about the cash account? Do we still show it as an asset but with brackets round it or should we put it directly under liabilities because it has a credit balance?

The best answer is to put it under liabilities but add a short description to make it more meaningful. We could also rename the profit & loss account to reflect its balance (ie. is it a profit or loss? - *figure 6.3*).

Balance Sheet as at 30th June			
Assets		**Liabilities**	
		Cash (shortfall)	70.00
		Equity	
		Loss for period	(40.00)
		Drawings	(30.00)
Balance	**0.00**		**0.00**

figure 6.3

Any account can be renamed as far as the balance sheet is concerned because it is only a report (ie. it is not an on-going part of the double-entry system, just a summary of all the accounts at a particular point in time).

A more obvious account which can have a debit or credit balance and therefore appear under assets or liabilities is a bank account.

This could be labelled 'Cash at bank' as an asset or 'Bank overdraft' as a liability.

You can use the guidelines (debits on the left, credits on the right) in the first place, then move things around and rename them to make it clearer to other people.

Another point to note is that the balances at the bottom of the balance sheet can be virtually meaningless depending on how the accounts are arranged. Our main concern is that they equal each other:

Assets = Liabilities + Equity.

Figures 6.1 & 6.2 highlight this perfectly: both have the same individual account balances but both have different overall balances. However, figure 6.2 tells us more about the business since we can see at a glance that the business has cash reserves of £10 (assets) and it owes this to the owner of the business (equity).

Chapter 16 in part two of this book goes into greater detail with regards to both assets and the layout of balance sheets.

Having entered our transactions into the journal, posted them to the ledger, produced a profit & loss account and finally a balance sheet we have effectively 'closed the books' for the year and are ready to open a new set for the following year. This is the subject of the next chapter.

7 • Opening and Closing the books

The process of transferring the balances of your revenue and expense accounts to the profit & loss account and subsequently producing a balance sheet at your year end is generally referred to as **closing the books**.

Starting them off again for the new year is known as **opening the books**. However, we shall **not** be using the **same** set of books. Instead, we will open a completely **new** set. This will allow us to store the original books (and paperwork) safely away.

Before we open the new set of books we need to carry out one more procedure: transfer the **profit & loss** and **drawings** accounts into another account (this is because the balances from the old books will be transferred to the new books and we do not want to carry forward the balances of last year's profit & loss and drawings accounts since they apply to that year only).

What we do with the profit (or loss) depends on the type of business we are running: sole-proprietors and partnerships (ie. the self-employed) are covered in this chapter and limited companies in part 2 - chapter 15.

The profit & loss and drawings accounts are held in the equity section of the balance sheet. They represent the owner's **capital** in the business (ie. how much the owner would get out of the business if everything was paid up and the business closed down). We shall therefore call the new account 'Capital' and **transfer** the profit & loss and drawings accounts into it.

This is exactly the same process we used to transfer the revenue and expense accounts to the profit & loss account: that is, zero the profit & loss and drawings accounts with a debit or credit and then credit or debit the capital account. Figure 7.1 shows the journal entries, figures 7.2, 7.3 and 7.4 show the profit & loss, drawings and capital accounts and figure 7.5 shows the final balance sheet.

Journal				
Date	Account	Reference	Debit	Credit
27th June	Cash	J1		10.00
27th June	Petrol	J1	10.00	
29th June	Sales	J2		50.00
29th June	Cash	J2	50.00	
30th June	Cash	(to Drawings)		30.00
30th June	Drawings	(from Cash)	30.00	
30th June	Petrol	(to P&L)		10.00
30th June	Profit & Loss	(from Petrol)	10.00	
30th June	Sales	(to P&L)	50.00	
30th June	Profit & Loss	(from Sales)		50.00
30th June	Profit & Loss	(to Capital)	40.00	
30th June	Capital	(from P&L)		40.00
30th June	Drawings	(to Capital)		30.00
30th June	Capital	(from Drawings)	30.00	

figure 7.1

Nominal Ledger	Profit & Loss Account		
Date	Reference	Debit	Credit
30th June	Sales		50.00
30th June	Petrol	10.00	
Totals		10.00	50.00
30th June	Balance b/d		40.00
30th June	(to Capital)	40.00	
Totals		40.00	40.00
30th June	Closed		

figure 7.2

Nominal Ledger	Drawings		
Date	Reference	Debit	Credit
30th June	Cash	30.00	
Totals		30.00	
30th June	Balance b/d	30.00	
30th June	(to Capital)		30.00
Totals		30.00	30.00
30th June	Closed		

figure 7.3

Nominal Ledger	Capital		
Date	Reference	Debit	Credit
30th June	Profit & Loss		40.00
30th June	Drawings	30.00	
Totals		30.00	40.00
30th June	Balance b/d		10.00

figure 7.4

Balance Sheet as at 30th June				
Assets	(Debit balances)	Liabilities		(Credit balances)
Cash Account	10.00			
		Equity		
		Capital		10.00
Balance	10.00			10.00

figure 7.5

The capital account represents all the money **left** in the business from profits since the business began. (If you make a £50 profit in the second year this will be added to the capital account so it will show a balance of £60 at the start of the third year - assuming you don't pay yourself any more drawings).

The first year's set of books are now complete and can be stored away.

To open the new year's set of books all we need is a copy of the final balance sheet (*figure 7.5*) so we can see which accounts still have a balance and must therefore be carried forward.

Like all transactions these balances are entered in the journal (a new one because we are starting a new year) where they are now referred to as **opening balances**.

The entries themselves are direct copies from the balance sheet. The cash account has a debit balance and the capital account has a credit balance so that is how they are entered (*figure 7.6*).

Journal				
Date	Account	Reference	Debit	Credit
1st July	Cash	(Opening balance)	10.00	
1st July	Capital	(Opening balance)		10.00

figure 7.6

If we wanted we could post these entries to the new ledger and produce an interim trial balance and balance sheet report but there is little point in this example because it is plain that the new set of books will balance (£10 debit = £10 credit).

Partnerships

The only difference between a sole-proprietor and a partnership is that there will be a drawings and capital account for each partner.

We will continue with the same example but imagine that the business was run by 2 people in partnership who share the profits equally. The first year's profit & loss shows a profit of £40, so we need two transfers from the profit & loss account for £20 each to two capital accounts. Figure 7.7 shows the resulting profit & loss account after these transfers have been entered in the journal and posted to the ledger.

Nominal Ledger	Profit & Loss Account		
Date	Reference	Debit	Credit
30th June	Sales		50.00
30th June	Petrol	10.00	
Totals		10.00	50.00
30th June	Balance b/d		40.00
30th June	(to Capital partner 1)	20.00	
30th June	(to Capital partner 2)	20.00	
Totals		40.00	40.00
30th June	Closed		

figure 7.7

Assuming that neither partner withdrew any drawings the resulting balance sheet would look like this (*figure 7.8*):

Balance Sheet as at 30th June			
Assets	(Debit balances)	Liabilities	(Credit balances)
Cash Account	40.00		
		Equity	
		Capital (partner 1)	20.00
		Capital (partner 2)	20.00
Balance	40.00		40.00

figure 7.8

8 • Notes concerning Part 1

The examples given relate to a business which started from scratch when the first transaction was made. It may well be that the business was already a going concern, in which case the first entries made in the journal would be the opening balances taken from the previous balance sheet (see page 38), or that the owner of the business started it by injecting some money into the business (this would be entered as a straightforward journal entry **from** the capital account **to** the bank account).

Most accounting periods for tax purposes cover one year. The year would normally be included in the date columns of the journal and ledger.

When the 'year end' is referred to we mean the date on which the books are closed (ie. the end of your accounting year). An accounting year can end on any date. However, many businesses use the traditional date of April the 5th.

Page 22 refers to items which should not be included directly in the profit & loss account. If your business involves the buying of goods for re-sale then a **trading account** will be needed before compiling the profit & loss account. If the business manufactures goods then a **manufacturing account** will be required as well (these are covered in chapters 13 & 14). Other items which are not included directly are major purchases bought for the business rather than for re-sale (eg. the office fax machine). These items are called 'fixed assets' and are covered in chapter 16.

9 • Notes for students

ISLE COLLEGE
RESOURCES CENTRE

Debits and Credits

Until chapter 5 we have been recording the credit entry of each journal transaction first, followed by the debit entry (this makes the logic easier to see); traditionally however, the debit entry is made first (*figure 8.1*).

Journal				
Date	Account	Reference	Debit	Credit
27th June	Petrol	J1	10.00	
27th June	Cash	J1		10.00
29th June	Cash	J2	50.00	
29th June	Sales	J2		50.00

figure 8.1

Balancing an account

Figure 3.4 shows the simplest way to balance a ledger account. However, many other text books not only show a different layout but also an alternative way to derive the balance (*figure 8.2*).

Ledger Cash Account					
Date	Reference	Debit	Date	Reference	Credit
29th June	J2	50.00	27th June	J1	10.00
			30th June	Balance c/d	40.00
Totals		50.00			50.00
30th June	Balance b/d	40.00			

figure 8.2

The results are just the same but the alternative way requires a separate working sheet because you cannot fill in the 'totals' line until you have added up both sides, subtracted one from the other and decided which side to put the balancing figure in. You must also remember to put the 'balance b/d' entry on the opposite side of the 'balance c/d' entry ('c/d'=carried down).

T Accounts

The layout of the account shown in figure 8.2 is called a **T** account (everything to do with a debit is shown on the left of the '**T**' and everything to do with credits on the right - this should be fairly obvious from the illustration).

The Cash Book

Another point of difference is the cash account. Rather than being part of the nominal ledger it can be kept in a separate journal (called the **cash book**). It includes the transactions of both **cash** and **bank** accounts.

It is usually laid out as shown in figure 8.2 but with extra columns to separate the cash from the bank.

Only one side of each transaction is posted to the nominal ledger since the final balances of the cash and bank columns represent the other side of the transactions and are looked at together with the nominal ledger accounts when compiling the trial balance and balance sheet.

An example will make it more obvious: receiving £20 from sales paid to the bank, transferring £15 from the bank to cash and buying £10 worth of petrol from cash (*figure 8.3*).

Cash Book			Debit Side					Credit Side	
Date	Account	Ref	Bank	Cash	Date	Account	Ref	Bank	Cash
26th June	Sales	CB1	20.00						
27th June		c		15.00	27th June		c	15.00	
					28th June	Petrol	CB2		10.00
					30th June		c/d	5.00	5.00
Totals			20.00	15.00				20.00	15.00
Balances b/d			5.00	5.00					

figure 8.3

The final balance of both the bank and cash accounts is £5. The reference 'c' for the £15 transfer represents the word **contra** which simply means a transfer of money from one account to another (ie. it is not 'new' money flowing into or out of the business).

Entry 'CB1' will be posted to the **credit** of the sales account (because it is shown as a **debit** in the bank column of the cash book) and for the same reason entry 'CB2' will be posted as a debit to the petrol account. Figure 8.4 shows the trial balance.

Trial Balance as at 30th June		
Account	Debit	Credit
Bank (from cash book)	5.00	
Cash (from cash book)	5.00	
Petrol (from nominal ledger)	10.00	
Sales (from nominal ledger)		20.00
Totals	20.00	20.00

figure 8.4

Typically discount columns would also be included in this system so that if you sent an invoice to a customer with a 10% discount if paid immediately (and they did) the discounted total could be included within the cash book to save further work. This method is known as the **three column cash book** (one for discounts, one for the bank and one for cash).

As you can see, this is a much harder method to implement (and remember) but it is the sort of thing you will come across if you are studying accounting as a student.

The idea of keeping a separate journal for bank and cash transactions is to enable more than one person to write up the accounts of a business but the cash book doesn't have to be of the 'three column' variety. Instead separate 'petty cash' and 'bank books' could be used with the same layout as our original journal.

These can be posted in their entirety to the nominal ledger or part-posted and used as accounts in their own right like the three column cash book.

The Journal Proper

When the journal is split into different sections (eg. petty cash book, bank book and journal) the journal itself is called the **Journal Proper**. In this case the journal proper is only used for transactions which cannot be entered in the other journals (eg. opening and closing balances and transfers between accounts).

The Nominal Ledger

We have kept all the accounts in the nominal ledger and used a single journal for all the transactions because it demonstrates the logic of double-entry book-keeping whichever way a set of accounts is prepared.

Traditionally the nominal ledger is only used for **nominal** accounts (ie. those accounts which do not relate directly to a person, business or specific asset or item of stock).

Real accounts (eg. a bank account) are held in their entirety in the cash book which is then looked upon as a part of the nominal ledger.

Personal accounts (eg. customers & suppliers) are held in their respective sales and purchase ledgers (see chapter 12).

Other accounts for items of stock, individual assets and investments are held in **inventories** (see chapter 18).

It would have been preferable in our examples to refer to the nominal ledger as the 'general' ledger (which is a more logical name). However, the term has become rather greyed and most accountants and computer software (in the UK) use the term 'nominal ledger' loosely (eg. they have no problem with 'real' accounts contained within it).

The Profit & Loss Account

In practice, most accountants prepare the profit & loss account as a report (like the balance sheet) rather than transferring all the revenue and expense account balances within the journal. The closing balances are calculated outside the double-entry framework and then entered as opening balances in the new set of books.

The Balance Sheet

Chapter 6 shows you how to compile a balance sheet. It has been laid out **horizontally** (assets on the left, liabilities on the right) because it makes it easy to compile (debit balances on the left, credit balances on the right).

In practice (especially for limited companies), it is laid out in a **vertical** format. This is shown and explained in chapter 16, page 122.

Despite popular belief, there are no rules regarding horizontal balance sheets. Some text books (and academics) insist that liabilities are shown on the left and assets on the right. Others argue for the opposite way.

The Institute of Chartered Accountants in England and Wales point out that as far as horizontal balance sheets are concerned, the 1985 finance act merely states that assets must be on one side and liabilities on the other, and that logically assets would appear on the left.

Companies House (a government department which stores the balance sheets of limited companies) has no preference either. However, they do prefer the **vertical** format since it is easier to photograph for archiving purposes (horizontal balance sheets tend to be printed in a landscape format - ie. sideways).

Note: All these terms (if they are new to you) are explained in detail in part 2 and are covered in the glossary at the end of this book.

10 • Reminders and Hints

A journal is just a book consisting of columns to record the day to day transactions of the business. It is used for **every** entry whether it is a new transaction (like buying some petrol) or one that involves transferring a balance from one account to another.

Each transaction involves a debit entry and a credit entry both of which will reference a different account. For **new transactions** the **credit** side refers to the account the money is coming **from**. The **debit** side refers to the account the money is going **to** (a transaction can also consist of **more** than two entries provided the debits equal the credits - more of which in part 2).

The **from/to** guide cannot (easily) be applied to **transfer** entries (like zeroing the sales account and transferring the balance to the profit & loss account), but it does not matter since one side of the transaction will credit a debit balance (or vice-versa) and the other side will be obvious (**the credits must equal the debits**).

Posting entries means making **exact** copies of each journal entry into a ledger account - if the journal entry was a debit then it will also be a debit in the ledger.

Balancing a ledger account means totalling its credit and debit columns, subtracting one from the other, then carrying forward the difference to the next line. The rule is: **put the balance in the debit column if the debits are greater than the credits** (and vice-versa).

A **journal** contains all your transactions in **date order**. A **ledger** is simply a copy of those transactions but in **account order**.

Part 2

VAT, creditors & debtors, stock, limited companies, assets & depreciation, adjustments, inventories, computers and more...

Introduction to part 2

There are three basic types of commercial business: those which sell a **service** (eg. an accountant or consultant), those which buy and **sell goods** (eg. a retailer or mail-order business), and those which **manufacture goods**.

There are also three basic ways in which a business can be owned: a **sole-proprietor** (the business is owned by one person who is self-employed), a **partnership** (the business is owned by more than one person, all of whom are self-employed), and a **limited company** (owned by its shareholders).

The basic principles of double-entry encompass them all, the main difference being that larger businesses will require more accounts and these will usually be split across a number of ledgers with the entries themselves split across more than one journal.

Two other aspects are common to most businesses: accounting for VAT, and goods or services bought and sold on credit.

Part 2 has therefore been arranged to cover the most common aspects first. All the chapters are worth looking at as many contain new concepts of relevance to most businesses.

11 • Accounting for VAT

Value Added Tax, or VAT as it is usually called is a sales tax which increases the price of goods.

At the time of writing the VAT standard rate is 17.5%. This applies to most goods except domestic fuel (eg. electricity, gas and oil) which is 5%. VAT is added to the net price so an item that sells at £10 will be priced £11.75 when standard rate VAT is added.

A few items are exempt from VAT and some are zero rated. Please consult the VAT guide '*VAT notice 700*' to see what is and is not subject to VAT.

Rather than going into great detail about VAT itself, we will stick to showing how to account for it within a double-entry system.

If you are not registered with UK Customs & Excise for VAT you will still need to be aware of the following points:

• You will need to check your sales figures periodically in order to assess whether you will be required by law to register. The current threshold (from April 1998) is £50,000. Check with Customs & Excise for the rules governing thresholds. (See 'Useful Contacts' - page 161).

• Always obtain a VAT receipt for any goods or equipment you buy which is of a capital nature (see **assets** - chapter 16) and make sure you keep the receipts safely. Should you become registered in the future you will be able to reclaim the VAT on these items (always check with Customs & Excise first as there are exceptions and the rules do change from time to time).

Until you reach the threshold and become registered you will not need to account for VAT.

The first transaction will be purchasing some petrol for £11.75 by cheque on the 15th April (the amount includes VAT at 17.5%).

Journal				
Date	Account	Reference	Debit	Credit
15th April	Bank	J1		11.75
15th April	Petrol	J1	11.75	
15th April	Petrol	J1		1.75
15th April	VAT	J1	1.75	

figure 11.1

Figure 11.1 is one way of entering the journal entries for the transaction; although it only involves 3 accounts (the **bank** to pay for it, the **petrol** account to record the expense, and a **VAT** account to record the VAT), we have needed to use four entries to account for it (the full value from **bank to petrol**, then the VAT portion from **petrol to the VAT** account).

A quick look at the two petrol entries will show a net balance of £10 to petrol. This is the **real** expense because when you pay VAT on a business purchase you will later reclaim it (**provided you are VAT registered**).

Figure 11.2 shows an alternative way of entering this transaction.

Journal				
Date	Account	Reference	Debit	Credit
15th April	Bank	J1		11.75
15th April	Petrol	J1	10.00	
15th April	VAT	J1	1.75	

figure 11.2

As you can see, we have reduced the number of entries by one and the debits still equal the credits so everything is in order.

If we now make a sale for £117.50 including VAT at 17.5% (£100+£17.50 VAT), post the journal entries to the ledger accounts, produce a profit & loss account and balance sheet you will see how VAT flows through the business (*figures 11.3 - 11.9*).

Journal				
Date	Account	Reference	Debit	Credit
15th April	Bank	J1		11.75
15th April	Petrol	J1	10.00	
15th April	VAT	J1	1.75	
20th April	Sales	J2		100.00
20th April	Bank	J2	117.50	
20th April	VAT	J2		17.50
1st May	Petrol	(to Profit & Loss)		10.00
1st May	Profit & Loss	(from Petrol)	10.00	
1st May	Sales	(to Profit & Loss)	100.00	
1st May	Profit & Loss	(from Sales)		100.00

figure 11.3

Nominal Ledger	Bank Account		
Date	Reference	Debit	Credit
15th April	J1		11.75
20th April	J2	117.50	
Totals		117.50	11.75
1st May	Balance b/d	105.75	

figure 11.4

Nominal Ledger	Petrol Account		
Date	Reference	Debit	Credit
15th April	J1	10.00	
1st May	(to Profit & Loss)		10.00
Totals	Closed		

figure 11.5

Nominal Ledger	Sales Account		
Date	Reference	Debit	Credit
20th April	J2		100.00
1st May	(to Profit & Loss)	100.00	
Totals	Closed		

figure 11.6

Nominal Ledger	VAT Account		
Date	Reference	Debit	Credit
15th April	J1	1.75	
20th April	J2		17.50
Totals		1.75	17.50
1st May	Balance b/d		15.75

figure 11.7

Nominal Ledger	Profit & Loss Account		
Date	Reference	Debit	Credit
1st May	Sales		100.00
1st May	Petrol	10.00	
Totals		10.00	100.00
1st May	Balance b/d		90.00

figure 11.8

Balance Sheet as at 1st May			
Assets	(Debit balances)	Liabilities	(Credit balances)
Bank Account	105.75	VAT owed	15.75
		Equity	
		Profit & Loss	90.00
Balance	105.75		105.75

figure 11.9

Looking at the balance sheet (*figure 11.9*) you can see that the VAT account has been put under liabilities. This is because the balance is a **credit** balance: more VAT has been received **from** sales than has been paid **to** expenses. We therefore owe Customs & Excise the balance.

When we get to the end of a VAT period we must pay Customs & Excise the balance so a journal entry is made to reflect this (*figure 11.10*).

Journal				
Date	Account	Reference	Debit	Credit
15th April	Bank	J1		11.75
15th April	Petrol	J1	10.00	
15th April	VAT	J1	1.75	
20th April	Sales	J2		100.00
20th April	Bank	J2	117.50	
20th April	VAT	J2		17.50
1st May	Petrol	(to Profit & Loss)		10.00
1st May	Profit & Loss	(from Petrol)	10.00	
1st May	Sales	(to Profit & Loss)	100.00	
1st May	Profit & Loss	(from Sales)		100.00
30th June	Bank	J3		15.75
30th June	VAT	J3	15.75	

figure 11.10

We paid the VAT by cheque hence the money came
from the bank (the **credit** side). It went **to** Customs &
Excise so the VAT account is debited.

If we then post these entries to the ledger, the VAT
account will show a zero balance (*figure 11.11*), and the
bank account will be reduced to £90 (*figure 11.12*). Figure
11.13 shows the final balance sheet.

Nominal Ledger	VAT Account		
Date	Reference	Debit	Credit
15th April	J1	1.75	
20th April	J2		17.50
Totals		1.75	17.50
1st May	Balance b/d		15.75
30th June	J3	15.75	
Totals		15.75	15.75
30th June	Balance b/d (zero)	0	0

figure 11.11

Nominal Ledger	Bank Account			
Date	Reference		Debit	Credit
15th April	J1			11.75
20th April	J2		117.50	
Totals			117.50	11.75
1st May	Balance b/d		105.75	
30th June	J3			15.75
Totals			105.75	15.75
30th June	Balance b/d		90.00	

figure 11.12

Balance Sheet as at 30th June			
Assets	(Debit balances)	Liabilities	(Credit balances)
Bank Account	90.00	VAT owed	
		Equity	
		Profit & Loss	90.00
Balance	90.00		90.00

figure 11.13

Whilst a look at the VAT account will tell you what you owe Customs & Excise (or what they owe you) at the end of a VAT period, it will not be easy to determine what to enter in the other boxes of a standard UK VAT Return form.

For example, some of your expenses may not be 'within the scope of VAT'. Items such as wages come under this category. This means that to find out the net value of all the expenses in a VAT period (the net value means the value before VAT has been added), we need to code each entry in some way. You can either include this code in the reference column or add a new column to the journal.

We shall do the latter to make it obvious (*figure 11.14*).

Journal					
Date	Account	Reference	Debit	Credit	VAT Code
15th April	Bank	J1		11.75	
15th April	Petrol	J1	10.00		I
15th April	VAT	J1	1.75		
20th April	Sales	J2		100.00	O
20th April	Bank	J2	117.50		
20th April	VAT	J2		17.50	

figure 11.14

This extra information is irrelevant to your accounts but will make life simpler when filling in your VAT return.

In this example we have chosen the character 'I' to represent Input VAT items (ie. purchases at the standard rate) and 'O' for Output VAT (ie. sales at the standard rate). We could just as easily use the codes 'P' and 'S' instead.

The current UK VAT return form requires you to specify the VAT exclusive totals of your sales and purchases. By coding each entry you can see at a glance which need to be added up in order to complete the form.

If you import or export goods to the EC (European Community) then these too will need identifying. You will also need to know the VAT registration number of an EC company if you export to them, so this could be added to the code or entered in a separate column (these are then detailed separately on another VAT form called an 'EC Sales List').

Furthermore, if your exports to an EC member country exceed the VAT registration threshold then you will need to register with that country for VAT.

In short, all that matters is that VAT relevant entries are coded in some way in the journal to ensure that you can produce the necessary reports when required.

VAT Scale Charge

If a car is used partly for business and you are claiming back the VAT on your petrol expenses then some of the reclaimed VAT will need to be paid back. There are a number of ways of doing this but the most common method is to repay a fixed amount for every VAT period.

This is known as the VAT Road Fuel Scale Charge and depends on the type of fuel (petrol or diesel), the size of engine in the vehicle and the length of your VAT period.

Currently (from 6th April 1998) for a 1600cc petrol engine car the scale charge is £39.91 every 3 months (assuming you are on a 3 month VAT period). We will use this as an example of how to enter such a transaction.

Instead of making an entry for every petrol receipt for the 3 months we will add them all together to keep the entries as simple as possible. Suppose the total petrol bought was £1175 including VAT (£1000 + £175 VAT). We credit the cash account £1175, debit the petrol account £1000, and debit the VAT account £175. We then enter the scale charge with a credit from the VAT account for £39.91 and a debit to the drawings account for the same amount (*figure 11.15*).

Journal					
Date	Account	Reference	Debit	Credit	VAT Code
15th April	Cash	J1		1175.00	
15th April	Petrol	J1	1000.00		I
15th April	VAT	J1	175.00		
20th April	VAT	Scale charge		39.91	
20th April	Drawings	Scale charge	39.91		

figure 11.15

Figure 11.16 shows the effect on the VAT account.

Nominal Ledger	VAT Account		
Date	Reference	Debit	Credit
15th April	J1	175.00	
20th April	Scale charge		39.91
Totals		175.00	39.91
1st May	Balance b/d	135.09	

figure 11.16

The VAT account is simple enough: we want to reclaim £175 VAT but we need to repay £39.91 due to the scale charge (for non-business use). The result is that we can only reclaim £135.09 for the period.

We have debited the drawings account with the scale charge (rather than petrol) because VAT is not an expense of the business. The net petrol expense therefore remains at £1000.

There is one more point to note: because the car is being used for both private and business use, a proportion of the petrol expense must be transferred from petrol to the drawings account. If we suppose the ratio was 75% business and 25% private then we would need to credit the petrol account £250 (25%) and debit the drawings account the same amount (figure 11.17).

Journal					
Date	Account	Reference	Debit	Credit	VAT Code
24th April	Petrol	(private use)		250.00	
24th April	Drawings	(private petrol)	250.00		

figure 11.17

The petrol account now has a balance of £750 which reflects the true amount we have spent on petrol for the business.

12 • Debtors and Creditors

Debtors

If you issue an invoice to a customer (you let them have some goods or a service on credit - ie. to be paid for later) then you will need to keep track of that **customer's account** as well as your general sales account.

Like any account this could be opened in the nominal ledger, but in order to keep the nominal ledger to a reasonable size (after all you may have 1000 customers or more) it is best to open a separate (or subsidiary) ledger.

A subsidiary ledger is just another book, but the accounts it holds relate only to a certain aspect of the business. Each subsidiary ledger is given a name to reflect what it holds; where customer accounts are concerned it is called the **Sales Ledger**.

The sales ledger consists of a page devoted to each customer. Typically the page will contain personal details like the customer's name and address which is then followed with the usual columns: date, reference, debit and credit.

Because we have used a subsidiary ledger to hold the customer accounts, it is also usual to open a **separate journal** to record these transactions (like everything else in double-entry all transactions are first entered in a journal).

The journal used for the sales ledger is usually called the **sales book**.

The very first thing you would do is send an invoice to the customer. The total of this invoice is then entered into the sales book, and subsequently posted to the relevant ledger accounts.

Suppose we send an invoice to J Smith for £117.50 including VAT at 17.5% and enter this into the sales book (*figure 12.1*).

Sales Book					
Date	**Account**	**Reference**	**Debit**	**Credit**	**VAT Code**
20th April	Sales	SB1		100.00	O
20th April	J Smith	SB1	117.50		
20th April	VAT	SB1		17.50	

figure 12.1

There are four important things to note:

1: The **sales book** will affect accounts in the **nominal ledger** (sales and VAT) as well as the **sales ledger** (J Smith).

2: The sales account has been **credited** because **all** sales whether they are paid immediately or on credit come **from** sales. If you are registered for VAT the sales account is credited with the net sales amount (ie. exclusive of VAT) because VAT is not part of the business's taxable revenue (see the previous chapter on accounting for VAT).

3: We have used a new reference ('**SB**1') to reflect that these entries have been entered in a different journal: the **S**ales **B**ook. We would also write this reference on our copy of the original invoice (to make it easy to trace should the need arise).

4: We have used multiple entries for a single transaction (two credits and a debit). This is fine since the two credits equal the debit.

Having entered an invoice, we will look at the other side of the sales ledger - what happens when a customer pays an invoice. This will require a further separate journal called the 'Receivables Book'.

The Receivables Book is used to record **payments received** from customers. Like the Sales Book, it will also affect accounts in the nominal ledger as well as the sales ledger.

Suppose J Smith pays £50 towards his outstanding invoice (*figure 12.2*).

Receivables Book				
Date	Account	Reference	Debit	Credit
22nd April	J Smith	SB1 (part payment)		50.00
22nd April	Bank	SB1 (part payment)	50.00	

figure 12.2

The **from** and **to** sides are easy to see - the money has come **from** J Smith (a **credit**) and gone **to** the bank (a **debit**). We have used the same reference as in the Sales Book because this payment relates to that invoice.

Figures 12.3 and 12.4 show the effect on the relevant ledger accounts when we post these entries to them.

Sales Ledger			
J Smith			
Date	Reference	Debit	Credit
20th April	SB1	117.50	
22nd April	SB1 (part payment)		50.00
Totals		**117.50**	**50.00**
22nd April	Balance b/d	**67.50**	

figure 12.3

(Note: from now onwards, the format of the ledger illustrations will change slightly: rather than being shown individually, each account will be included as a section within each ledger - see figure 12.4 overleaf).

Nominal Ledger			
Bank Account			
Date	**Reference**	**Debit**	**Credit**
22nd April	SB1 (part payment)	50.00	
Sales Account			
Date	**Reference**	**Debit**	**Credit**
20th April	SB1		100.00
VAT Account			
Date	**Reference**	**Debit**	**Credit**
20th April	SB1		17.50

figure 12.4

If we produce a normal trial balance using just the
nominal ledger, we will have a problem. The debits do
not equal the credits because we haven't included J
Smith's account from the sales ledger (*figure 12.5*).

Trial Balance as at 20th April		
Account	**Debit**	**Credit**
Bank	50.00	
Sales		100.00
VAT		17.50
Totals	**50.00**	**117.50**

figure 12.5

Since the trial balance is only a report, we could simply
include J Smith's balance within it (*figure 12.6*).

Trial Balance as at 20th April		
Account	**Debit**	**Credit**
Bank	50.00	
Sales		100.00
VAT		17.50
J Smith (Sales Ledger)	67.50	
Totals	**117.50**	**117.50**

figure 12.6

However, if you have many customers this would
become unwieldy.

As far as the balance sheet is concerned, we are only interested in the overall balance of the sales ledger (not the individual balances). We could add up all the balances manually and include that in the trial balance direct from the sales ledger, but this would require a good deal of extra work (and we would need to do it from scratch every time we wanted to see how much was owed).

The answer is to open two new accounts. One in the **Sales Ledger**, and the other in the **Nominal Ledger**. From time to time these two accounts (called **control accounts**) will be updated. The Nominal Ledger will then hold the overall Sales Ledger balance and our trial balance will be complete.

The **Sales Ledger** account will simply be called **Control Account** (because there will only ever be one control account in the sales ledger no matter how many customer accounts there are).

The **Nominal Ledger** account will be called **Debtors control** since it will represent the money your customers owe you (ie. the debtors of the business).

In order to update the control accounts we need to get the totals from the **sales** and **receivables** books. This would normally be done on a monthly basis to keep the entries to a minimum.

All we do is draw a line under the last journal posted in each book and add up the debit and credit columns (*figures 12.7 & 12.8*).

Sales Book

Date	Account	Reference	Debit	Credit	VAT Code
20th April	Sales	SB1		100.00	O
20th April	J Smith	SB1	117.50		
20th April	VAT	SB1		17.50	
Totals for April			117.50	**117.50**	

figure 12.7

Receivables Book

Date	Account	Reference	Debit	Credit
22nd April	J Smith	SB1		50.00
22nd April	Bank	SB1	50.00	
Totals for April			**50.00**	50.00

figure 12.8

We need to know how much has come **from** sales on credit, therefore we are only interested in the **Sales Book credit** column.

We also need to see how much of this has been paid, so we only need look at the **Receivables Book debit** column.

Having established this we can enter the journal entries for the control accounts. These entries are made in the general journal (*figure 12.9*).

Journal

Date	Account	Reference	Debit	Credit
22nd April	Sales Ledger Control	April Invoices		117.50
22nd April	Debtors control	(Sales Ledger)	117.50	
22nd April	Sales Ledger Control	April Receipts	50.00	
22nd April	Debtors control	(Sales Ledger)		50.00

figure 12.9

The above can be reduced to three entries as shown in figure 12.10 if you like. The only thing that matters is that the debits equal the credits.

Journal				
Date	Account	Reference	Debit	Credit
22nd April	Sales Ledger Control	April Invoices		117.50
22nd April	Sales Ledger Control	April Receipts	50.00	
22nd April	Debtors control	(Sales Ledger)	67.50	

figure 12.10

If we post these entries and produce a trial balance we can see that everything balances (*figures 12.11 to 12.13*).

Sales Ledger			
J Smith			
Date	Reference	Debit	Credit
20th April	SB1	117.50	
22nd April	SB1 (part payment)		50.00
Totals		117.50	50.00
22nd April	Balance b/d	67.50	
Control Account			
Date	Reference	Debit	Credit
22nd April	April Invoices		117.50
22nd April	April Receipts	50.00	
Totals		50.00	117.50
22nd April	Balance b/d		67.50

figure 12.11

Nominal Ledger			
Bank			
Date	Reference	Debit	Credit
22nd April	SB1 (part payment)	50.00	
Sales			
Date	Reference	Debit	Credit
20th April	SB1		100.00
VAT			
Date	Reference	Debit	Credit
20th April	SB1		17.50
Debtors control			
Date	Reference	Debit	Credit
22nd April	(from Sales Ledger)	67.50	

figure 12.12

Trial Balance as at 22nd April		
Account	Debit	Credit
Bank	50.00	
Sales		100.00
VAT		17.50
Debtors control	67.50	
Totals	**117.50**	**117.50**

figure 12.13

As an exercise, if we prepared a trial balance for just the sales ledger we would also see that this balances (*figure 12.14*).

Sales ledger trial balance as at 22nd April		
Account	Debit	Credit
J Smith	67.50	
Control		67.50
Totals	**67.50**	**67.50**

figure 12.14

This method involves the double-entry principle from beginning to end and produces what is known as **self-balancing** ledgers - ie. we can produce a trial balance for any of the ledgers and each will balance.

The idea of control accounts is not particularly easy to grasp, so a summary will help:

Each subsidiary ledger (the **Sales Ledger** in this example) will include two extra journals: one to record invoices issued on credit (the **Sales Book**), and the other to record the payment of those invoices (the **Receivables Book**).

Two control accounts (sometimes referred to as **Total accounts**) will also be associated with it. One in the **subsidiary ledger**, and the other in the **Nominal Ledger**.

From time to time (usually every month), the subsidiary
ledger journal entries for that period are added up, and
posted from one control account to the other. Whenever
this is done, you are only adding up the new entries for
the period. Although you will be making a few extra
entries each month to update the control accounts, you
will be reducing the possibility of mistakes.

Creditors

The **creditor** side of the business (where we want to keep
track of our **suppliers** and what we owe them) makes use
of another subsidiary ledger called the **Purchase Ledger**.

Just like the sales ledger the entries are first written into
journals called the **Purchases book** and the **Payments
book**.

The purchases book is used to record incoming bills **from**
our suppliers and the payments book is used to record
the payments of these bills **to** our suppliers.

The principle is identical, it is only the labels which are
different (ie. **Creditors** instead of **Debtors** for the control
account in the nominal ledger).

By way of illustrating the purchase ledger and associated
control accounts we shall open accounts for four
suppliers and make a number of entries in the journals.

Purchases Book

Date	Account	Reference	Debit	Credit	VAT Code
1st April	**A Jones**	PB1		23.75	
1st April	Petrol	PB1	20.00		I
1st April	VAT	PB1	3.75		
15th April	**D Honey**	PB2		117.50	
15th April	Rent	PB2	100.00		I
15th April	VAT	PB2	17.50		
20th April	**Post Office**	PB3		30.00	
20th April	Postage	PB3	30.00		E
22nd April	**Vik King**	PB4		250.00	
22nd April	Printing	PB4	180.00		
22nd April	Cardboard	PB4	10.00		
22nd April	Packing	PB4	60.00		
Totals for April			**421.25**	421.25	

figure 12.15

We have entered four transactions and used a new reference to show that these entries relate to the **P**urchases **B**ook. We would also write this reference on each of the bills sent to us.

Transactions 'PB1' and 'PB2' involve input VAT so we have entered the letter 'I' for VAT return purposes (see chapter 11).

'PB3' is a bill for postage from the Post Office (however unlikely this may be!) hence there is no VAT (postage stamps are exempt hence the VAT code E).

'PB4' is another example of a multiple entry - we ordered £250 worth of goods from Vik King, but we want to break down the purchase into different sections so we can separate our printing costs from packing etc.

We will now enter our payments for April (*figure 12.16*). We have used the same reference as the original bill and for further clarity we have appended a cheque number to it (where one has been used).

Payables Book

Date	Account	Reference	Debit	Credit
2nd April	Bank	PB1/00001		10.00
2nd April	A Jones	PB1/00001	10.00	
20th April	Cash	PB3		30.00
20th April	Post Office	PB3 (cash)	30.00	
Totals for April			40.00	**40.00**

figure 12.16

'PB1/00001' is a part payment to A Jones (for the petrol). The money has come **from** the bank therefore we **credit** the bank. It has gone **to** A Jones so we **debit** the Jones account.

'PB3' is a cash payment made on the same day we bought the stamps from the Post Office (in reality there was no credit involved!, but this still serves a purpose - we can enter non-credit items into the sales and purchase ledgers if we want to keep track of everything we sell or receive from individual customers and suppliers).

Having totalled our purchases and payments for April we can also enter the journals for the purchase and nominal ledger control accounts (*figure 12.17*).

Journal

Date	Account	Reference	Debit	Credit
22nd April	Purchase Ledger Control	April Bills	421.25	
22nd April	Creditors control	(Purchase Ledger)		421.25
22nd April	Purchase Ledger Control	April Payments		40.00
22nd April	Creditors control	(Purchase Ledger)	40.00	

figure 12.17

We can now post the whole lot to the ledgers and produce a trial balance (*figures 12.18 to 12.20*).

Purchase Ledger			
A Jones			
Date	**Reference**	**Debit**	**Credit**
1st April	PB1		23.75
2nd April	PB1/00001	10.00	
Totals		**10.00**	**23.75**
22nd April	Balance b/d		**13.75**
D Honey			
Date	**Reference**	**Debit**	**Credit**
15th April	PB2		117.50
Totals			**117.50**
22nd April	Balance b/d		**117.50**
Post Office			
Date	**Reference**	**Debit**	**Credit**
20th April	PB3		30.00
20th April	PB3 (cash)	30.00	
Totals		**30.00**	**30.00**
22nd April	Balance b/d (zero)		0.00
Vik King			
Date	**Reference**	**Debit**	**Credit**
22nd April	PB4		250.00
Totals			**250.00**
22nd April	Balance b/d		**250.00**
Control Account			
Date	**Reference**	**Debit**	**Credit**
22nd April	April Bills	421.25	
22nd April	April Payments		40.00
Totals		**421.25**	**40.00**
22nd April	Balance b/d	**381.25**	

figure 12.18

Nominal Ledger

Bank

Date	Reference	Debit	Credit
2nd April	PB1/00001		10.00

Cash

Date	Reference	Debit	Credit
20th April	PB3		30.00

Petrol

Date	Reference	Debit	Credit
1st April	PB1	20.00	

Rent

Date	Reference	Debit	Credit
15th April	PB2	100.0	

Postage

Date	Reference	Debit	Credit
20th April	PB3	30.00	

Printing

Date	Reference	Debit	Credit
22nd April	PB4	180.00	

Cardboard

Date	Reference	Debit	Credit
22nd April	PB4	10.00	

Packing

Date	Reference	Debit	Credit
22nd April	PB4	60.00	

VAT

Date	Reference	Debit	Credit
1st April	PB1	3.75	
15th April	PB2	17.50	
Totals		21.25	
22nd April	Balance b/d	21.25	

Creditors control

Date	Reference	Debit	Credit
22nd April	(from Purchase Ledger)		421.25
22nd April	(from Purchase Ledger)	40.00	
Totals		40.00	421.25
22nd April	Balance b/d		381.25

figure 12.19

Trial Balance as at 22nd April		
Account	Debit	Credit
Bank		10.00
Cash		30.00
Petrol	20.00	
Rent	100.00	
Postage	30.00	
Printing	180.00	
Cardboard	10.00	
Packing	60.00	
VAT	21.25	
Creditors control		381.25
Totals	**421.25**	**421.25**

figure 12.20

To finish this chapter we will add in the debtors section covered earlier and produce a profit & loss and balance sheet.

Only two of the above accounts will be affected: namely the bank and VAT accounts. The sales and debtors accounts will also join the list. We can work out the bank and VAT account balances by referring to figure 12.13: the bank accounts balance will be £40 debit (£50-£10) and the VAT balance will be £3.75 (£21.25-£17.50).

Figure 12.21 shows the final trial balance.

Trial Balance as at 22nd April		
Account	Debit	Credit
Bank	40.00	
Cash		30.00
Sales		100.00
Petrol	20.00	
Rent	100.00	
Postage	30.00	
Printing	180.00	
Cardboard	10.00	
Packing	60.00	
VAT	3.75	
Debtors control	67.50	
Creditors control		381.25
Totals	**511.25**	**511.25**

figure 12.21

Figure 12.22 shows the profit & loss account (we will assume the journal entries have been made correctly):

Nominal Ledger			
Profit & Loss Account			
Date	Reference	Debit	Credit
22nd April	Sales		100.00
22nd April	Petrol	20.00	
22nd April	Rent	100.00	
22nd April	Postage	30.00	
22nd April	Printing	180.00	
22nd April	Cardboard	10.00	
22nd April	Packing	60.00	
Totals:		400.00	100.00
22nd April	Balance b/d	300.00	

figure 12.22

Finally figure 12.23 shows the balance sheet:

Balance Sheet as at 22nd April			
Assets	(Debit balances)	Liabilities	(Credit balances)
Bank Account	40.00	Cash (overdrawn)	30.00
VAT to reclaim	3.75	Creditors	381.25
Debtors	67.50		
		Equity	
		Profit & Loss	(300.00)
Balance	111.25		111.25

figure 12.23

Control accounts can be set up for any subsidiary ledgers provided you use two separate journals to record the ins and outs of the ledger.

The main advantages of subsidiary ledgers and control accounts are:

1: More than one person can look after the books.
2: Each ledger can be balanced on its own.
3: Mistakes can be spotted earlier.
4: The trial balance and balance sheet are easier to compile.

13 • Stock and the Trading Account

The first part of this book showed the flow of transactions from the journal to the ledger, then the profit & loss account and finally the balance sheet. However, if your business involves buying goods for re-sale then another aspect comes into play - the **trading account**.

The trading account, like the profit & loss account, is an interim account usually made up when the business's books are about to be closed for the year.

Once the trading account has been compiled the balance is transferred to the profit & loss account. The trading account must therefore be created first.

The basic equation used for the trading account is:

SALES - COST OF SALES = GROSS PROFIT

Sales refers to the value of your sales for the current accounting year (as shown in your sales account in the nominal ledger).

COST OF SALES is the total of the following items:

opening stock + purchases + expenses - closing stock

Opening Stock: This is the value of your stock at the start of the accounting year (ie. the closing stock value bought forward from the previous year).

Purchases: This is the value of new stock bought for re-sale during the current year.

Expenses: This is a bit of a grey area as some expenses are incurred for running the administrative side of the business and others relate directly to the sales or trading side; for example, wages may be paid to shop staff as well as administrative staff - in theory the shop staff wages will be posted to the trading account whereas the administrative staff costs will be posted direct to the profit & loss account.

Splitting your expenses between the trading and profit & loss accounts will not affect the **net** profit or loss (which is shown in the profit & loss account) but it will give you a clearer picture of the trading side of the business.

Closing Stock: This is the value of all the stock you have left at the end of the accounting year. Your stock can be valued in many ways (see chapter 19, page 150). However, the most common method is to look at the original cost and current market value, then choose the lowest. This valuation **will** affect the net profit or loss for the current year: a higher valuation will result in an increased profit (and vice-versa).

The opening and closing stock values must be included because some of the sales may be from stock bought in previous years and some of the stock may be unsold at the end of the current year. (See page 87).

Your **gross profit** therefore reflects the profit made from buying and selling goods and the direct expenses incurred to do this.

To illustrate the trading account we shall look at a business which started from scratch and then follow it through its first and second years. A minimum number of transactions will be made so the concept can be clearly seen.

Year 1 - Starting the business

Only one transaction is needed; paying £1000 from the bank account to purchase some goods for re-sale (*figure 13.1*). Like the revenue and expense accounts, the purchases account will be zeroed each year - in other words it will only be used to record the **current** year's purchases of stock.

Journal - Year 1				
Date	Account	Reference	Debit	Credit
27th June	Bank	J1		1000.00
27th June	Purchases	J1	1000.00	

figure 13.1

Figure 13.2 shows the nominal ledger after these entries have been posted.

Nominal Ledger - Year 1			
Bank			
Date	Reference	Debit	Credit
27th June	J1		1000.00
Purchases			
Date	Reference	Debit	Credit
27th June	J1	1000.00	

figure 13.2

Nothing else happened in the business during its first year so we are ready to create the trading account.

As far as year 1 is concerned two transfer transactions are needed in the journal to compile the trading account (*figure 13.3*).

The first transfer will credit purchases £1000 (in order to zero it for year 2) and debit the trading account the same amount.

The second will credit the trading account and debit a
new account called 'Stock'. This is the closing stock
balance which we will value at cost.

Journal - Year 1				
Date	Account	Reference	Debit	Credit
27th June	Bank	J1		1000.00
27th June	Purchases	J1	1000.00	
30th June	Purchases	(to Trading account)		1000.00
30th June	Trading account	(from Purchases)	1000.00	
30th June	Trading account	(to closing Stock)		1000.00
30th June	Stock	(from Trading account)	1000.00	

figure 13.3

All we are really doing in this case is transferring
purchases to the trading account and then transferring it
again into the stock account.

Nominal Ledger - Year 1

Bank

Date	Reference	Debit	Credit
27th June	J1		1000.00

Purchases

Date	Reference	Debit	Credit
27th June	J1	1000.00	
30th June	(to Trading account)		1000.00
Totals		1000.00	1000.00
30th June	Closed		

Trading account

Date	Reference	Debit	Credit
30th June	Purchases	1000.00	
30th June	Closing Stock		1000.00
Totals		1000.00	1000.00
30th June	Balance b/d	0.00	0.00

Stock

Date	Reference	Debit	Credit
30th June	Closing balance	1000.00	

figure 13.4

Figure 13.4 shows the ledger after the journal entries have been posted.

The balance b/d figure in the trading account shows the gross profit (zero in this case).

Normally we would then transfer the trading account to the profit & loss account but there is little point in doing this since there is no profit or loss.

Only two accounts have a non-zero balance so we will end year 1 with just the balance sheet (*figure 13.5*).

Balance Sheet - at end of year 1			
Assets	(Debit balances)	**Liabilities**	(Credit balances)
Stock	1000.00	Bank Overdraft	1000.00
		Equity	
Balance	**1000.00**		**1000.00**

figure 13.5

Year 2 - the full equation

We start the second year's set of books by entering the opening balances in a new journal (*figure 13.6*).

Journal - Year 2				
Date	**Account**	**Reference**	**Debit**	**Credit**
1st July	Bank	(Opening balance)		1000.00
1st July	Stock	(Opening balance)	1000.00	

figure 13.6

During year 2 the business purchases a further £500 of stock and sells some of the stock for £1600.

The business also incurs costs of £20 because the goods need delivering to the customer (by post in this example).

Two extra accounts will be required to cope with these new transactions: one for sales and another for postage.

Figure 13.7 shows the journal updated with the new transactions and figure 13.8 (overleaf) shows the ledger accounts after all the entries have been posted.

Journal - Year 2				
Date	Account	Reference	Debit	Credit
1st July	Bank	(Opening balance)		1000.00
1st July	Stock	(Opening balance)	1000.00	
2nd July	Bank	J1		500.00
2nd July	Purchases	J1	500.00	
2nd July	Sales	J2		1600.00
2nd July	Bank	J2	1600.00	
3rd July	Bank	J3		20.00
3rd July	Postage	J3	20.00	

figure 13.7

Nominal Ledger - Year 2			
Bank			
Date	Reference	Debit	Credit
1st July	(Opening balance)		1000.00
2nd July	J1		500.00
2nd July	J2	1600.00	
3rd July	J3		20.00
Totals		1600.00	1520.00
3rd July	Balance b/d	80.00	
Purchases			
Date	Reference	Debit	Credit
2nd July	J1	500.00	
Sales			
Date	Reference	Debit	Credit
2nd July	J2		1600.00
Postage			
Date	Reference	Debit	Credit
3rd July	J3	20.00	
Stock			
Date	Reference	Debit	Credit
1st July	Opening balance	1000.00	

figure 13.8

This is all that happened in year 2, so we can now create the trading account.

We need to transfer the purchase, postage and sales account balances to the trading account as well as the opening and closing stock figures to complete it.

The **opening** and **closing** stock figures are held in a single account called 'stock'. This is the hardest part to understand since an account can only have one balance yet we need to extract two balances from the one stock account in order to compile the trading account.

What actually happens is this: the opening stock balance is transferred **from stock** to the trading account (at this point the stock balance will be zero). We then do a stock take (which means physically looking at our stock and valuing it) and transfer this value from the trading account back **to stock.**

In essence then, the opening stock balance will be the **only** entry in the stock account until the year end. It is then transferred to the trading account and a new value (the closing balance) is transferred back again (and so on year after year).

The only grey area is the closing stock valuation. Even if we knew how much we had sold (and therefore how much remained) we would still perform a manual stock take to check for damaged or missing items (all of which can be recorded in the journal - see the notes at the end of this chapter).

Whatever the reason for the valuation the books will always balance because a higher valuation will automatically result in a higher gross profit and vice-versa (logically, the stock account is on the debit side of the balance sheet - an asset, and the trading account is on the credit side).

As mentioned earlier, chapter 19 - page 150 discusses stock valuations in more detail.

Journal - Year 2				
Date	Account	Reference	Debit	Credit
1st July	Bank	(Opening balance)		1000.00
1st July	Stock	(Opening balance)	1000.00	
2nd July	Bank	J1		500.00
2nd July	Purchases	J1	500.00	
2nd July	Sales	J2		1600.00
2nd July	Bank	J2	1600.00	
3rd July	Bank	J3		20.00
3rd July	Postage	J3	20.00	
4th July	Stock	(to Trading account)		1000.00
4th July	Trading Account	(from opening Stock)	1000.00	
4th July	Purchases	(to Trading Account)		500.00
4th July	Trading Account	(from Purchases)	500.00	
4th July	Postage	(to Trading Account)		20.00
4th July	Trading Account	(from Postage)	20.00	
4th July	Sales	(to Trading Account)	1600.00	
4th July	Trading Account	(from Sales)		1600.00
4th July	Stock	(from Trading account)	700.00	
4th July	Trading Account	(to closing Stock)		700.00

figure 13.9

Figure 13.9 shows the journal entries for the trading account.

You can enter the transfers in any order you like provided they are all entered in one go prior to posting them to the ledger.

Remember that we are zeroing the stock, purchase, postage and sales accounts so it is easy to see whether they need to be entered as debits or credits, and finally we are taking the closing stock **from** the trading account **to** the stock account.

Figure 13.10 overleaf shows the updated ledger accounts.

Nominal Ledger - Year 2

Bank

Date	Reference	Debit	Credit
1st July	Opening balance		1000.00
2nd July	J1		500.00
2nd July	J2	1600.00	
3rd July	J3		20.00
Totals		1600.00	1520.00
3rd July	Balance b/d	80.00	

Purchases

Date	Reference	Debit	Credit
2nd July	J1	500.00	
4th July	(to Trading account)		500.00

Postage

Date	Reference	Debit	Credit
3rd July	J3	20.00	
4th July	(to Trading account)		20.00

Sales

Date	Reference	Debit	Credit
2nd July	J2		1600.00
4th July	(to Trading account)	1600.00	

Trading Account

Date	Reference	Debit	Credit
4th July	Opening stock	1000.00	
4th July	Purchases	500.00	
4th July	Postage	20.00	
4th July	Sales		1600.00
4th July	Closing Stock		700.00
Totals		1520.00	2300.00
4th July	Balance b/d (gross profit)		780.00

Stock

Date	Reference	Debit	Credit
1st July	Opening balance	1000.00	
4th July	(to Trading account)		1000.00
4th July	Closing balance	700.00	
Totals		1700.00	1000.00
4th July	Balance b/d	700.00	

figure 13.10

We have not bothered totalling the purchase, postage
and sales accounts since it is obvious their balances are
zero (they are now reflected in the trading account).

Having completed the trading account, we can transfer
the balance to the profit & loss account, and finally
transfer it again to the capital account. Figure 13.11
shows the journal entries (dated 5th July).

Journal - Year 2				
Date	Account	Reference	Debit	Credit
1st July	Bank	(Opening balance)		1000.00
1st July	Stock	(Opening balance)	1000.00	
2nd July	Bank	J1		500.00
2nd July	Purchases	J1	500.00	
2nd July	Sales	J2		1600.00
2nd July	Bank	J2	1600.00	
3rd July	Bank	J3		20.00
3rd July	Postage	J3	20.00	
4th July	Stock	(to Trading account)		1000.00
4th July	Trading Account	(from opening Stock)	1000.00	
4th July	Purchases	(to Trading Account)		500.00
4th July	Trading Account	(from Purchases)	500.00	
4th July	Postage	(to Trading Account)		20.00
4th July	Trading Account	(from Postage)	20.00	
4th July	Sales	(to Trading Account)	1600.00	
4th July	Trading Account	(from Sales)		1600.00
4th July	Stock	(from Trading account)	700.00	
4th July	Trading Account	(to closing Stock)		700.00
5th July	Trading Account	(to Profit & Loss)	780.00	
5th July	Profit & Loss	(from Trading account)		780.00
5th July	Profit & Loss	(to Capital)	780.00	
5th July	Capital	(from Profit & Loss)		780.00

figure 13.11

Nominal Ledger - Year 2			
Trading Account			
Date	**Reference**	**Debit**	**Credit**
4th July	Opening stock	1000.00	
4th July	Purchases	500.00	
4th July	Postage	20.00	
4th July	Sales		1600.00
4th July	Closing Stock		700.00
Totals		**1520.00**	**2300.00**
4th July	Balance b/d (gross profit)		780.00
5th July	(balance to Profit & Loss)	780.00	
	Closed		
Profit & Loss			
Date	**Reference**	**Debit**	**Credit**
5th July	(Gross profit from Trading)		780.00
5th July	(balance to Capital)	780.00	
	Closed		
Capital			
Date	**Reference**	**Debit**	**Credit**
5th July	(from Profit & Loss)		**780.00**

figure 13.12

Figure 13.12 shows the final trading, profit & loss, and capital accounts. Figure 13.13 shows the finished balance sheet.

Balance Sheet - at end of year 2			
Assets	(Debit balances)	**Liabilities**	(Credit balances)
Bank	80.00		
Stock	700.00	**Equity**	
		Capital	780.00
Balance	**780.00**		**780.00**

figure 13.13

Notes to chapter 13

Stock Valuation Adjustments

Page 81 mentions some reasons why a stock valuation may be different from its original cost price and that you may want the reason recorded in the books.

A good example is that of goods found to be missing during a stock take.

As always, the entries are made in the journal. Since the stock valuation directly affects both the trading and stock accounts, that is where we will post them.

Figure 13.14 shows how the journal entries relating to figure 13.11 would have been entered if the closing stock figure of £700 included the fact that £100 worth was found to be missing.

Journal				
Date	Account	Reference	Debit	Credit
4th July	Stock	(from Trading account)	800.00	
4th July	Trading Account	(to closing Stock unadjusted)		800.00
4th July	Stock	(from Trading account)		100.00
4th July	Trading Account	(to missing Stock adjustment)	100.00	

figure 13.14

This produces the same result, but tells us more about the business (ie. the stock should have been worth £800 but we have devalued it because £100 worth has disappeared).

The Inland Revenue will be happier if you document details like this since a lower valuation will result in a lower profit (and therefore less tax) and they may want to know the reason why.

This type of transaction is known as an **adjustment** and is one of many that may be required at the year end to reflect a true picture of the business (see chapter 17).

If you subsequently made a claim for the goods (assuming they were stolen and you were insured) this would also need to be recorded in the journal. This is a straightforward entry from an account named 'Insurance claims' (or something similar) to your bank account. The 'insurance claims' account is treated as a sale and would be transferred to the trading account along with your other sales at the year end (in effect you have 'sold' the goods to the insurance company).

Current purchases and the ongoing stock account

This chapter has covered an important concept. It is not easy to grasp, but an explanation of the logic will help: anything you buy for the business will either be 'used up' (eg. sold) by the end of the year, or not.

If it is not 'used up', then we **must** account for what remains at the end of the year (hence the opening and closing stock account balances).

To see why, we will look at a very simple example of a business which purchases two televisions for £100 each, but only sells one of them (at £200, say) during the first year.

If we forget about the closing stock valuation, and close the purchase account at the year end, the trading account will show a balance of zero (£200 of purchases, and £200 of sales). Assuming nothing else happened during the year, the balance sheet would also show a zero balance.

Everything balances, **except** for the fact that the business still has one television left in its warehouse which has not been accounted for. If the owner of the business simply took the television home (to 'account' for it!), this would be fraud (the owner has gained a television without any record of it being shown as sold).

If the accounts were prepared properly (ie. by entering a closing stock value of £100), the business would show a profit of £100 (purchases bought **and sold** during the year: £100, sales during the year: £200). The balance sheet would show £100 on the asset side (the remaining television) and £100 under equity (the profit).

If the business neither buys nor sells anything during year 2, the opening stock value will be posted to the trading account, and posted back again at the same value (showing neither a profit or loss - which is as it should be).

However, if the television was valued at £150 at the end of year 2, then a £50 profit would be shown (opening balance £100, closing balance £150). Stock valuations at the end of each accounting year are therefore vital not only for showing the true picture of the business, but also from the way they affect a business's profit (or loss).

Note: there is a section within the self-assessment tax return covering goods taken from a business by the owner (in case it was overlooked on the accounting side), but if you do remove stock for your own use, it is better to account for it in the first place by making a journal entry crediting the purchase (or stock) account and debiting your drawings (or capital account) - you can then ignore that section of the self-assessment form.

14 • The Manufacturing Account

Having covered both service and trading businesses there is one more type to take into account: a business which manufactures its own goods for re-sale.

A business of this type will require a **manufacturing account** as well as a trading and profit & loss account.

Just like the trading account the manufacturing account is an interim account: its balance is transferred to the trading account which in turn is transferred to the profit & loss account. The manufacturing account must therefore be compiled before the others.

The manufacturing account differs from the trading account in one very important area. It is only concerned with what it **costs** to produce the goods (its balance will be an expense of the business). The trading account, on the other hand, includes both the costs **and** the sales. Its balance can end up on either side (a profit or a loss).

Like traders, manufacturers also buy stock, but in this case the term refers to the **raw materials** used to manufacture goods.

At the end of the year we are also likely to have a stock of partly finished goods (called **work in progress**), and a stock of finished (ie. manufactured) goods.

Three stock accounts are therefore required if we are to show an accurate picture of the business.

We also need an account to record new purchases of raw materials for the current year (this is the same principle as the trading account: the stock account rolls on year after year, the purchases account records only the current year's purchases of stock).

We must also ensure that our **expenses** are broken down into the categories necessary to separate manufacturing costs from the trading and administration costs of the business.

To illustrate this, we will use an example of a manufacturer who makes bricks.

The **raw materials** stock account will keep track of the value of the clay bought and how much remains after it has been used to manufacture the bricks.

At the end of the year, some of the clay will have been formed into bricks but not yet 'fired' in the furnace. This value will be held in the second stock account (**work in progress**). It represents the value of partly finished bricks.

A certain number of bricks will have been finished completely, but not yet sold at the end of the year. This value is held in the third stock account, which we shall call **Stock (manufactured)**.

Like the trading account we need to track a business over two years to see the full effect of the opening and closing stock accounts.

Year 1

During the year we buy £2000 worth of clay and pay the factory workers £10,000 in wages (*figure 14.1*).

Journal - Year 1

Date	Account	Reference	Debit	Credit
27th June	Bank	J1		2000.00
27th June	Purchases	J1	2000.00	
27th June	Bank	(to pay factory wages)		10000.00
30th June	Wages	(paid from bank)	10000.00	

figure 14.1

At the end of year 1 we transfer the purchases into the manufacturing account. We also transfer part of our wage costs into the manufacturing account: we decide that £5000 worth has been used to form the clay into bricks prior to firing.

We then do a stock take of raw materials left, which we value at £1000 (ie. we have used half the stock during the year), and transfer this value from the manufacturing account to the raw materials stock account (*figure 14.2*).

Journal - Year 1

Date	Account	Reference	Debit	Credit
27th June	Bank	J1		2000.00
27th June	Purchases	J1	2000.00	
27th June	Bank	(to pay factory wages)		10000.00
30th June	Wages	(paid from bank)	10000.00	
31st July	Purchases	(to manufacturing account)		2000.00
31st July	Manufacturing Account	(from purchases)	2000.00	
31st July	Wages	(to manufacturing account)		5000.00
31st July	Manufacturing Account	(from wages)	5000.00	
31st July	Manufacturing Account	(to raw materials)		1000.00
31st July	Raw Materials	(closing balance - from manuf.)	1000.00	

figure 14.2

Figure 14.3 (overleaf) shows the nominal ledger after the journal has been posted.

Nominal Ledger - Year 1

Bank

Date	Reference	Debit	Credit
27th June	J1		2000.00
27th June	(to pay factory wages)		10000.00
Totals			**12000.00**
31st July	Balance b/d (overdraft)		**12000.00**

Purchases

Date	Reference	Debit	Credit
27th June	J1	2000.00	
31st July	(to Manufacturing account)		2000.00

Wages

Date	Reference	Debit	Credit
30th June	(paid from bank)	10000.00	
31st July	(to Manufacturing account)		5000.00
Totals		**10000.00**	**5000.00**
31st July	Balance b/d	**5000.00**	

Manufacturing account

Date	Reference	Debit	Credit
31st July	Purchases	2000.00	
31st July	Wages	5000.00	
31st July	Closing Raw Materials		1000.00
Totals		**7000.00**	**1000.00**
31st July	Balance b/d (work in progress)	**6000.00**	

Raw Materials Account

Date	Reference	Debit	Credit
31st July	Closing balance	**1000.00**	

figure 14.3

We haven't finished the manufacturing account yet, but the entries posted so far gives us the value of the partly finished bricks (work in progress). We started with £2000 worth of clay. We spent £5000 on wages into transforming the clay into bricks ready to be fired. We had £1000 worth of unused clay left at the end of the year. The balance is £6000, and this represents what it has cost us to get to this state of manufacture.

Because it is the end of the year, this £6000 balance must now be transferred to the work in progress account.

We also have one more expense to transfer; the remainder of the wages. This represents the wages paid to the workers responsible for finishing the bricks. Figure 14.4 shows the journal entries.

Journal - Year 1				
Date	Account	Reference	Debit	Credit
27th June	Bank	J1		2000.00
27th June	Purchases	J1	2000.00	
27th June	Bank	(to pay factory wages)		10000.00
30th June	Wages	(paid from bank)	10000.00	
31st July	Purchases	(to manufacturing account)		2000.00
31st July	Manufacturing Account	(from purchases)	2000.00	
31st July	Wages	(to manufacturing account)		5000.00
31st July	Manufacturing Account	(from wages)	5000.00	
31st July	Manufacturing Account	(to raw materials)		1000.00
31st July	Raw Materials	(closing balance - from manuf.)	1000.00	
31st July	Manufacturing Account	(to work in progress)		6000.00
31st July	Work in Progress	(closing balance - from manuf.)	6000.00	
31st July	Wages	(to manufacturing account)		5000.00
31st July	Manufacturing Account	(from wages)	5000.00	

figure 14.4

The wages account is now closed and the Work in Progress account will have a balance of £6000 debit, so we only need show the effect on the manufacturing account (*figure 14.5*).

Nominal Ledger - Year 1			
Manufacturing account			
Date	Reference	Debit	Credit
31st July	Purchases	2000.00	
31st July	Wages	5000.00	
31st July	Closing Raw Materials		1000.00
Totals		**7000.00**	**1000.00**
31st July	Balance b/d (work in progress)	6000.00	
31st July	(balance to Work in Progress)		6000.00
31st July	Wages	5000.00	
Totals		**11000.00**	**6000.00**
31st July	Balance b/d (cost of manufactured stock)	**5000.00**	

figure 14.5

At the end of year 1, we have £1000 of clay left, £6000 of partly finished bricks, and £5000 of fully finished bricks (the final balance of the manufacturing account).

All the valuations have been at cost. The only grey area is the closing value of raw materials (being clay, it can only be an estimate). As figure 14.5 shows, once the raw materials have been valued, the other valuations are purely mathematical (but see the notes at the end of this chapter).

The balance of the manufacturing account (£5000) would normally be transferred to the trading account. However, since it will then be transferred out again as closing stock (manufactured), the business will neither show a profit or a loss, so we may as well transfer it direct to the stock (manufactured) account.

Figure 14.6 shows the balance sheet at the end of year 1.

Balance Sheet - at end of year 1			
Assets	(Debit balances)	Liabilities	(Credit balances)
Raw Materials	1000.00	Bank Overdraft	12000.00
Work in Progress	6000.00	Equity	
Stock (manufactured)	5000.00		
Balance	12000.00		12000.00

figure 14.6

Year 2

During year 2 we purchase a further £1000 worth of clay and concentrate more on finishing the bricks than producing more work in progress. To this end, the wages bill will remain at £10,000, but we estimate that £8,000 of it was for finishing the bricks (with only £2000 for producing more partly finished stock). The closing raw materials will be valued at £1800. We also manage to sell £14,000 of finished bricks during the year.

Figure 14.7 (overleaf) shows all the journal entries for year 2 up to the manufacturing account. They have been split into a number of sections to make it easier to follow.

Journal - Year 2				
Date	Account	Reference	Debit	Credit
1st August	Bank	(Opening balance)		12000.00
1st August	Raw Materials	(Opening balance)	1000.00	
1st August	Work in Progress	(Opening balance)	6000.00	
1st August	Stock (manufactured)	(Opening balance)	5000.00	
2nd August	Bank	J1		1000.00
2nd August	Purchases	J1	1000.00	
2nd August	Bank	(to pay factory wages)		10000.00
2nd August	Wages	(paid from bank)	10000.00	
2nd August	Sales	J2		14000.00
2nd August	Bank	J2	14000.00	
3rd August	Raw Materials	(to Manufacturing Account)		1000.00
3rd August	Manufacturing Account	(from opening Raw Materials)	1000.00	
3rd August	Purchases	(to Manufacturing Account)		1000.00
3rd August	Manufacturing Account	(from Purchases)	1000.00	
3rd August	Wages	(to Manufacturing Account)		2000.00
3rd August	Manufacturing Account	(from wages)	2000.00	
3rd August	Raw Materials	(from Manufacturing Account)	1800.00	
3rd August	Manufacturing Account	(to closing Raw Materials)		1800.00
3rd August	Work in Progress	(to Manufacturing Account)		6000.00
3rd August	Manufacturing Account	(from opening Work in Progress)	6000.00	
4th August	Manufacturing Account	(to closing Work in Progress)		8200.00
4th August	Work in Progress	(from Manufacturing Account)	8200.00	
4th August	Wages	(to Manufacturing Account)		8000.00
4th August	Manufacturing Account	(from wages)	8000.00	

figure 14.7

The first four entries (dated 1st August) are the opening balances for year 2 taken from year 1's balance sheet.

The next six entries show the new transactions during year 2 (£1000 of clay, £10,000 wages, and £14,000 sales).

The third section (dated 3rd August) shows the transfer entries needed to compile the manufacturing account up to the work in progress balance. If we balance the manufacturing account at this point, it will give us the work in progress closing balance. This balance, together with the remaining wages is shown in the last section (dated 4th August).

The manufacturing account is shown in figure 14.8 (overleaf).

Nominal Ledger - Year 2			
Manufacturing Account			
Date	Reference	Debit	Credit
3rd August	Opening Raw Materials	1000.00	
3rd August	Purchases	1000.00	
3rd August	Wages	2000.00	
3rd August	Closing Raw Materials		1800.00
3rd August	Opening Work in Progress	6000.00	
Totals		10000.00	1800.00
4th August	Balance b/d (closing work in progress)	8200.00	
4th August	(balance to work in progress)		8200.00
4th August	Wages	8000.00	
Totals		16200.00	8200.00
4th August	Balance b/d (cost of manufactured stock)	8000.00	

figure 14.8

We have highlighted the work in progress balance as well as the final balance for clarity.

The important thing to notice in year 2 is that the manufacturing account includes both the raw material and work in progress opening **and** closing balances. This format will now apply year after year.

We are now ready to compile the trading account. We will transfer the **Sales** account first. The opening **Stock (manufactured)** account is then transferred. This is followed by the balance from the **Manufacturing account**.

We now do a stock take of finished bricks and transfer that from the **trading account** to the **Stock (manufactured)** account (which is its closing balance for the year). We will calculate the valuation by assuming we sell the bricks at double their cost price. Ignoring sales for a moment, at the end of the year we had £13,000 worth of finished bricks (£5000 opening balance plus £8,000 of newly finished bricks). We sold £7,000 worth of bricks (for £14,000), therefore £13,000 minus £7,000 leaves a balance of £6,000, so this will be our valuation. Figure 14.9 (overleaf) shows the journal so far.

Journal - Year 2				
Date	Account	Reference	Debit	Credit
1st August	Bank	(Opening balance)		12000.00
1st August	Raw Materials	(Opening balance)	1000.00	
1st August	Work in Progress	(Opening balance)	6000.00	
1st August	Stock (manufactured)	(Opening balance)	5000.00	
2nd August	Bank	J1		1000.00
2nd August	Purchases	J1	1000.00	
2nd August	Bank	(to pay factory wages)		10000.00
2nd August	Wages	(paid from bank)	10000.00	
2nd August	Sales	J2		14000.00
2nd August	Bank	J2	14000.00	
3rd August	Raw Materials	(to Manufacturing Account)		1000.00
3rd August	Manufacturing Account	(from opening Raw Materials)	1000.00	
3rd August	Purchases	(to Manufacturing Account)		1000.00
3rd August	Manufacturing Account	(from Purchases)	1000.00	
3rd August	Wages	(to Manufacturing Account)		2000.00
3rd August	Manufacturing Account	(from wages)	2000.00	
3rd August	Raw Materials	(from Manufacturing Account)	1800.00	
3rd August	Manufacturing Account	(to closing Raw Materials)		1800.00
3rd August	Work in Progress	(to Manufacturing Account)		6000.00
3rd August	Manufacturing Account	(from opening Work in Progress)	6000.00	
4th August	Manufacturing Account	(to closing Work in Progress)		8200.00
4th August	Work in Progress	(from Manufacturing Account)	8200.00	
4th August	Wages	(to Manufacturing Account)		8000.00
4th August	Manufacturing Account	(from wages)	8000.00	
5th August	Sales	(to trading account)	14000.00	
5th August	Trading Account	(from sales)		14000.00
5th August	Stock (manufactured)	(to trading account)		5000.00
5th August	Trading Account	(opening stock - manufactured)	5000.00	
5th August	Manufacturing Account	(to trading account)		8000.00
5th August	Trading Account	(balance from manufacturing)	8000.00	
5th August	Trading Account	(to stock - manufactured)		6000.00
5th August	Stock (manufactured)	(closing balance from trading)	6000.00	

figure 14.9

These last entries will close (ie. zero) the sales and manufacturing accounts, and update the stock of manufactured bricks account, so we only need show the effect on the trading account (*figure 14.10*).

Nominal Ledger - Year 2			
Trading Account			
Date	Reference	Debit	Credit
5th August	Sales		14000.00
5th August	Opening Stock (manufactured)	5000.00	
5th August	Cost of newly manufactured goods	8000.00	
5th August	Closing Stock (manufactured)		6000.00
Totals		13000.00	20000.00
5th August	Balance b/d (gross profit)		7000.00

figure 14.10

In practice, we would also transfer any trading expense accounts to the trading account before arriving at the gross profit (eg. warehouse expenses - where we store the finished bricks, and any other expenses to do with the trading side of the business).

The trading account can now be closed by transferring its balance (the gross profit) to the profit & loss account. In our example, this would result in a net profit of £7,000. In practice, the general business administrative expenses would also be transferred to the profit & loss before arriving at the net profit.

Rather than showing what would now be a rather large nominal ledger, we will go direct to the closing balance sheet for year 2 (*figure 14.11*).

Balance Sheet - at end of year 2			
Assets	(Debit balances)	**Liabilities**	(Credit balances)
Raw Materials	1800.00	Bank Overdraft	9000.00
Work in Progress	8200.00	**Equity**	
Stock (manufactured)	6000.00	Profit for the year	7000.00
Balance	**16000.00**		**16000.00**

figure 14.11

This formula then continues year after year: opening raw materials and work in progress to the manufacturing account. Purchases and expenses to the manufacturing account. Closing raw materials and work in progress back again. Balance of the manufacturing account to the trading account together with sales and opening finished stock. Trading expenses to the trading account. Closing finished stock back again. Balance of the trading account (gross profit) to the profit & loss account together with the administrative and other remaining expenses. Finally, the balance of the profit & loss is posted to an equity account (eg. the owner's capital account) where it is carried forward to the following year with all the other balance sheet accounts.

Notes to Chapter 14

Manufacturing expenses and Work in Progress

In our example, we decided to split the factory workers wages between those moulding the clay into bricks, and those finishing the bricks in the furnace. This gives us a believable picture of 'work in progress' as well as the cost of finished stock.

In practice, the manufacturing expenses will be split across a range of different accounts. Some can be considered direct or **prime costs**, and others can be considered as 'fixed'. The 'direct' costs are generally variable (eg. factory workers wages - workers can be made redundant or added to depending on the workload). Fixed costs are the overheads of the factory (eg. the factory manager's salary, rent, lighting etc.). Work in progress can then be assessed on many different aspects.

Increasing the closing **work in progress** valuation will ultimately **decrease** the **profit** unless the increase is matched with a decrease in the closing raw materials valuation.

Manufacturing, Trading, and Profit & Loss accounts

Chapters 13 & 14 have covered the above accounts in detail. They all have one thing in common: they are made up from other accounts.

We could have ignored the manufacturing and trading accounts and posted everything direct to the profit & loss account (the result would be the same). We could even have changed the profit & loss account's name to reflect this fact.

In practice, many accountants will simply compile **reports** from the accounts which make up the manufacturing, trading and profit & loss accounts rather than include them as accounts in their own right in the ledger.

Purchase accounts for stock

In theory, the current purchase accounts used for each stock account are unnecessary: we could post new purchases of stock direct to the stock account (the end result would be no different, provided the stock balance was transferred to the manufacturing or trading account, and the final valuation posted back again).

The only reason for using separate purchase accounts is for easy analysis by the owner of the business. If you take the case of a wheelbarrow manufacturer, separate purchase accounts could be opened for the purchase of wheels, the barrow's, and the nuts and bolts. All three purchase accounts would be posted to the single raw materials account at the end of the year, thus enabling the manufacturer to analyse immediately how much had been spent on each aspect of the wheelbarrow.

Manufacturing and Trading businesses

If a business manufactures goods but also buys in other stock for re-sale, then it is usual to keep the stock of manufactured goods separate from the stock for re-sale.

The trading account will therefore contain the opening balances of both types of stock (and subsequent closing balances). See chapter 13 for a full description of the trading account.

15 • Limited Companies

We could fill this entire book on limited companies, but since we are only concerned with the principles of double-entry we will outline just the basic differences between un-limited businesses (ie. sole-proprietors and partnerships) and limited companies.

The owner(s) of an **un-limited** business pay **Income Tax** on the profits of the business regardless of what they take out of the business in the way of drawings (in other words if a business has sales of £20,000 and expenses of £6,000 the taxable profit will be £14,000 - even if they pay themselves the £14,000 as wages).

A **limited** company on the other hand is owned by its shareholders. Every person working for the company **including its directors** are employees of the company and their wages will be treated as expenses to the company (with Income Tax deducted as they earn). Any profits left over are then subject to a tax called **Corporation Tax** (or **CT**).

Some of the profits of a limited company are paid to the shareholders (these are called **dividends**) and the remainder is transferred to one or more **reserve accounts** which are carried forward to the following year.

These reserve accounts are used to enable the company to meet future commitments (eg. to ensure a reasonable dividend if there is less profit the following year, or to replace or repair capital equipment, or to pay any corporation tax due for the year).

Transferring the balance of the Profit & Loss account to the dividend and reserve accounts could be achieved by journal entries direct from the Profit & Loss account, but depending on the number of accounts used this may make the Profit & Loss account difficult to read.

The balance is therefore usually transferred in one go to an interim account called an **appropriation account** from where it can be distributed accordingly.

Corporation Tax is normally due within 9 months from the end of an accounting year (which is why a reserve account is set up for it), however if a dividend is paid (and this can happen more than once a year) some of the corporation tax must be paid in advance. This is called **Advanced Corporation Tax** (or **ACT**).

This is done to ensure that shareholders are taxed at source (for the same reason that bank and building society interest is taxed before you receive it).

Whilst corporation tax varies depending on the size of the profits (the minimum for 1997/98 is 21%), ACT usually reflects the current lower income tax rate (currently 20% for 1997/98).

If a company makes a profit of £1200 and decides it can afford to pay dividends totalling £1000, the ACT due will be £200 (ie. 20% of £1000). The shareholders will actually receive £800 in cash plus a form called a **tax credit** showing the amount of tax paid (eg. if there were two shareholders they would each get a £100 tax credit plus £400 in cash).

The tax credit can then be reclaimed by the shareholder if they are not liable for tax.

Once the corporation tax has been calculated, the ACT can be deducted from it. In this example the CT due is 21% of £1200 which is £252. Because £200 has already been paid, the final tax bill to the company will be £52.

To summarise: at the end of the year the company will have paid £800 to the shareholders and £200 to the Inland Revenue in ACT. It will have £200 left over, £52 of which will be transferred to a CT reserve account and £148 to a general reserve. The CT reserve will be zeroed when the tax is actually paid 9 months later and the £148 general reserve can be used again if necessary for re-distribution to shareholders, or for any other purpose in the following year.

(**Note:** ACT will be abolished from April 1999 and the lower rate for corporation tax will be reduced to 20%).

To show this in double-entry terms we will use an example of a service company (business consultants, say) started by two directors which issues 100 shares at £1 each.

The directors ('F Smith' and 'J Smith') have an equal stake in the company so each buys 50 shares. Figure 15.1 shows the opening journal entries.

Journal				
Date	Account	Reference	Debit	Credit
5th July	Share Capital (F Smith)	(to Bank)		50.00
5th July	Share Capital (J Smith)	(to Bank)		50.00
5th July	Bank	(from Share Capital)	100.00	

figure 15.1

We have made separate entries of £50 for each shareholder but paid both into the bank on one paying-in slip therefore a single entry of £100 has been made to the bank (the debit equals the credits, so this is fine).

During the first year the company charges a client £1000 for consulting fees and incurs no costs. It will therefore make a profit of £1000 which is transferred to the appropriation account. No dividends are paid in the first year so part of the balance is transferred to the general reserve account and the remainder to an account for corporation tax (21% of £1000). Figure 15.2 shows the full journal for the first year.

Journal - Year 1				
Date	Account	Reference	Debit	Credit
5th July	Share Capital (F Smith)	(to Bank)		50.00
5th July	Share Capital (J Smith)	(to Bank)		50.00
5th July	Bank	(from Share Capital)	100.00	
6th July	Consulting fees	J1		1000.00
6th July	Bank	J1	1000.00	
7th July	Consulting fees	(to Profit & Loss)	1000.00	
7th July	Profit & Loss	(from Consulting fees)		1000.00
8th July	Profit & Loss	(to Appropriation account)	1000.00	
8th July	Appropriation account	(from Profit & Loss)		1000.00
9th July	Appropriation account	(to General/CT Reserves)	1000.00	
9th July	General Reserve	(from Appropriation account)		790.00
9th July	CT Reserve	(from Appropriation account)		210.00

figure 15.2

Figure 15.3 shows the first year's balance sheet.

Balance Sheet - at end of year 1			
Assets	(Debit balances)	**Liabilities**	(Credit balances)
Bank Account	1100.00	Share Capital	100.00
		General Reserve	790.00
		CT Reserve	210.00
Balance	**1100.00**		**1100.00**

figure 15.3

During the second year the company makes a further profit of £5000 and decides to pay the shareholders dividends totalling £4000. It also pays the corporation tax due from the first year.

Figure 15.4 shows the second year's complete journal entries.

Journal - Year 2				
Date	Account	Reference	Debit	Credit
5th July	Bank	(Opening balance)	1100.00	
5th July	Share Capital	(Opening balance)		100.00
5th July	General Reserve	(Opening balance)		790.00
5th July	CT Reserve	(Opening balance)		210.00
6th July	Consulting fees	J1		5000.00
6th July	Bank	J1	5000.00	
6th July	Bank	(to pay CT from year 1)		210.00
6th July	CT Reserve	(paid from Bank)	210.00	
7th July	Consulting fees	(to Profit & Loss)	5000.00	
7th July	Profit & Loss	(from Consulting fees)		5000.00
8th July	General Reserve	(to Appropriation account)	790.00	
8th July	Appropriation account	(from General Reserve)		790.00
8th July	Profit & Loss	(to Appropriation account)	5000.00	
8th July	Appropriation account	(from Profit & Loss)		5000.00
9th July	Appropriation account	(to Dividends)	3200.00	
9th July	Dividends	(from Appropriation account)		3200.00
9th July	Appropriation account	(to CT Reserve)	840.00	
9th July	CT Reserve	(from Appropriation account)		840.00
9th July	Appropriation account	(to General Reserve)	1750.00	
9th July	General Reserve	(from Appropriation account)		1750.00
10th July	Bank	(to pay Dividends F Smith)		1600.00
10th July	Bank	(to pay Dividends J Smith)		1600.00
10th July	Dividends (F Smith)	(paid from Bank)	1600.00	
10th July	Dividends (J Smith)	(paid from Bank)	1600.00	
10th July	Bank	(to pay ACT from CT Reserves)		800.00
10th July	CT Reserve	(paid ACT from Bank)	800.00	

figure 15.4

Figure 15.5 (on the next page) shows the full ledger at the end of year 2.

ISLE COLLEGE
RESOURCES CENTRE

Nominal Ledger - Year 2

Bank

Date	Reference	Debit	Credit
5th July	Opening balance	1100.00	
6th July	J1	5000.00	
6th July	to pay CT from year 1		210.00
10th July	to pay Dividends to F Smith		1600.00
10th July	to pay Dividends to J Smith		1600.00
10th July	to pay ACT		800.00
Totals		6100.00	4210.00
10th July	Balance b/d	1890.00	

Share Capital

Date	Reference	Debit	Credit
5th July	Opening balance		100.00

Consulting fees

Date	Reference	Debit	Credit
6th July	J1		5000.00
7th July	(balance to Profit & Loss)	5000.00	

Profit & Loss account

Date	Reference	Debit	Credit
7th July	Consulting fees		5000.00
8th July	(balance to Appropriation account)	5000.00	

Appropriation account

Date	Reference	Debit	Credit
7th July	from General Reserve		790.00
8th July	from Profit & Loss		5000.00
9th July	to Dividends	3200.00	
9th July	to CT Reserve	840.00	
Totals		4040.00	5790.00
9th July	Balance b/d	1750.00	
9th July	(balance to General Reserve)		1750.00

Dividends

Date	Reference	Debit	Credit
9th July	from Appropriation account		3200.00
10th July	Paid F Smith from Bank	1600.00	
10th July	Paid J Smith from Bank	1600.00	

General Reserve

Date	Reference	Debit	Credit
5th July	Opening balance		790.00
7th July	to Appropriation account	790.00	
9th July	from Appropriation account		1750.00
Totals		790.00	2540.00
10th July	Balance b/d		1750.00

CT Reserve

Date	Reference	Debit	Credit
5th July	Opening balance		210.00
6th July	paid from bank	210.00	
9th July	from Appropriation account		840.00
10th July	Paid ACT from Bank	800.00	
Totals		1010.00	1050.00
10th July	Balance b/d		40.00

figure 15.5

Figure 15.6 shows the final balance sheet.

Balance Sheet - at end of year 2			
Assets	(Debit balances)	**Liabilities**	(Credit balances)
Bank Account	1890.00	Share Capital	100.00
		General Reserve	1750.00
		CT Reserve	40.00
Balance	**1890.00**		**1890.00**

figure 15.6

Limited companies and the Balance Sheet

The balance sheets of sole-proprietors and partnerships is not governed by law (providing of course it shows a fair and accurate representation of the business) whereas a limited company's balance sheet is.

This is because the shareholders (and anyone else who has an interest in the company) have a right to see how the business is doing.

The government has laid down certain guidelines on company balance sheets which you will need to know.

These guidelines have been amended and added to over the years via the various government Finance Acts.

Having said this though, there is nothing to stop a limited company from producing an internal balance sheet if it wishes to see the results displayed in a different way: it is only the balance sheet sent to Companies House that should conform to the rules. (**Companies House** is the government department responsible for storing the balance sheets and annual reports of limited companies).

There are two basic layouts: **horizontal**, and **vertical**.

We have been using the **horizontal** layout so far (because it makes the logic easier to understand).

In practice, a **vertical** layout is preferred (especially by Companies House - see page 46). Figure 15.7 shows the same balance sheet from figure 15.6 in a vertical layout.

Balance Sheet - at end of year 2	
Assets	
Bank Account	1890.00
Total Assets	**1890.00**
Liabilities	
Share Capital	100.00
General Reserve	1750.00
CT Reserve	40.00
Total Liabilities	**1890.00**

figure 15.7

Chapter 16, page 122 shows this type of layout in greater detail.

Another difference is that traditionally, sole-proprietors and partnerships show their most liquid accounts first whereas companies show them last. A 'liquid' account is one where the money can be realised very quickly (eg. money in the bank).

ISLE COLLEGE
RESOURCES CENTRE

16 • Assets and Depreciation

The **asset** side of an average balance sheet contains many different types of asset (eg. petty cash, vehicles etc.).

These assets are usually summarised into two groups: **Current Assets** and **Fixed Assets**.

Current Assets include money in the bank, petty cash, money received but not yet banked (termed **cash in hand** or **undeposited funds**), money owed to the business by its customers, raw materials for manufacturing, and stock bought for re-sale.

They are termed 'current' because they are **active** accounts. Money flows in and out of them each financial year, and we will need frequent reports of their balances if the business is to survive (eg. 'do we need more stock and have we got enough money in the bank to buy it?').

Just about everything we have done so far has involved a current asset account of one sort or another, so the rest of this chapter is devoted to assets of the 'fixed' variety; what they are, and why they need to be accounted for in a different way.

Fixed Assets consist of anything which a business owns or buys for use within the business and which still **retains a value at year end**. They usually consist of major items like land, buildings, equipment and vehicles.

A tank of petrol or a ream of paper for the photocopier are also assets but they tend to last less than a year and once bought they tend to retain little value. As such these types of item are termed **expenses** and are accounted for in full in the Profit & Loss account.

The term 'fixed' can therefore be translated as 'long term', and by that we mean an item which will last longer than a year and which will still retain a significant value.

The point being made is that anything you buy for use within a business is an asset, but some are long term ('fixed'), and some are short term (expenses).

The reason we must treat fixed assets differently from expenses can be summed up in the following example:

If you buy a new vehicle for £8000 and treat it as an expense you will be claiming the whole value against the year's profit. If at the end of the year the car is worth £6000 then in reality you have only used up £2000 of its value during the year. You will therefore be over-stating your expenses by £6000. A quick look at the balance sheet would show an £8000 overdraft under liabilities and an £8000 loss under equity. The books balance in themselves but we still have an asset worth £6000 which is not shown in the accounts at all!

A distinction must therefore be made if a true picture of the business is to be reflected in the Profit & Loss account and balance sheet.

The problem then is how to account for fixed assets.

The first thing you will need is a separate account for them. Most small businesses will open an account in the nominal ledger for each asset (larger businesses will use a separate ledger to keep track of their fixed assets - this type of ledger is usually called an **inventory** - see chapter 18).

If we go back to the £8000 vehicle example, the buying of the vehicle in the first place is simple enough: **credit** the bank (or wherever the money is coming **from**) and debit the vehicle account (*figure 16.1*).

Journal - Year 1				
Date	Account	Reference	Debit	Credit
5th July	Bank	(to buy vehicle ABC 123)		8000.00
5th July	Vehicle (ABC 123)	(paid by Bank)	8000.00	

figure 16.1

We have included the vehicles registration number ('ABC 123') as part of the account name so we can distinguish it from any other vehicles we buy.

If at the end of the year the vehicle is worth £6000 then we will need a further new account to record the £2000 difference in the value of the vehicle. This difference is called **depreciation** so we will call the new account **Depreciation (motor pool)**.

The term 'motor pool' is an accounting convention but it adequately describes the fact that we only need a single depreciation account no matter how many vehicles a business owns.

The depreciation itself is flowing **from** the vehicle **to** the depreciation account, so we know that the **to** side of the transaction will **debit** the depreciation account. However, if we complete the transaction by crediting the vehicle account we will lose sight of the original cost of the vehicle: the balance sheet will only show the current depreciated balance. If you were thinking of selling the business (or obtaining a loan), one of the first questions will be "what is the state of your fixed assets and how much will it cost to replace them when they wear out?".

It is prudent therefore, to leave the vehicle account's original balance alone.

Another problem is that depreciation accumulates year after year but the depreciation account is in effect an expense of the business, therefore, (like all expense accounts) it will be closed at year end.

So, to sum up, we need to transfer the depreciation from the asset but we can't use the asset's account. We also need to carry forward the depreciation to the next year but we can't use the depreciation account because it will be zero at year end when we close it.

The solution is to open a second depreciation account. This account will be used specifically to record the current and future depreciation of the vehicle (ABC 123), so we shall call it 'Accumulated Depreciation (ABC 123)' which we shall abbreviate to 'Acc. Depr. (ABC123)' in the following illustrations.

Each year the depreciation will therefore be recorded in the journal with a **credit** from the **Acc. Depr. (ABC123)** account and a **debit** to the **Depreciation (motor pool)** account (*figure 16.2*).

Journal - Year 1				
Date	**Account**	**Reference**	**Debit**	**Credit**
5th July	Bank	(to buy vehicle ABC 123)		8000.00
5th July	Vehicle (ABC 123)	(paid by Bank)	8000.00	
6th July	Acc. Depr. (ABC 123)	(to depreciation motor pool)		2000.00
6th July	Depreciation (motor pool)	(from vehicle ABC 123)	2000.00	

figure 16.2

The depreciation (motor pool) account will then be credited (to close it) by transferring its balance to the profit & loss account (*figure 16.3*).

Journal - Year 1

Date	Account	Reference	Debit	Credit
5th July	Bank	(to buy vehicle ABC 123)		8000.00
5th July	Vehicle (ABC 123)	(paid by Bank)	8000.00	
6th July	Acc. Depr. (ABC 123)	(to depreciation motor pool)		2000.00
6th July	Depreciation (motor pool)	(from vehicle ABC 123)	2000.00	
7th July	Depreciation (motor pool)	(to profit & loss)		2000.00
7th July	Profit & Loss account	(from depreciation motor pool)	2000.00	

figure 16.3

Figure 16.4 shows the effect on the accounts after the journal entries have been posted.

Nominal Ledger - Year 1

Bank

Date	Reference	Debit	Credit
5th July	to buy vehicle ABC 123		8000.00
Totals			8000.00
7th July	Balance b/d		8000.00

Vehicle (ABC 123)

Date	Reference	Debit	Credit
5th July	paid by bank	8000.00	
Totals		8000.00	
7th July	Balance b/d	8000.00	

Acc. Depr. (ABC 123)

Date	Reference	Debit	Credit
6th July	to depreciation motor pool		2000.00
Totals			2000.00
7th July	Balance b/d		2000.00

Depreciation (motor pool)

Date	Reference	Debit	Credit
6th July	from acc. depr. ABC 123	2000.00	
7th July	balance to Profit & Loss		2000.00
7th July	Closed		

Profit & Loss Account

Date	Reference	Debit	Credit
7th July	from depreciation (motor pool)	2000.00	
Totals		2000.00	
7th July	Balance b/d	2000.00	

figure 16.4

The Profit & Loss account shows a £2000 loss (more money has gone to expenses in the form of depreciation than has been received from sales).

This makes sense because we started off with £8000 worth of assets but by the end of the year they were only worth £6000.

If we also made sales for the year of £10,000 then we would be showing a profit of £8000 (£10,000 sales less £2000 loss due to depreciation).

This profit is known as the **book value**. Whilst you can depreciate your assets by any amount you like (provided it is a fair assessment on your part), for **tax purposes** the depreciation is added back again (this 'adding back' is not part of the double-entry system so no journal entries are needed).

The Inland Revenue then allows a certain proportion of the value of your fixed assets to be deducted from the taxable profit when it comes to calculating income tax (or corporation tax for Limited Companies). These deductions are called **Capital Allowances**.

Since we are showing a loss of £2000 in figure 16.4 we won't be claiming any capital allowances this year.

The result of this is that the book value of your fixed assets may be entirely different from the value held by the Inland Revenue. In this example, the book value of the vehicle is £6000 but the Inland Revenue will still hold the original value of £8000.

If the capital allowance on fixed assets is 25% (which is typical) and we make a profit in the following year, we will claim 25% off the Inland Revenue value (ie. £2000).

The book value (showing the true position to the business) is reduced by 25% each year regardless of any capital allowances taken, so the asset will have a book value of £4500 at the end of the second year (25% off £6000) whereas the Inland Revenue will hold a value of £6000.

One problem remains: what happens if we sell or 'write off' a fixed asset?

• **If an asset is written off** it means we have decided that it no longer has any value. This is dealt with by a credit from the asset's accumulated depreciation account and a debit to the depreciation expense account (motor pool). In other words, we will be including the remainder of the asset's value as an expense in one go.

The amount to debit and credit is the difference between its original cost price and its accumulated depreciation (eg. if the asset cost £8000 and its depreciation was £7800, we would credit the accumulated depreciation account £200).

Since both the vehicle account and accumulated depreciation account will then equal each other (£8000 in this example), we can close them both by debiting the accumulated depreciation account and crediting the asset's account with the original value of the asset.

• **If we sold the asset at its current book value** then we must account for the money received with a debit to the bank (or cash) account and a credit from the asset's accumulated depreciation account. We can then close the asset and its accumulated depreciation account as described in the previous paragraph. Unlike writing off an asset, the depreciation (motor pool) account won't be affected in this case because there is no loss involved.

• **If we sold the asset at a loss** (on its current book value) we must still account for the money received (as in the previous paragraph). We can then use the method described earlier to write off the remaining value.

• **If we sold the asset at a profit** we would credit the accumulated depreciation account by the amount necessary to balance it with its associated asset account (we can then write them off as previously described). We also need to account for the profit so we would credit a **capital gains account**. Finally we would debit the bank account for the full selling price.

The capital gains account only applies to this year because it is a **revenue account** and its balance must be transferred to the profit & loss account to close it (the term 'revenue' means sales or income of the business).

Just like depreciation, capital gains or losses for the year will be removed from the profit & loss balance when it comes to calculating income tax, but we needn't do anything in the books to show this since it is not part of the double-entry system.

Any **loss** or **gain** on a fixed asset when it is disposed of, is dealt with by the Inland Revenue via something called a **balancing charge**. This is necessary since the rules for calculating capital gains are different from income tax.

A balancing charge can best be explained by a simple example: If you bought a vehicle for £8000 and claimed a capital allowance for the first year of £2000, then sold it at the start of the second year for £4000, it would result in an overall loss of £2000 on the asset. This loss is accounted for on your self-assessment Income Tax return by entering it in the 'balancing charge' box (using brackets to show it is a loss - ie. negative).

Gains and losses on fixed assets shown in a Profit & Loss account are usually referred to as 'extraordinary items', and accountants will generally highlight them because they may well increase or decrease the profit, yet have no bearing on the business's normal trading figures. If a limited company sells an asset for a vast profit, the profits shown as far as the books are concerned will be greatly inflated. Since this is unlikely to happen every year it needs to be pointed out to the shareholders.

Strictly speaking, when a fixed asset is sold or disposed of the date of the sale should be taken into account when working out the final depreciation: if an asset is bought for £8000, depreciates by 25% to £6000 by the end of year 1 and is subsequently written off **half way** through year 2, then we need to account for 6 months depreciation before calculating the final loss on disposal of the vehicle.

To see this in action we will continue with our first example. Figure 16.5 shows the balance sheet at the end of year 1 (taken from the nominal ledger in figure 16.4).

Balance Sheet - end of year 1			
Fixed Assets		**Liabilities**	
Vehicle (ABC 123)	8000.00	Bank overdraft	8000.00
Less acc. depr.	(2000.00)		
Total Fixed Assets	6000.00		
		Equity	
		Capital (loss on depreciation)	(2000.00)
Balance	**6000.00**		**6000.00**

figure 16.5

We have assumed that just before we compiled the balance sheet we transferred the loss from the profit & loss account to the owner's capital account (hence the 'Capital' entry under equity).

The vehicles original value has been kept intact, the accumulated depreciation has then been deducted and we have shown the balance on a new line ('Total Fixed Assets').

In practice, we are likely to have many other fixed assets. We do not want to clutter up the balance sheet with all this detail, therefore fixed assets are usually included as a **separate report** with just the overall balances shown in the balance sheet.

If a large company owns many fixed assets (eg. 20 company cars) then the separate report will only include the total value of these (the 'motor pool') and their associated depreciation accounts. It will also do the same for the other types of fixed asset (eg. buildings and land, equipment, and fixtures & fittings). It all depends on what type of (and how many) fixed assets you own.

Continuing with our example, we will sell the vehicle for £3000 half way through year 2. This means we need to calculate 6 months of depreciation in order to work out how much is being written off after the sale.

The equation is fairly simple:

12.5% of £6000=**£750** (this is 6 months depreciation based on a rate of 25% per year).

£6000-£750=**£5250** (the value of the vehicle less depreciation just before we sell it).

£5250-£3000=**£2250** (this is the value of the vehicle less the selling price which gives us the value to be written off in order to close the asset's account).

Journal - Year 2				
Date	Account	Reference	Debit	Credit
5th January	Bank	(opening balance)		8000.00
5th January	Vehicle (ABC 123)	(opening balance)	8000.00	
5th January	Acc. Depr. (ABC 123)	(opening balance)		2000.00
5th January	Capital	(opening balance)	2000.00	
5th July	Vehicle (ABC 123)	(accumulated depreciation)		2000.00
5th July	Acc. Depr. (ABC 123)	(balance to vehicle ABC 123)	2000.00	
6th July	Vehicle (ABC 123)	(current depreciation)		750.00
6th July	Depreciation (motor pool)	(from vehicle ABC 123)	750.00	
6th July	Vehicle (ABC 123)	(sold vehicle)		3000.00
6th July	Bank	(from selling vehicle ABC 123)	3000.00	
7th July	Depreciation (motor pool)	(to Profit & Loss)		750.00
7th July	Profit & Loss	(from depreciation - motor pool)	750.00	
7th July	Vehicle (ABC 123)	(loss on sale)		2250.00
7th July	Profit & Loss	(loss on sale of vehicle ABC 123)	2250.00	
8th July	Profit & Loss	(balance to capital account)		3000.00
8th July	Capital	(from Profit & Loss)	3000.00	

figure 16.6

The full journal for year 2 is shown above (*figure 16.6*).

The first section (dated 5th January) covers the opening balances for the year.

The second section (5th July) shows the accumulated depreciation account transferred to the vehicle account.

The third section (6th July) shows the 6 months depreciation of the vehicle (£750) and selling of the vehicle (£3000). We have credited the vehicles account directly because the account is being closed this year.

The fourth section (7th July) shows the transfer of current depreciation to the profit & loss account. It also shows the loss we sustained from selling the vehicle below its book value.

The last section (8th July) shows the transfer of the profit & loss account to the capital account.

Figure 16.7 shows the complete ledger after the journal entries have been posted.

Nominal Ledger - Year 2			
Bank			
Date	Reference	Debit	Credit
5th January	Opening balance		8000.00
6th July	Selling a vehicle	3000.00	
Totals		3000.00	8000.00
8th July	Balance b/d		5000.00

Vehicle (ABC 123)			
Date	Reference	Debit	Credit
5th January	Opening balance	8000.00	
5th July	Accumulated depreciation		2000.00
6th July	Current depreciation		750.00
6th July	Sold vehicle		3000.00
7th July	Loss on sale		2250.00
Totals		8000.00	8000.00
8th July	Closed		

Acc. Depr. (ABC 123)			
5th January	Opening balance		2000.00
5th July	Balance to vehicle ABC 123	2000.00	
	Closed		

Depreciation (motor pool)			
6th July	Vehicle ABC 123	750.00	
7th July	balance to Profit & Loss		750.00
	Closed		

Profit & Loss Account			
Date	Reference	Debit	Credit
7th July	Depreciation (motor pool)	750.00	
7th July	Loss on sale of vehicle ABC 123	2250.00	
8th July	balance to capital account		3000.00
Totals		3000.00	3000.00
8th July	Closed		

Capital Account			
5th January	Opening balance	2000.00	
8th July	From Profit & Loss	3000.00	
Totals		5000.00	
8th July	Balance b/d	5000.00	

figure 16.7

As you can see, the bank overdraft has been reduced to £5000 (because it gained £3000 by the sale of the vehicle) and this is reflected by an overall loss of £5000 in the owner's equity (the capital account).

The Profit & Loss account shows a loss of £3000 for the year but it is obvious this was through no particular fault of the owner's trading ability: it is clear it was derived through depreciation and the writing off of an asset.

There is no point in illustrating the balance sheet here because it will only contain 2 accounts and they balance each other out (bank and capital).

The assets side of the balance sheet would normally be expanded by using different headings to separate the current assets from the fixed assets. The same is true of liabilities. These can be split into **current liabilities** and **long term liabilities**.

Figure 16.8 has no bearing on the figures we have produced so far, but shows a typical layout including both current and fixed assets and current and long term liabilities.

Balance Sheet					
Assets			**Liabilities**		
Current			**Current**		
Petty Cash	150.00		VAT Accruals		500.00
Bank	562.00		Creditors		1600.00
Cash in hand	250.00		**Total Current Liabilities**		**2100.00**
Pre-payments	50.00				
Debtors	250.00		**Long term (see note 2)**		
Total Current Assets	**1262.00**		Mortgage		23000.00
Fixed (see note 1)			**Total Liabilities**		**25100.00**
Office	25000.00				
Vehicles	6000.00		**Equity**		
Equipment	2000.00		Profit & Loss		5662.00
Fixtures & Fittings	1500.00		Capital		5000.00
Total Fixed Assets	**34500.00**		**Total Equity**		**10662.00**
Balance	**35762.00**				**35762.00**

figure 16.8

Where it states 'see note 1' and 'see note 2' in figure 16.8, it is referring to the reports we mentioned earlier (page 118). These reports would accompany the balance sheet and contain more detail on the fixed assets and long term liabilities.

Current liabilities are similar to current assets in that they are active accounts: money flows in and out of them during the year and we need to check the balances often to ensure we can cover our debts.

Long term liabilities cover items like mortgages and other long term loans (ie. those that are taken out for more than a year).

Vertical Balance Sheets

Figure 16.8 is an example of an **horizontal** balance sheet. As explained previously, we have used this layout because it makes it easy to compile (debit balances on the left and credit balances on the right).

Figure 16.9 on the next page shows an alternative display. It is known as a **vertical** balance sheet. In practice, it is the most common layout (see chapter 9, pages 45/6).

Balance Sheet (vertical layout)		
Assets		
Current		
Petty Cash	150.00	
Bank	562.00	
Cash in hand	250.00	
Pre-payments	50.00	
Debtors	250.00	
Total Current Assets		**1262.00**
Fixed (see note 1)		
Office	25000.00	
Vehicles	6000.00	
Equipment	2000.00	
Fixtures & Fittings	1500.00	
Total Fixed Assets		**34500.00**
Total Assets		**35762.00**
Liabilities		
Current		
VAT Accruals	500.00	
Creditors	1600.00	
Total Current Liabilities	**2100.00**	
Long term (see note 2)		
Mortgage	**23000.00**	
Total Liabilities		**25100.00**
Equity		
Profit & Loss	5662.00	
Capital	5000.00	
Total Equity		**10662.00**
Total Liabilities & Equity		**35762.00**

figure 16.9

A vertical balance sheet is useful if you want to include
the previous year's results for comparison. You just add
extra columns and include the year at the top.

A large companies balance sheet will devote a page or more to each section and include many extra reports (known as 'notes to the accounts'). The idea is to present the information in as concise a way as possible in the balance sheet, then break it down into more manageable chunks via extra reports.

Depreciation methods

So far we have used the 'declining balance method'. We fix a percentage for depreciation and use this every year. The value of the asset keeps declining but until we dispose of it, it will never get to zero.

The other main method is the 'straight line method'. Instead of a percentage, an actual amount is deducted each year for depreciation based on the estimated life of the asset: if you buy an asset for £1000 and decide it will last for five years then the depreciation will be fixed at £200 a year (£1000/5=£200). At the end of five years the asset will have a book value of zero and can be written off directly from its accumulated depreciation account.

There are many other methods, but whichever way you choose will be entirely independent of the rates allowed by the Inland Revenue for capital allowances.

Note: First year capital allowances were doubled (to 50%) for the 1997/98 tax year and have been set at 40% for a year from July 1998 (ie. it can only be applied to newly purchased fixed assets - and then, only for a year. Allowances on assets bought before April 1997 and those more than one year old remain at 25%). As far as your books are concerned, assets should still be shown to depreciate at a rate equivalent to their real loss in value (eg. 25%).

17 • Adjustments

Before you close your books at the end of a year certain adjustments may need to be made in order to reflect a true profit or loss.

Most of these adjustments will be made to your expenses.

There are many possibilities, but what matters is the reason for an adjustment.

Pre-payments

An example of a **pre-payment** adjustment is insurance where the yearly premium covers part of one year and part of the next. Suppose your accounting year runs from July to June the following year, but your buildings insurance runs from January to December. When you enter the expense in January only six months of it will be used for the current year; the other six months worth will pertain to the following year's expenses.

We therefore need to split the expense between an 'Insurance Account' (for this year's portion) and another to cover the portion for next year (called 'Pre-paid Insurance' or something similar). Only the portion in the Insurance account will appear in this year's Profit & Loss account.

The Pre-paid account will be shown as a current asset in the balance sheet and carried forward to the following year.

At the start of the following year we will transfer the Pre-paid account's balance to the Insurance account so it will be included in that year's Profit & Loss as an expense.

Figure 17.1 shows the journal entries for the first year.
The first transaction credits the bank account and debits
the insurance account for the full amount. The second
transaction transfers half from insurance to pre-payments.
The third transaction closes the Insurance account by
transferring it to the Profit & Loss account and the last
transaction closes the Profit & Loss account by
transferring it to the owner's Capital account.

Journal - Year 1				
Date	Account	Reference	Debit	Credit
1st January	Bank	(to insurance)		100.00
1st January	Insurance	(from bank)	100.00	
30th June	Insurance	(to pre-payments)		50.00
30th June	Pre-payments	(6 months insurance)	50.00	
30th June	Insurance	(to Profit & Loss)		50.00
30th June	Profit & Loss	(from Insurance)	50.00	
30th June	Profit & Loss	(to Capital)		50.00
30th June	Capital	(from Profit & Loss)	50.00	

figure 17.1

Figure 17.2 shows the first year's balance sheet.

Balance Sheet - end of year 1			
Assets		**Liabilities**	
Pre-payments	50.00	Bank overdraft	100.00
		Equity	
		Capital	(50.00)
Balance	**50.00**		**50.00**

figure 17.2

At the start of the following year the pre-payments
account will be entered in the journal as an opening
balance and then immediately transferred to the
Insurance account (figure 17.3 shows only the relevant
journal entries).

Journal - Year 2				
Date	Account	Reference	Debit	Credit
1st July	Bank	(opening balance)		100.00
1st July	Pre-payments	(opening balance)	50.00	
1st July	Capital	(opening balance)	50.00	
1st July	Pre-payments	(to insurance)		50.00
1st July	Insurance	(from pre-payments)	50.00	

figure 17.3

The result of this is that the insurance premium paid last year has now been accounted for in full as an expense (albeit over two years).

You can apply this example to any expense item which is paid for in one year but not used up until the following (or later) year. Another example of a pre-payment which may need adjusting is rent paid in advance.

It is important to decide if an expense covers more than one year and therefore treat part of it as a pre-payment for the following year otherwise you will be overstating your expenses.

Provisions

Another adjustment that may need to be made is a **Provision**.

Provisions include items where an expense has been incurred but the supplier has not yet sent an invoice to you.

A typical example is where you use an accountant to look after your books. The accountant will not be able to work out your bill until the books have been finalised; but the books can't be finalised until the bill is known!, so an estimate is entered instead. This estimate is included as an expense item in the Profit & Loss account; therefore a 'provision' is being made for it.

At some point during the following year you will receive the proper invoice. The estimate and final invoice are then subtracted from one another and the difference can be entered as a credit or debit depending on whether the estimate was more or less than the final invoice.

We will illustrate this with a simple example: you have sales for year 1 of £10,000 and the accountant estimates that the bill for book-keeping will be £500. Figure 17.4 shows the journal entries and figure 17.5 shows the balance sheet.

Journal - Year 1				
Date	Account	Reference	Debit	Credit
1st January	Sales	(to bank)		10000.00
1st January	Bank	(from sales)	10000.00	
31st December	Creditors (accountant)	(provision for Book-keeping)		500.00
31st December	Book-keeping provision	(from year 1 estimate)	500.00	
31st December	Book-keeping provision	(to Profit & Loss)		500.00
31st December	Sales	(to Profit & Loss)	10000.00	
31st December	Profit & Loss	(sales less expenses)		9500.00
31st December	Profit & Loss	(to Capital)	9500.00	
31st December	Capital	(from Profit & Loss)		9500.00

figure 17.4

Balance Sheet - end of year 1			
Assets		Liabilities	
Bank	10000.00	Creditors (accountant)	500.00
		Equity	
		Capital	9500.00
Balance	10000.00		10000.00

figure 17.5

The accountant is a creditor of the business because the estimate will not be paid until the final bill is sent.

During year 2 you receive the final bill for £550 and decide to pay it. The accountant has under-estimated the bill so a journal entry is made to account for the extra £50 expense (*figure 17.6*).

Journal - Year 2				
Date	Account	Reference	Debit	Credit
1st January	Bank	(opening balance)	10000.00	
1st January	Creditors	(opening balance)		500.00
1st January	Capital	(opening balance)		9500.00
1st July	Creditors (accountant)	(to Book-keeping year 1)		50.00
1st July	Book-keeping	(from year 1 difference)	50.00	
2nd July	Bank	(to pay accountant)		550.00
2nd July	Creditors (accountant)	(from bank)	550.00	
31st December	Book-keeping	(to Profit & Loss)		50.00
31st December	Profit & Loss	(from Book-keeping)	50.00	
31st December	Profit & Loss	(to Capital)		50.00
31st December	Capital	(from Profit & Loss)	50.00	

figure 17.6

One transaction is needed to cover the difference between the estimate and final bill (entered on 1st July) and another to actually pay it (entered on 2nd July).

The Profit & Loss account shows a £50 loss (due to the under-estimate of the charges for year 1) and this has been transferred to the Capital account. The Creditors' account has a zero balance because you have now paid the accountant. Figure 17.7 shows the final balance sheet.

Balance Sheet - end of year 2			
Assets		Liabilities	
Bank	9450.00		
		Equity	
		Capital	9450.00
Balance	9450.00		9450.00

figure 17.7

This assumes of course that the accountant doesn't make a charge for keeping your books for year 2 (otherwise a further provision will be entered for year 2 and so on).

A further example of a provision concerns staff wages. If your financial year ends half way through a pay period then provision should be made to cover the portion of the wages due up to the end of the year. This operates in exactly the same way as the previous example.

Bad Debts 1 (Real or likely bad debts)

If you think a customer is unlikely to pay an invoice or a customer has been declared bankrupt and there is no money left to pay the debt then a bad debts account can be opened to cover it as an expense against the current year's profits. This is known as a **direct write-off**.

When the original invoice was sent, a credit will have been made from the sales account and a debit to the customer's account. To write-off the bad debt, a credit is made to the customer's account, and a debit to an account called 'Bad Debts'. This is then transferred to the Profit & Loss account where it is seen as an expense of the business.

The result is that the bad debt has been included in the year's profit & loss figures and closed. The customer's account will also have been closed (assuming it was the only debt from that customer).

If a sales ledger and associated control accounts are being used (see chapter 12) then a further journal entry is needed to credit the sales ledger control account and debit the nominal ledger debtors' account.

If during the following or later year the debt is recovered from the customer then all we need do is enter the original transaction again in the new set of books, crediting sales and debiting the customer as in a normal credit transaction. (To make it clear we could also include the original invoice number in the reference and add a further comment to explain it).

Bad Debts 2 (General reserve for bad debts)

Provision can also be made to cover a general estimate of bad debts for the year. This is different from 'direct write-offs' explained on the previous page since it cannot be set directly against your tax liability for the year.

If after a period of trading you discover that on average 5% (or whatever) of your credit sales are usually written off as bad debts then a bad debts **reserve** account can be opened in order to give a more accurate indication of your real sales for the year.

You will also need a bad debts expense account (as described on the previous page: 'Bad Debts 1') in order to keep the general reserve account separate from it.

The real bad debts should be subtracted from the estimate to get a more accurate total.

Because we are not dealing with a specific customer you only need to credit the reserve account and debit the profit & loss account (if the estimate is greater than the actual bad debts, and vice-versa if more real bad debts were sustained than the estimate). In subsequent years the bad debts reserve account will only need slight adjustments to keep within the percentage.

Keeping a reserve account for bad debts is only of any value if it represents a significant amount of your sales, and even then only if your business suffers from the odd major or minor increase in bad debts. This is because the bad debts expense account already shows the true figures, so all a reserve account will do is even out the estimated profit or loss.

An example will help to clarify both types of bad debt account.

In the first year you issue 3 invoices totalling £10,000. The first invoice (for £500) is to a customer who is subsequently declared bankrupt with no assets during that year.

The second invoice for £9,250 is part-paid during the year. The third invoice, for £250, will not be paid because you have heard that the customer is in financial trouble. You therefore decide to write it off (the first and third invoices represent 'bad debt 1' examples).

Due to market research you have also decided that 10% of your sales are unlikely to be paid due to bad debts (this is the 'bad debt 2' example).

We will also assume that you are using a sales ledger and control accounts to track the individual customers.

Your first entries will therefore be made in the **sales book** (*figure 17.8*).

Sales Book - Year 1				
Date	Account	Reference	Debit	Credit
20th April	Sales	SB1		500.00
20th April	A Smith	SB1	500.00	
20th April	Sales	SB2		9250.00
20th April	B Smith	SB2	9250.00	
20th April	Sales	SB3		250.00
20th April	C Smith	SB3	250.00	
Total sales for April			10000.00	10000.00

figure 17.8

B Smith then pays off £9000 of the £9,250 invoice. This is made in the **receivables book** (*figure 17.9*).

Receivables Book - Year 1

Date	Account	Reference	Debit	Credit
22nd April	B Smith	SB2 (part-paid)		9000.00
22nd April	Bank	SB2 (part-paid)	9000.00	
Total paid in April			**9000.00**	9000.00

figure 17.9

We are now in a position to update the control accounts for the sales and nominal ledgers. £1000 more has been invoiced than has been received so we credit the sales ledger control account and debit the nominal ledger debtors control account (this is entered in the **journal** - *figure 17.10*).

Journal - Year 1

Date	Account	Reference	Debit	Credit
30th April	Sales Ledger Control	April invoices less receipts		1000.00
30th April	Debtors Control	(from Sales Ledger)	1000.00	

figure 17.10

'A Smith' is then declared bankrupt so we credit the 'A Smith' account (to close it) and debit the bad debts expense account using the **sales book**. We also decide that 'C Smith' is unlikely to pay up so we do the same thing (*figure 17.11*).

Sales Book - Year 1

Date	Account	Reference	Debit	Credit
20th April	Sales	SB1		500.00
20th April	A Smith	SB1	500.00	
20th April	Sales	SB2		9250.00
20th April	B Smith	SB2	9250.00	
20th April	Sales	SB3		250.00
20th April	C Smith	SB3	250.00	
Totals for April			**10000.00**	**10000.00**
1st May	A Smith	SB1		500.00
1st May	Bad Debts (bankrupt)	SB1	500.00	
1st May	C Smith	SB2		250.00
1st May	Bad Debts (probable)	SB2	250.00	
Totals for May			**750.00**	**750.00**

figure 17.11

Further entries are also needed in the **journal** to update the control accounts and transfer the sales and bad debts to the Profit & Loss account (*figure 17.12*).

Journal - Year 1				
Date	Account	Reference	Debit	Credit
30th April	Sales Ledger Control	April invoices less receipts		1000.00
30th April	Debtors Control	(from Sales Ledger)	1000.00	
1st May	Sales Ledger Control	May invoices less receipts	750.00	
1st May	Debtors Control	(from Sales Ledger)		750.00
1st May	Sales	(to Profit & Loss)	10000.00	
1st May	Profit & Loss	(from Sales)		10000.00
1st May	Bad Debts	(to Profit & Loss)		750.00
1st May	Profit & Loss	(from Bad Debts)	750.00	

figure 17.12

Figure 17.13 shows the sales ledger.

Sales Ledger			
A Smith			
Date	Reference	Debit	Credit
20th April	SB1	500.00	
1st May	SB1 (bad debt-bankrupt)		500.00
Totals		500.00	500.00
1st May	**Closed**		
B Smith			
Date	Reference	Debit	Credit
20th April	SB2	9250.00	
22nd April	SB2 (part-paid)		9000.00
Totals		9250.00	9000.00
1st May	Balance b/d	**250.00**	0.00
C Smith			
Date	Reference	Debit	Credit
20th April	SB3	250.00	
1st May	SB3 (bad debt-probable)		250.00
Totals		250.00	250.00
1st May	**Balance b/d (zero)**	0	0
Control Account			
Date	Reference	Debit	Credit
30th April	April invoices less receipts		1000.00
1st May	May invoices less receipts	750.00	
Totals		750.00	1000.00
1st May	Balance b/d	0.00	**250.00**

figure 17.13

Figure 17.14 shows the nominal ledger.

Nominal Ledger

Bank

Date	Reference	Debit	Credit
22nd April	SB2	9000.00	

Sales

Date	Reference	Debit	Credit
20th April	SB1		500.00
20th April	SB2		9250.00
20th April	SB3		250.00
Totals			10000.00
1st May	Balance b/d		10000.00
1st May	Transferred to Profit & Loss	10000.00	

Bad Debts

Date	Reference	Debit	Credit
1st May	SB1 (A Smith - bankrupt)	500.00	
1st May	SB3 (C Smith - probable)	250.00	
Totals		750.00	
1st May	Balance b/d	750.00	
1st May	Transferred to Profit & Loss		750.00

Profit & Loss

Date	Reference	Debit	Credit
1st May	from Sales		10000.00
1st May	from Bad Debts	750.00	
Totals		750.00	10000.00
1st May	Balance b/d		9250.00

Debtors control

Date	Reference	Debit	Credit
30th April	(from Sales Ledger)	1000.00	
1st May	(from Sales Ledger)		750.00
Totals		1000.00	750.00
1st May	Balance b/d	250.00	

figure 17.14

We can now show how the bad debts reserve account fits into the picture: we estimated that 10% of the sales are unlikely to be recovered which represents a value of £1000 in this example. £750 has already been written off therefore a reserve of £250 needs to be set up.

This is a straightforward transaction entered in the journal which credits the bad debts reserve account and debits the Profit & Loss account.

Figure 17.15 shows the final nominal ledger for year 1.

Nominal Ledger			
Bank			
Date	**Reference**	**Debit**	**Credit**
22nd April	SB2	9000.00	
Sales			
Date	**Reference**	**Debit**	**Credit**
20th April	SB1		500.00
20th April	SB2		9250.00
20th April	SB3		250.00
Totals			10000.00
1st May	Balance b/d		10000.00
1st May	Transferred to Profit & Loss	10000.00	
Bad Debts			
Date	**Reference**	**Debit**	**Credit**
1st May	SB1 (A Smith - bankrupt)	500.00	
1st May	SB3 (C Smith - probable)	250.00	
Totals		750.00	
1st May	Balance b/d	750.00	
1st May	Transferred to Profit & Loss		750.00
Bad Debts Reserve			
Date	**Reference**	**Debit**	**Credit**
1st May	Estimated bad debts		250.00
Profit & Loss			
Date	**Reference**	**Debit**	**Credit**
1st May	Sales		10000.00
1st May	Bad Debts	750.00	
1st May	Bad Debts Reserve	250.00	
Totals		1000.00	10000.00
1st May	Balance b/d		9000.00
Debtors control			
Date	**Reference**	**Debit**	**Credit**
30th April	(from Sales Ledger)	1000.00	
1st May	(from Sales Ledger)		750.00
Totals		1000.00	750.00
1st May	Balance b/d	250.00	

figure 17.15

The bad debts **reserve** cannot be included as an expense against income tax therefore it must be added back again before the tax liability can be calculated. However, this aspect is not part of the double-entry system so no journal entries are needed (suitable boxes are included in the income tax self-assessment forms for these figures which is why we need to keep the real bad debts separate from the general reserve).

Figure 17.16 shows the year 1 balance sheet (we have transferred the profit to the capital account).

Balance Sheet - end of year 1			
Assets		**Liabilities**	
Bank	9000.00	Bad Debts Reserve	250.00
Debtors	250.00		
		Equity	
		Capital	9000.00
Balance	**9250.00**		**9250.00**

figure 17.16

During year 2 we make credit sales for a further £10,000 and suffer no losses due to bad debts. £9,000 of the sales are duly paid during the year so the bank account will show a balance of £18,000. The debtors' account will increase to £1,250 and the capital account will increase to £19,000 (opening balance of £9,000 plus a new profit of £10,000 with no bad debts or expenses).

As you can see, the books balance (assets of £18,000 in the bank plus £1,250 of debtors on one side, and liabilities of £250 reserves plus an equity of £19,000 on the other).

If we still estimate that 10% of the credit sales will turn out to be bad debts then we need to increase the reserve by £750 to cover this, so a journal entry is made crediting the reserve and debiting the Profit & Loss account.

Figure 17.17 shows the final balance sheet for year 2.

Balance Sheet - end of year 2			
Assets		Liabilities	
Bank	18000.00	Bad Debts Reserve	1000.00
Debtors	1250.00		
		Equity	
		Capital	18250.00
Balance	19250.00		19250.00

figure 17.17

Other Reserves

Reserve accounts can be set up for many things in order
to show a truer picture of a business. The important thing
to remember is that they have no effect on the tax
liability even if they are included in the Profit & Loss
account.

Typical examples are reserves for replacing capital items
such as vehicles and equipment and reserves to cover
legal expenses.

Whatever reserves you may want to set up they all use
the same logic as the bad debt reserve ie. credit the
reserve account and debit the capital, Profit & Loss or
any other equity account (in the case of a limited
company the debit will be a distribution from the
appropriation account - see chapter 15).

These accounts are generally used for information only;
therefore, if a reserve of £1000 has been set up to replace
an asset, then, when the asset is finally bought, a real
transaction will be needed (ie. credit the bank and debit
the asset's account) and an adjustment will also be
needed to correct the reserve account (ie. debit the
reserve and credit the relevant equity or capital account).

Accruals

An example of an adjustment which can occur on both the income and expense side of your books concerns **Accruals**.

If you have some money held in a deposit account, then that money will earn interest. If at the end of the year you have not received a statement for the deposit account then you will need to account for the interest accruing to the end of the year (hence the term 'Accrual').

The same applies if you have borrowed some money.

This works in exactly the same way as a provision; ie. you need to make provision for the interest owing, then make an adjustment in the following year to account for any difference.

Your final VAT return for the year is an accrual since it probably won't be paid until a month after the year has ended but provision for it will need to be entered before the books are closed.

Goodwill

A goodwill account can be set up if you decide that a business is worth more than that shown in the equity section of the balance sheet. In other words, if the business was to be sold as a going concern and the equity was say, £10,000 but you actually valued the business (because of its turnover and customer loyalty) at £12,000 then the extra £2000 can be shown on the balance sheet under a 'goodwill' account.

All we need do is make a journal entry crediting your capital account and debiting the goodwill account (ie. we are increasing the assets of the business and also your equity in it).

This can also be applied to partnerships, in which case the goodwill aspect can be kept in a separate capital account for each partner. This will help keep track of the goodwill portion of a partner's capital, especially if the portions are not equal.

Only a single goodwill **asset** account needs to be kept in either case.

As a simple example, suppose a business was started by two partners with no money and no assets, but for whatever reason they decided that it had a goodwill value of £1000. Furthermore they also decided on a 40/60 percentage split of the goodwill between the partners.

Figure 17.18 shows the journal, figure 17.19 shows the ledger and figure 17.20 shows the balance sheet.

Journal				
Date	Account	Reference	Debit	Credit
30th April	Goodwill	to partners capital	1000.00	
30th April	Partner A (40% goodwill)	from goodwill		400.00
30th April	Partner B (60% goodwill)	from goodwill		600.00

figure 17.18

Nominal Ledger			
Goodwill			
Date	Reference	Debit	Credit
30th April	to partners	1000.00	
Partner A (40% goodwill)			
Date	Reference	Debit	Credit
30th April	from Goodwill		400.00
Partner B (60% goodwill)			
Date	Reference	Debit	Credit
30th April	from Goodwill		600.00

figure 17.19

Balance Sheet			
Assets		Liabilities	
Goodwill	1000.00		
		Equity	
		Partner A (40% goodwill)	400.00
		Partner B (60% goodwill)	600.00
Balance	1000.00		1000.00

figure 17.20

If you re-value the goodwill at any time then further journal entries can be made to adjust it (eg. if the partners change the portions to 50% each then a journal transaction would be entered to credit partner A £100 and debit partner B the same amount).

If the partners eventually have separate capital accounts too, then typically the balance sheet would show the total equity with a note pointing to a further document showing the breakdown of each partner's capital.

Whatever form this extra document takes is fine since both it and the balance sheet are only reports (they are not a fundamental part of the double-entry system itself). All that matters is that enough accounts are used in the first place to make the reports easier to compile.

Suspense Accounts

If a trial balance shows a very slight error which can't immediately be accounted for, a single entry can be made in the journal to credit or debit an account called a suspense account in order to force the trial balance to balance. When the error is found, the suspense account can then be debited or credited back to zero, and reversing and correcting entries can be made to amend the mistake.

If the trial balance is fine, but one of the balances is not correct (and you don't know why) then a suspense account can be used to debit or credit the offending account - a typical example is petty cash: the account shows, say, a £50 debit balance, but the actual cash within it amounts to £45. In this case you would credit petty cash £5 and debit the suspense account £5. When you discover the reason for the missing £5, you can credit the suspense account and debit the correct account.

You can call a suspense account anything you like provided its use is made obvious.

18 • Inventories

An Inventory is a subsidiary ledger which is used to keep track of individual items. They can be opened for any number of things (eg. stock for re-sale, assets, investments, raw materials for manufacturing etc.).

They can work in the same way as other subsidiary ledgers (eg. sales and purchase ledgers) using control accounts to keep track of their overall value in the nominal ledger, but more typically they are **not** included directly within a double-entry system.

A stock control system is just such an example, the reason being that connecting it to the nominal ledger using control accounts requires a great deal of extra work not least because each transaction involves not only the **value** but also the **quantity** of stock bought or sold.

Stock control systems vary from business to business depending on the nature of the business, but as far as double-entry is concerned we already have the most important data regardless of whether a separate system is in use: this is the **stock account** described in chapter 13.

The same can be said for fixed assets described in chapter 16: it is far easier to use a few nominal ledger accounts to keep track of the overall value of a companies' vehicles, equipment and depreciation and keep a separate record of each asset somewhere else than attempt to link them together via control accounts.

It can be done of course, but it will only be of benefit (time-wise) if a computer is being used for the accounts (see chapter 20).

19 • Hints and Tips

Reconciling bank accounts

The term 'Reconciling' simply means checking a set of figures in the accounts with another set produced by someone else.

A typical example is checking your bank account entries in the nominal ledger with the statement of account sent by your bank.

Reconciling has nothing whatsoever to do with double-entry book-keeping but is one of the most important things any business should carry out to ensure their records are correct.

The simplest way of reconciling a bank account is to compare the account in your nominal ledger with the statement from the bank. Go through each entry in the ledger and mark it in some way if it also appears on the bank statement. You will also need to mark the entry on the bank statement too. What matters is that each reconciled entry agrees with both the reference (eg. cheque number) and amount on the statement.

Once you have finished, every entry should have a mark against it in both the ledger and the bank statement. This is an excellent double check on your book-keeping, it may also show up errors by the bank!

If an entry in the ledger doesn't appear on the bank statement it could be due to a number of reasons:

1. The payee hasn't yet cashed it.

2. The cheque has been lost in the post.

3. The entry in the ledger is a mistake.

In case 1, you simply wait until it appears on one of the following bank statements. If it still hasn't been cashed after six months then the original entry will need to be reversed and a new cheque written and entered again in the journal (see chapter 4 for details about reversing entries). The same applies to reason 2 though you need not wait six months since you can advise your bank to cancel the cheque. The reason for the six month period is simply that a cheque becomes worthless if it hasn't been cashed within that time limit.

If you discover the entry was a mistake (case 3 above) all you need is a reversing entry to correct it (see chapter 4).

If an entry appears on both the ledger and statement but is for the wrong amount then a reversing and correcting entry should be made (see chapter 4).

Finally, if an entry appears on the bank statement but **not** in the ledger, then you need to check that all the journal entries have been posted, if it still doesn't appear then either the bank has made a mistake or you have forgotten to enter the transaction in the ledger.

The Cash in Hand account

If you regularly receive a number of cheques, cash or credit card payments and pay them into a bank account in one go then it is a very good idea to open a **Cash in Hand account** in the nominal ledger. This account is sometimes referred to as an **Undeposited funds** account.

Whenever you receive a payment (which will eventually be banked) always debit the cash in hand account instead of the bank. When you eventually pay the money into the bank, credit cash in hand and debit the bank with the full amount paid in.

The logic of this is that you are paying the money into a temporary area (cash in hand) where it accumulates until you finally pay it into the bank in one go. This procedure has three important advantages and one minor disadvantage:

1. You will know how much there is (or should be!) to go into the bank by checking the cash in hand account's balance.

2. It will help when reconciling the bank account since the single transfers from cash in hand to the bank will tie in with the bank statement.

3. You can use the paying in slip's reference on the journal entry to the bank which will also help when reconciling.

The disadvantage is that you will need to enter an extra journal transaction each time you bank some money.

Bounced cheques/Unpaid cheques

If you pay a customers cheque into the bank and it is returned to you unpaid for some reason then you will need to reverse the original entry (see chapter 4). This will effectively make the customer a debtor again if the original entry for payment was made in the receivables book (see chapter 12). If you decide to try paying it in again then another entry will need to be made in the receivables book to show that the customer has paid.

If you are using the Cash in Hand account (see page 145) and decide to try paying in the cheque again you will still need a reversing entry but you will also need to credit the bank and debit the cash in hand account (you need to do this so that your ledger bank account will match the next bank statement when reconciling).

If the cheque is returned again (or has the words 'return to drawer' written on it - which means the bank is very unlikely to cash it), then you may need to look at this as a bad debt. A reversing entry will therefore be required (see chapter 4) as well as a transfer between the customers account and the bad debts account (see page 130).

Loans to the business

If the business receives a commercial loan (commercial means the lender will be charging interest on the loan) then a loan account will need to be opened in the nominal ledger (this is no different to any other account and you can call it what you like). The loan account will be credited with the amount, and the bank or wherever you pay it to will be debited.

You will also need an expense account to track the interest payable on the loan.

Every time a payment is made, two transactions will occur:

1. Debit the expense account and credit the loan account for the interest.

2. Debit the loan account and credit the bank account (or whichever account is being used to pay the loan) for the total paid.

Discounts

If you issue an invoice which includes a discount for
early payment (known as Early Settlement Discount) the
original invoice will still be entered in the sales book
with the full un-discounted amount.

If the customer takes up the discount, then two
transactions are needed:

1. Credit the customer's account for the discounted total
and debit the bank account (or whichever account you
are paying the money into).

2. Credit the customer's account with the actual discount
and debit the sales account.

It would also be useful to add a comment (a 'narrative' in
accounting terms) to the second transaction stating that it
was a discount (this will distinguish it from say, a credit
note for returned goods). Figure 19.1 shows the sales and
receivables books after all the transactions have taken
place (see chapter 12 for details on the sales ledger and
sales and receivables books).

Sales Book

Date	Account	Reference	Debit	Credit
20th April	Sales	SB1		100.00
20th April	J Smith	SB1	100.00	

Receivables Book

Date	Account	Reference	Debit	Credit
22nd April	J Smith	SB1		90.00
22nd April	Bank	SB1	90.00	
22nd April	J Smith	SB1-discount taken		10.00
22nd April	Sales	SB1-discount taken	10.00	

figure 19.1

The original invoice for £100 included a 10% discount if paid early (say, within 7 days), hence J Smith took advantage of this and paid £90. A look at J Smith's account will show a zero balance, but it will be obvious that the entries which made it up started with an invoice for £100 and within 2 days J Smith had paid up and taken the discount.

The sales account will show £90 credit and the bank will mirror this. The exact same applies in reverse if you take up a discount offered by a supplier.

Dedicated discount accounts can be opened instead (eg. debit the discount account instead of sales). Both are posted to the trading account to arrive at the net sales.

Discounts and VAT

Current legislation in the UK permits a business to calculate VAT on the discounted total of an invoice (eg. if you issue an invoice for £100 + VAT @ 17.5%, but offer an early settlement discount of 10%, then regardless of whether the discount is taken the final invoice total will be £100 + 17.5% VAT on £90 = £115.75). This means that whether the discount is taken or not, no adjustment is needed on the VAT portion of it.

Credit notes

If a customer returns some goods, you will issue the customer with a **credit note**. A credit note is a sales invoice in reverse (ie. a statement showing that you owe the customer some money, rather than the other way round). You will still use the same sales ledger journals but the customer will be credited and sales debited (see chapter 12 for details on the sales ledger and sales and receivables books).

If you receive a credit note from a supplier then you will debit the supplier's account and credit the original expense or stock account.

Stock valuation

Chapter 13 briefly refers to the valuation of stock at year end. There are four generally accepted methods of valuing stock (there are many others too, but we will stick to the main ones):

1. **Cost**: The stock left at the end of the year is valued at what it cost to buy. This can be hard to calculate if the stock was bought in different periods and at different prices since you need to keep track of each batch and how many are left in each one.

2. **FIFO**: First In First Out. This method assumes that you sell your stock in the order in which you bought it, ie. if you bought 100 widgets at £1 each in January, then another 100 at £1.10 in February, sold 100 in January and none in february the valuation would be 100 left at £1.10 each.

3. **LIFO**: Last In First Out. This is FIFO in reverse. Using the FIFO example, the final valuation would be 100 left at £1 each.

4. **Average**: The total price paid for the stock is divided by the total quantity bought. The result is then multiplied by the total quantity left at year end. Using the FIFO example, the final valuation would be 100 left at £1.05 each.

Whichever method you choose, a stock valuation should also be calculated at current market values because the golden rule is to choose whichever yields the lowest valuation. In other words if you choose the **average** method but find the current market value is lower then use the current market value (if the cost of widgets had dropped to 50p each by the year end it would be prudent to value the stock at 100 x 50p, instead of 100 x £1.05).

Flow of Funds

Figures 19.2 & 19.3 show the first and second year's balance sheets of the manufacturing example used in chapter 14.

Balance Sheet - at end of year 1			
Assets	(Debit balances)	**Liabilities**	(Credit balances)
Raw Materials	1000.00	Bank Overdraft	12000.00
Work in Progress	6000.00	**Equity**	
Stock (manufactured)	5000.00		
Balance	**12000.00**		**12000.00**

figure 19.2

Balance Sheet - at end of year 2			
Assets	(Debit balances)	**Liabilities**	(Credit balances)
Raw Materials	1800.00	Bank Overdraft	9000.00
Work in Progress	8200.00	**Equity**	
Stock (manufactured)	6000.00	Profit for the year	7000.00
Balance	**16000.00**		**16000.00**

figure 19.3

By comparing them, we can produce a 'flow of funds' statement. This is **not** to be confused with a 'cash flow' statement (explained on page 153).

The term 'funds' includes cash, but also refers to cash on credit (eg. your creditors and debtors).

By looking at the **increases** and **decreases** of the assets and liabilities over a period of time we can make assumptions about how the business is progressing.

The statement can be prepared vertically or horizontally. For our purposes, we shall show the horizontal version using the formula below:

If an **asset** account has **increased** (or a **liability** account has **decreased**) it is seen as a **use** of funds, and the **difference** is placed on the left side of the statement.

If a **liability** account has **increased** (or an **asset** account has **decreased**) it is seen as a **source** of funds, and the **difference** is placed on the right hand side.

The bank overdraft (a **liability**) has **decreased** by £3000, therefore it is placed on the left hand side. The three stock accounts (**assets**) have **increased**, so they too are placed on the left. The profit (a **liability**) has **increased**, so it is placed on the right (*figure 19.4*).

Flow of funds statement - year 2			
Uses		**Sources**	
Bank (reducing overdraft)	3000.00	Profit for the year	7000.00
Raw Materials	800.00		
Work in Progress	2200.00		
Stock (manufactured)	1000.00		
Balance	**7000.00**		**7000.00**

figure 19.4

In this example we only have one **source**: the profit for the year. We can immediately see how we have **used** this source of funds: £3000 has gone to the bank, and the rest has been split across (and thus increased) the balance in the three stock accounts.

Questions can now be asked about the business: could we have made a better return on the funds had we used the £3000 for another purpose (rather than reducing the bank overdraft)?. Have we produced more work in progress than we needed to? - and could these funds have been better spent on something else?

The flow of funds statement for year 1 will be identical to the balance sheet in figure 19.2. By comparing both year's flow of funds, we can see that the company is improving: the overdraft is reducing, profits are up, and funding for the three stock accounts is being reduced.

This is a very simple example. Because nothing was sold during the first year, the assumptions made in the last paragraph are a little premature. By the end of year three, the flow of funds statement would be far more meaningful.

Cash flow & Cash flow forecasting

The 'cash flow' of a business is a statement which analyses the income and expenditure of a business over a period of time. It is usually broken down into monthly segments. Each month, the opening cash balance is entered (this includes money in the bank, petty cash, cash in hand etc.). The revenue for the month is then added to this, and the expenses and purchases subtracted. The closing balance shows the cash situation at the end of the month. This then becomes the opening balance for the following month, and so on.

Cash flow forecasting is exactly the same, except that it is an estimate of income and expenditure in the future. The initial opening cash balance will be based on today's real figures, and the income and expenditure for each future month is usually based on existing figures with an adjustment made either way depending on how you see the future (eg. if sales have increased by 10% in the past year, then you will add 10% to your last sales figure to arrive at an estimate of future sales). This will give you an idea of the sort of funding you may need in the future.

20 • Computer Programs

This chapter does not cover specific computer accounting programs, instead it gives an overview of their general design.

A computer system

A computer system consists of **hardware** and **software**. The term **hardware** is used to describe the physical parts of a computer (the computer itself, the screen, the keyboard, the printer and many other devices). The **software** consists of the programs which are installed into the computer to make it do something useful (eg. an accounting program for your accounts and a 'word-processor' for writing letters).

The interface

The most important part of any software is the **interface**. This is the part which interacts with you on the computer screen.

If the interface is well designed you will have few problems, if it is poor you will keep referring to the manual. Try out as many programs as you can and compare their interfaces (eg. if you are VAT registered, does it have an obvious VAT section?, and if so, does it produce a dedicated report which at least tells you what to enter in each box of your VAT return).

The software

The best way to get to grips with a program is to run it alongside your previous system for a while. However, deciding on which program to buy in the first place can be a little daunting. The following list of questions should narrow down the choice a little (bear in mind your future as well as current requirements).

• Is there a limit on the maximum amounts I can enter (eg. £99,999.99)?, and what happens if I accidentally enter a larger figure? (try it out if you can - this is always a good test).

• Is there a limit on the number of transactions it can handle?

• Is there a limit on the number of accounts it can hold in each of the ledgers? (the nominal ledger is not usually a problem, but the sales ledger may be if you have 10,000 customers).

• Can I edit unposted journal entries? (if the answer is 'yes', then how easy is it to edit? - software varies enormously. You should be able to move freely around the entries within the same 'window' you entered them and alter what you like).

• Can I post the journal in batches, or must I post each transaction as I enter it?. Once an entry has been posted most programs will not allow you to change them. The best programs will allow you to enter and edit as many transactions as you like before posting them in one go to the ledger.

• Can I enter transactions in any date order, and will it sort them for me automatically? (this is useful if you tend to write up your accounts on a weekly basis. However, the program should check that you are not trying to enter something into a previous period).

• Can it handle batch invoice printing, and if so, can I edit and add to previously prepared but un-printed invoices? (this is vital if your customers order things on, say, a daily basis, but you do not normally send an invoice until the end of the month).

• Can I include free text within an invoice, or is it stock based only? (most software can be tailored to suit service and retail businesses, but it is worth checking).

• Can I design my own forms (eg. invoices), or do I have to buy pre-printed stationary? (it is also worth checking if you can include graphics within the design - eg. your logo).

• Can I export the information to other programs? (this may be a vital requirement if you decide to change your software - it could save you typing in the details of all your customers again).

• Can I use the program to run more than one set of accounts? (vital if you intend to use the program to look after other people's books).

• Is the program multi-user? (can one person produce invoices while another updates the purchase ledger? - do not be confused with the term 'multi-tasking', this is entirely different).

• How much do upgrades cost? (upgrades are usually essential - not only to fix problems within the software but also to keep it up to date with current accounting requirements. A typical example is the VAT return, this has altered 3 times since 1990).

• Can it handle more than one currency? (this may not seem important now, but in the near future you may have to account for the new european single currency as well as your own).

• Is the software supported by a telephone help-line, and if so what does it cost? Try telephoning the help-line (before you buy): how long do they take to answer?

Year 2000 (the millennium problem)

All modern computers have an internal clock which can cope with the millennium (and therefore, beyond), but some software is available which uses 2 digits for the year part of a date. These should be carefully scrutinised since the year 2000 will be shown as '00' on screen - this may be interpreted as the year 1900.

Most software will require a year start and end date for your accounts, so a program which uses 2 digits for the year will be obvious from the word go. The question is: will a '00' entry be sorted before or after the 1999 entries.

Double-entry accounting systems

Most programs include the nominal, sales and purchase ledgers. However, these may be sold separately as modules. This is especially true of programs designed for larger companies.

Many programs will require you to set up a 'chart of accounts' for the nominal ledger. These accounts are usually numbered according to their place in the balance sheet: accounts 1000 to 1999 for asset accounts, 2000 to 2999 for liability accounts, 3000 to 3999 for equity accounts, 4000 to 4999 for revenue accounts, and 5000 to 5999 for expense accounts.

The main purpose of this is to allow the software to place the accounts in the correct position on the balance sheet regardless of a credit or debit balance (brackets or minus signs will automatically be placed around a total where necessary).

Some of the best software lets you select an account type (instead of a number) - this is much easier to grasp. You can add accounts whenever you like, and inform the software that it is an asset, revenue or any other type of account.

Most programs run within a 'windows' environment. That is, different parts of the program can be displayed in a separate area of the screen simultaneously (eg. you can view your stock inventory and an invoice at the same time).

The main interface (sometimes referred to as the 'main menu') usually contains a set of basic options which let you into different parts of a program.

To keep the screen as uncluttered as possible these options tend to be kept to a minimum (eg. the ledgers and associated journals). Other options, such as a trial balance are usually hidden away within one of the main options. The most suitable programs are those which let you access your most used options with the minimum of fuss.

When entering transactions you may find that the 'thinking' has been done for you; for example when making a payment, the payments book may be presented on screen as a 'cheque' - all you do is fill in the amount and enter the name of the person or account you are paying.

This of course is fine, but if you regularly use more than one bank account you may find yourself having to access further menus to change the account to be debited every time you change cheque books.

Another problem associated with this type of interface is where the purchases book is displayed as a purchase order. Can you debit more than one expense account if, for instance, you are purchasing a number of different office supplies which you will later need to analyse?

The same applies to the sales book. This is usually displayed as an invoice. You may want to split the credit side of an invoice across multiple sales accounts (eg. stock sold and carriage). Your invoice may also contain a mixture of VAT codes. Can the software handle this without the need for separate invoices?

There are ways of getting round these problems though. For instance, crediting a single sales account in the sales book when producing an invoice, then subsequently debiting the sales account and crediting your 'real' set of sales accounts using the general journal. The same can be applied to purchases.

Some accounts may be hidden from you. A typical example is a subsidiary ledger control account - it will be present within the software, but you are only shown its associated nominal ledger control account (eg. 'Debtors', or 'Accounts Receivable').

A computer accounting program will always have advantages over a manual system. The physical posting of entries (ie. copying) is done for you, adding up and balancing ledger accounts is automatic, and reports usually require nothing more than a key or mouse button press.

Inventories

Computer accounting programs are also useful for inventories. They can be kept and automatically updated within the system. For instance, stock can be picked directly from the stock inventory when producing an invoice. The stock valuation can automatically be taken from the inventory at year end (some programs allow you to choose which method the valuation is based upon - though most use 'averaging').

Where an inventory is included, you will often find at least one extra journal. In the case of a stock inventory an 'adjustment' journal may be used to alter the quantities of stock (say, to a 'damaged' or 'written off' stock account), another may be used to allow transfers of stock from one record to another (eg. a manufacturer may make wheelbarrows, once the component parts have been assembled into the wheelbarrow, a transfer will be made from 'wheels' and other associated stock to a new record which holds the complete product).

Useful Contacts

CCTA Government Information Service:
Internet: **http://www.open.gov.uk/**
This is the UK government's world wide web site. It contains a great deal of information useful to businesses.

Companies House:
55-71 City Road
London
EC1Y 1BB
Tel: 0171 253 9393
Internet: **http://www.companies-house.gov.uk/**
Their web site is full of useful information about limited and public limited companies.

Customs & Excise:
Dorset House
Stamford Street
London
SE1 9PY
Tel: 0171 928 3344
Internet: **http://www.open.gov.uk/**
HM Customs & Excise have business centres in almost every major town in the UK. If you need advice on VAT, contact the London office, who will give you the address of your local centre.

Inland Revenue:
Victoria Street
Shipley
West Yorkshire
BD98 8AA
Tel: 01274 530750
Internet: **http://www.open.gov.uk/**
This is one of two IR collection centres which can deal with public enquiries.

Self Assessment Help Line: 0345 161514
Telephone the above number if you need help when filling in a self assessment income tax return.

The Institute of Chartered Accountants in England and Wales:
PO Box 433
Chartered Accountants Hall
Moorgate Place
London
EC2P 2BJ
Tel: 0171 920 8100
Internet: **http://www.icaew.co.uk/**

Royal Society of Arts: Courses in Accounting
RSA Examinations Board
Westwood Way
Coventry
CV4 8HS
Tel: 01203 470033
The RSA run several courses on accounting. These are available throughout the UK.

Her Majesty's Stationery Office (HMSO):
The trading side of HMSO was sold in 1996 to the National Publishing Group who trade as The Stationery Office Limited:
The Stationary Office Publications Centre
Orders Department
PO Box 276
London
SW8 5DT
Tel: 0171 873 9090
Internet: **http://www.the-stationery-office.co.uk/**
There are many books and leaflets available from The Stationery Office which are of use to businesses. Their web site is an excellent place to start if you are looking for specific information.

Glossary of Terms

Account: A section in a ledger devoted to a single aspect of a business (ie. a Bank Account).

Accounting equation: The formula used to prepare a balance sheet: **assets=liability+equity** (see chapter 6).

Accounts Payable: See *'Creditors (control account)'.*

Accounts Payable Ledger: See *'Purchase Ledger'.*

Accounts Receivable: See *'Debtors (control account)'.*

Accounts Receivable Ledger: See *'Sales Ledger'.*

Accruals: If during the course of a business certain charges are incurred but no invoice is received then these charges are referred to as accruals (they 'accrue' or increase in value). A typical example is interest payable on a loan where you have not yet received a bank statement. These items (or an estimate of their value) should still be included in the profit & loss account. When the real invoice is received, an adjustment can be made to correct the estimate. Accruals can also apply to the income side. (See chapter 17).

Accrual method of accounting: Most businesses use the accrual method of accounting (because it is usually required by law). When you issue an invoice on credit (ie. regardless of whether it is paid or not), it is treated as a taxable supply on the date it was issued for income tax purposes (or corporation tax for limited companies). The same applies to bills received from suppliers. (This does not mean you pay income tax immediately, just that it must be included in that year's profit & loss account).

Accumulated Depreciation Account: This is an account held in the nominal ledger which holds the depreciation of a fixed asset until the end of the asset's useful life (either because it has been scrapped or sold). It is credited each year with that year's depreciation, hence the balance increases (ie. accumulates) over a period of time. Each fixed asset will have its own accumulated depreciation account (see chapter 16).

Advanced Corporation Tax (ACT): This is corporation tax paid in advance when a limited company issues a dividend. ACT is then deducted from the total corporation tax due when it has been calculated at year end. ACT will be abolished from April 1999. See *'Corporation Tax'*.

Appropriation Account: An account in the nominal ledger which shows how the net profits of a business (usually a partnership or limited company) have been used.

Assets: Assets represent what a business owns or is due. Equipment, vehicles, buildings, creditors, money in the bank, cash are all examples of the assets of a business.

Audit: The process of checking every entry in a set of books to make sure they agree with the original paperwork (eg. checking a journal's entries against the original purchase and sales invoices).

Audit Trail: A list of transactions in the order they occurred.

Bad Debts Account: An account in the nominal ledger to record the value of un-recoverable debts from customers. Real bad debts or those that are likely to happen can be deducted as expenses against tax liability (provided they refer specifically to a customer). (See chapter 17).

Bad Debts Reserve Account: An account used to record an estimate of bad debts for the year (usually as a percentage of sales). This cannot be deducted as an expense against tax liability. (See chapter 17).

Balance Sheet: A summary of all the accounts of a business. Usually prepared at the end of each financial year. (See chapter 6).

Balancing Charge: When a fixed asset is sold or disposed of, any loss or gain on the asset can be reclaimed against (or added to) any profits for income tax purposes. This is called a balancing charge.

Bill: A term typically used to describe a purchase invoice (eg. an invoice from a supplier).

Bought Ledger: See *Purchase Ledger*.

Capital: An amount of money put into the business (often by way of a loan) as opposed to money earned by the business.

Capital account: A term usually applied to the owners equity in the business.

Capital Allowances: The depreciation on a fixed asset is shown in the Profit & Loss account, but is added back again for income tax purposes. In order to be able to claim the depreciation against any profits the Inland Revenue allow a proportion of the value of fixed assets to be claimed before working out the tax bill. These proportions (usually calculated as a percentage of the value of the fixed assets) are called Capital Allowances. (See pages 114 and 124).

Capital Assets: See *'Fixed Assets'*.

Capital Gains Tax: When a fixed asset is sold at a profit, the profit may be liable to a tax called Capital Gains Tax. Calculating the tax can be a complicated affair (capital gains allowances, adjustments for inflation and different computations depending on the age of the asset are all considerations you will need to take on board).

Cash Accounting: This term describes an accounting method whereby only invoices and bills which have been **paid** are accounted for. However, for most types of business, as far as the Inland Revenue are concerned as soon as you issue an invoice (**paid or not**), it is treated as revenue and must be accounted for. An exception is VAT: Customs & Excise normally require you to account for VAT on an accrual basis, however there is an option called 'Cash Accounting' whereby only paid items are included as far as VAT is concerned (eg. if most of your sales are on credit, you may benefit from this scheme - contact your local Customs & Excise office for the current rules and turnover limits).

Cash Book: A journal where a business's cash sales and purchases are entered. A cash book can also be used to record the transactions of a bank account. The side of the cash book which refers to the cash or bank account can be used as a part of the nominal ledger (rather than posting the entries to cash or bank accounts held directly in the nominal ledger - see *'Three column cash book'*).

Cash Flow: A report which shows the flow of money in and out of the business over a period of time (see page 153).

Cash Flow Forecast: A report which estimates the cash flow in the future (usually required by a bank before it will lend you money, or take on your account). (See page 153).

Cash in Hand: An account used to show the current total of money received (ie. not yet banked or spent). Cash used in this context includes money, cheques, credit card payments, bankers drafts etc. This type of account is also commonly referred to as an 'Undeposited funds' account.

Chart of Accounts: A list of all the accounts held in the nominal ledger.

Closing the books: A term used to describe the journal entries necessary to close the sales and expense accounts of a business at year end by posting their balances to the profit & loss account, and ultimately to close the profit & loss account too by posting its balance to a capital or other account (see chapter 7).

Companies House: The title given to the government department which collects and stores information supplied by limited companies. A limited company must supply Companies House with a statement of its final accounts every year (eg. trading and profit & loss accounts, and balance sheet). (See page 161).

Contra: This word describes transactions which transfer a balance from one account to another (eg. transferring money from the bank to the cash account, or where a customer is also a supplier, the difference in what you owe each other can be balanced by a transfer so that only one of you needs send a cheque to balance both accounts). A contra entry therefore shows money flowing within the business rather than new money coming in or going out of the business.

Control Account: An account held in a ledger which summarises the balance of all the accounts in the same or another ledger. Typically each subsidiary ledger will have a control account which will be mirrored by another control account in the nominal ledger (see *'Self-balancing ledgers'*).

Corporation Tax (CT): The tax paid by a limited company on its profits. At present this is calculated at year end and due within 9 months of that date. From April 1999 advanced corporation tax will be abolished (see *'Advanced Corporation Tax'*) and large companies will instead pay CT in instalments. Small and medium-sized companies will be exempted from the instalment plan. The main rate of corporation tax is 31p for 1997/8, reducing to 30p from April 1999. The small companies rate is 21p for 1997/98, reducing to 20p from April 1999. (See chapter 15).

Cost of finished goods: The value (at cost) of newly manufactured goods shown in a business's manufacturing account. The valuation is based on the opening raw materials balance, less direct costs involved in manufacturing, less the closing raw materials balance, and less any other overheads. This balance is subsequently transferred to the trading account.

Credit: A column in a journal or ledger to record the 'From' side of a transaction (eg. if you buy some petrol using a cheque then the money is paid **from** the bank to the petrol account, you would therefore credit the bank when making the journal entry).

Credit Note: A sales invoice in reverse. A typical example is where you issue an invoice for £100, the customer then returns £25 worth of the goods, so you issue the customer with a credit note to say that you owe the customer £25.

Creditors: A list of suppliers to whom the business owes money.

Creditors (control account): An account in the nominal ledger which contains the overall balance of the Purchase Ledger. (See chapter 12).

Current Assets: These include money in the bank, petty cash, money received but not yet banked (see '*cash in hand*'), money owed to the business by its customers, raw materials for manufacturing, and stock bought for re-sale. They are termed 'current' because they are **active** accounts. Money flows in and out of them each financial year and we will need frequent reports of their balances if the business is to survive (eg. 'do we need more stock and have we got enough money in the bank to buy it?').

Current Liabilities: These include bank overdrafts, short term loans (less than a year), and what the business owes its suppliers. They are termed 'current' for the same reasons outlined under *current assets* in the previous paragraph.

Customs & Excise: The government department responsible for collecting VAT. (See *Value Added Tax*). (See page 161 for contact details).

Debenture: This is a type of share issued by a limited company. It is the safest type of share in that it is really a loan to the company and is usually tied to some of the company's assets so should the company fail, the debenture holder will have first call on any assets left after the company has been wound up.

Debit: A column in a journal or ledger to record the 'To' side of a transaction (eg. if you are paying money into your bank account you would debit the bank when making the journal entry).

Debtors: A list of customers who owe money to the business.

Debtors (control account): An account in the nominal ledger which contains the overall balance of the Sales Ledger. (See chapter 12).

Depreciation: The value of assets usually decreases as time goes by. The amount or percentage it decreases by is called depreciation. This is normally calculated at the end of every accounting period (usually a year) at a typical rate of 25% of its last value. It is shown in both the profit & loss account and balance sheet of a business. (See chapter 16).

(references in italics refer to other entries in the glossary)

Dividends: These are payments to the shareholders of a limited company.

Double-entry book-keeping: A system which accounts for every aspect of a transaction - where it came **from** and where it went **to**. This **from** and **to** aspect of a transaction (called **crediting** and **debiting**) is what the term double-entry means.

Drawings: The money taken out of a business by its owner(s) for personal use. This is entirely different to wages paid to a business's employees or the wages or remuneration of a limited company's directors (see *'Wages'*).

Entry: Part of a transaction recorded in a journal or posted to a ledger.

Equity: The value of the business to the owner of the business (which is the difference between the business's assets and liabilities).

Expenses: Goods or services purchased directly for the running of the business. This does **not** include goods bought for re-sale or any items of a capital nature (see *'Stock'* and *'Fixed Assets'*).

FIFO: First In First Out. A method of valuing stock (see page 150).

Fiscal year: The term used for a business's accounting year. The period is usually twelve months which can begin during any month of the calendar year (eg. 1st April 1998 to 31st March 1999).

Fixed Assets: These consist of anything which a business owns or buys for use within the business and which still **retains a value at year end**. They usually consist of major items like land, buildings, equipment and vehicles but can include smaller items like tools. (see *'Depreciation'*)

Fixtures & Fittings: This is a class of fixed asset which includes office furniture, filing cabinets, display cases, warehouse shelving and the like.

Flow of Funds: This is a report which shows how a balance sheet has changed from one period to the next. See chapter 19, page 151 for a full example.

General Ledger: See *'Nominal Ledger'*.

Goodwill: This is an extra value placed on a business if the owner of a business decides it is worth more than the value of its assets. It is usually included where the business is to be sold as a going concern. (See chapter 17).

Gross loss: The balance of the trading account assuming it has a debit balance.

Gross profit: The balance of the trading account assuming it has a credit balance.

Historical Cost: This refers to the valuation of assets and liabilities. These can be valued at what they originally cost, or what they would cost to replace at today's prices. The 'historical cost' means the original price.

(references in italics refer to other entries in the glossary)

Impersonal Accounts: These are accounts not held in the name of persons (ie. they do not relate directly to a business's customers and suppliers). There are two types, see *'Real'* and *'Nominal'*.

Imprest System: A method of topping up petty cash. A fixed sum of petty cash is placed in the petty cash box. When the petty cash balance is nearing zero, it is topped up back to its original level again (known as 'restoring the Imprest').

Income: Money received by a business from its commercial activities. See *'Revenue'*.

Inland Revenue: The government department responsible for collecting income tax from individuals, and corporation tax from limited companies.

Integration Account: See *'Control Account'*.

Inventory: A subsidiary ledger which is usually used to record the details of individual items of stock. Inventories can also be used to hold the details of other assets of a business.

Invoice: A term describing an original document either issued by a business for the sale of goods on credit (a sales invoice) or received by the business for goods bought (a purchase invoice).

Journal(s): A book or set of books where your transactions are first entered.

Journal entries: A term used to describe the transactions recorded in a journal.

Journal Proper: A term used to describe the main or general journal where other journals specific to subsidiary ledgers are also used.

Ledger: A book in which entries posted from the journals are re-organised into accounts.

Liabilities: This includes bank overdrafts, loans taken out for the business and money owed by the business to its suppliers. Liabilities are included on the right hand side of the balance sheet and normally consist of accounts which have a credit balance.

LIFO: Last In Last Out. A method of valuing stock (see page 150).

Long term liabilities: These usually refer to long term loans (ie. a loan which lasts for more than one year such as a mortgage).

Loss: See *'Net loss'*.

Matching principle: A method of analysing the sales and expenses which make up those sales to a particular period (eg. if a builder sells a house then the builder will tie in all the raw materials and expenses incurred in building and selling the house to one period - usually in order to see how much profit was made).

Manufacturing account: An account used to show what it cost to produce the finished goods made by a manufacturing business (see chapter 14).

Net loss: The value of expenses less sales assuming that the expenses are greater (ie. if the profit & loss account shows a debit balance).

Net profit: The value of sales less expenses assuming that the sales are greater (ie. if the profit & loss account shows a credit balance).

Net worth: See *'Equity'*.

Nominal Accounts: A set of accounts held in the nominal ledger. They are termed 'nominal' because they don't usually relate to an individual person. The accounts which make up a Profit & Loss account are nominal accounts (as is the Profit & Loss account itself), whereas an account opened for a specific customer is usually held in a subsidiary ledger (the sales ledger in this case) and these are referred to as *'personal'* accounts.

Nominal Ledger: A ledger which holds all the nominal accounts of a business. Where the business uses a subsidiary ledger like the sales ledger to hold customer details, the nominal ledger will usually include a control account to show the total balance of the subsidiary ledger (a control account can be termed 'nominal' because it doesn't relate to a specific person).

Opening the books: Every time a business closes the books for a year, it opens a new set. The new set of books will be empty, therefore the balances from the last balance sheet must be copied into them (via journal entries) so that the business is ready to start the new year. (See chapter 7).

Ordinary Share: This is a type of share issued by a limited company. It carries the highest risk but usually attracts the highest rewards.

Original book of entry: A book which contains the details of the day to day transactions of a business (see *'Journal'*).

Overheads: These are the costs involved in running a business. They consist entirely of expense accounts (eg. rent, insurance, petrol, staff wages etc.).

P.A.Y.E: 'Pay as you earn'. The name given to the Income Tax system where an employee's tax and national insurance contributions are deducted before the wages are paid.

Personal Accounts: These are the accounts of a business's customers and suppliers. They are usually held in the Sales and Purchase Ledgers.

Petty Cash: A small amount of money held in reserve (normally used to purchase items of small value where a cheque or other form of payment is not suitable).

Petty Cash Slip: A document used to record petty cash payments where an original receipt was not obtained (sometimes called a petty cash voucher).

Posting: The copying of entries from the journals to the ledgers.

Preference Shares: This is a type of share issued by a limited company. It carries a medium risk but has the advantage over ordinary shares in that preference shareholders get the first slice of the dividend 'pie' (but usually at a fixed rate).

Pre-payments: One or more accounts set up to account for money paid in advance (eg. insurance, where part of the premium applies to the current financial year, and the remainder to the following year). (See chapter 17).

Prime book of entry: See *'Original book of entry'*.

Profit: See *'Gross profit'*, *'Net profit'*, and *'Profit & Loss Account'*.

Profit & Loss Account: An account made up of revenue and expense accounts which shows the current profit or loss of a business (ie. whether a business has earned more than it has spent in the current year). (See chapter 5).

Provisions: One or more accounts set up to account for expected future payments (eg. where a business is expecting a bill, but hasn't yet received it). (See chapter 17).

Purchase Invoice: See *'Invoice'*.

Purchase Ledger: A subsidiary ledger which holds the accounts of a business's suppliers. A single control account is held in the nominal ledger which shows the total balance of all the accounts in the purchase ledger. (See chapter 12).

Raw Materials: This refers to the materials bought by a manufacturing business in order to manufacture its products (see chapter 14).

Real accounts: These are accounts which deal with money such as bank and cash accounts. They also include those dealing with property and investments. In the case of bank and cash accounts they can be held in the nominal ledger, or balanced in a journal (eg. the cash book) where they can then be looked upon as a part of the nominal ledger when compiling a balance sheet. Property and investments can be held in subsidiary ledgers (with associated control accounts if necessary) or directly in the nominal ledger itself.

Receipt: A term typically used to describe confirmation of a payment - if you buy some petrol you will normally ask for a receipt to prove that the money was spent legitimately.

Reconciling: The procedure of checking entries made in a business's books with those on a statement sent by a third person (eg. checking a bank statement against your own records - see chapter 19).

Reserve accounts: Reserve accounts are usually set up to make a balance sheet clearer by reserving or apportioning some of a business's capital against future purchases or liabilities (such as the replacement of capital equipment or estimates of bad debts).

A typical example is a limited company where they are used to hold the residue of any profit after all the dividends have been paid. This balance is then carried forward to the following year to be considered, together with the profits for that year, for any further dividends.

Retail: A term usually applied to a shop which re-sells other people's goods. This type of business will require a trading account as well as a profit & loss account.

Retained earnings: This is the amount of money held in a business after its owner(s) have taken their share of the profits.

Revenue: The sales and any other taxable income of a business (eg. interest earned from money on deposit).

Sales: Income received from selling goods or a service. See *'Revenue'*.

Sales Invoice: See *'Invoice'*.

Sales Ledger: A subsidiary ledger which holds the accounts of a business's customers. A control account is held in the nominal ledger (usually called a debtors' control account) which shows the total balance of all the accounts in the sales ledger. (See chapter 12).

Self Assessment: A new style of income tax return introduced for the 1996/1997 tax year. If you are self-employed, or receive an income which is un-taxed at source, you will need to register with the Inland Revenue so that the relevant self assessment forms can be sent to you. The idea of self assessment is to allow you to calculate your own income tax.

Self-balancing ledgers: A system which makes use of control accounts so that each ledger will balance on its own. A control account in a *subsidiary ledger* will be mirrored with a *control account* in the nominal ledger.

Self-employed: The owner (or partner) of a business who is legally liable for all the debts of the business (ie. the owner(s) of a non-limited company).

Service: A term usually applied to a business which sells a service rather than manufactures or sells goods (eg. an architect or a window cleaner).

Shareholders: The owners of a limited company.

Shares: These are documents issued by a company to its owners (the shareholders) which state how many shares in the company each shareholder has bought and what percentage of the company the shareholder owns. Shares can also be called *'Stock'*.

Sole trader: See *'Sole-proprietor'*.

Sole-proprietor: The self-employed owner of a business (see *'Self-employed'*).

Source document: An original invoice, bill or receipt to which journal entries refer.

Stock: This can refer to the shares of a limited company (see *'Shares'*) or goods manufactured or bought for re-sale by a business.

Stock control account: An account held in the nominal ledger which holds the value of all the stock held in the inventory subsidiary ledger.

Stockholders: See *'Shareholders'*.

Stock Taking: Physically checking a business's stock for total quantities and value.

Stock valuation: Valuing a stock of goods bought for manufacturing or re-sale (see page 150).

Subsidiary ledgers: Ledgers opened in addition to a business's nominal ledger. They are used to keep sections of a business separate from each other (eg. a Sales ledger for the customers, and a Purchase ledger for the suppliers). (See *'Control Accounts'*)

Suspense Account: A temporary account used to force a trial balance to balance if there is only a small discrepancy (or if an account's balance is simply wrong, and you don't know why). A typical example would be a small error in petty cash. In this case a transfer would be made to a suspense account to balance the cash account. Once the person knows what happened to the money, a transfer entry will be made in the journal to credit or debit the suspense account back to zero and debit or credit the correct account. (See chapter 17).

T Account: A particular method of displaying an account where the debits and associated information are shown on the left, and credits and associated information on the right. (See chapter 9).

Three column cash book: A journal which deals with the day to day cash and bank transactions of a business. The side of a transaction which relates directly to the cash or bank account is usually balanced within the journal and used as a part of the nominal ledger when compiling a balance sheet (ie. only the side which details the sale or purchase needs to be posted to the nominal ledger).

Trading account: An account which shows the gross profit of a manufacturing or retail business. (See chapter 13).

Transaction: Two or more entries made in a journal which when looked at together reflect an original document such as a sales invoice or purchase receipt.

Trial Balance: A statement showing all the accounts used in a business and their balances. (See chapter 4).

Turnover: The income of a business over a period of time (usually a year).

Undeposited Funds Account: See *'Cash in Hand'*.

Value Added Tax (VAT): Value Added Tax, or VAT as it is usually called is a sales tax which increases the price of goods. At the time of writing the VAT standard rate is 17.5%, there is also a rate for fuel which is 5% (this refers to heating fuels like coal, electricity and gas and **not** 'road fuels' like petrol which is still rated at 17.5%).

VAT is added to the price of goods so an item that sells at £10 will be priced £11.75 when 17.5% VAT is added. (See chapter 11).

Wages: Payments made to the employees of a business for their work on behalf of the business. These are classed as expense items and must not be confused with 'drawings' taken by sole-proprietors and partnerships (see *'Drawings'*).

Work in Progress: The value of partly finished (ie. partly manufactured) goods. (See chapter 14).

Index

Business
Accounts